Music Hall: Performance and Style

⌐

Popular Music in Britain

Series Editors:	Dave Harker and Richard Middleton
Dave Harker:	*Fakesong: The Manufacture of British 'folksong' 1700 to the present day*
Dave Laing:	*One Chord Wonders: Power and Meaning in Punk Rock*
J S Bratton (ed.):	*Music Hall: Performance and Style*

Music Hall

Performance and Style

Edited by J. S. Bratton

Open University Press
Milton Keynes · Philadelphia

Open University Press
Open University Educational Enterprises Limited
12 Cofferidge Close
Stony Stratford
Milton Keynes MK11 1BY, England

and
242 Cherry Street
Philadelphia, PA 19106, USA

First Published 1986

British Library Cataloguing in Publication Date

Music hall: performance and style. —
   (Popular music in Britain)
   1. Music-halls (Variety-theaters, cabarets, etc.) — Great Britain — History
   I. Bratton, J.S.   II. Series
   792.7'0941   PN1968.G7

   ISBN 0 335 15277 5
   ISBN 0 335 15131 0 Pbk

Library of Congress cataloging in Publication Data
Main entry under title:
Music hall.
   (Popular music in Britain)
   1. Music, Popular (Songs, etc.)—Great Britain—History and criticism.
   2. Songs, English—Great Britain—History and criticism.   3. Music-halls
   (Variety–theaters, cabarets, etc.)—Great Britain.   4. Musical revue,
   comedy, etc.—Great Britain.   5. Great Britain—Popular culture.   6. Great
   Britain—Social life and customs.
I. Bratton, J. S. (Jacquelin S.) II. Series.
ML3650.M88 1986   784.5'00941   86–1260

   ISBN 0–335–15131–0 (pbk.)
   ISBN 0–335–15277–5

Text design by
Typeset by Marlborough Design, Oxford, Oxon
Printed in Great Britain at the Alden Press

Contents

Editorial Preface

What *is* British popular music? Does such a thing exist? What makes certain music and songs popular? And who made the musical cultures of these islands? What did Scots, Welsh, Irish and North American people have to do with the process? What part did people in the English regions play — the Geordies, Cockneys, midlanders and all the rest? Where did the Empire fit in? How did European 'high' culture affect what most people played and sang? And how did all these factors vary in significance over time? In the end, just how much do we know about the history of musical culture on these tiny patches of land? The truth is that we know very little, and this realisation led to this series.

The history of British people and culture has been dominated by capitalism for centuries; and capitalism helped to polarise people into classes not only economically, but culturally too. Music was never *simply* music: songs were never *simply* songs. Both were produced and use by particular people in particular historical periods for particular reasons, and we have recognised that in the way in which we have put this series together.

Every book in this series aims to exemplify and to foster interdisciplinary research. Each volume studies not only 'texts' and performances, but institutions and technology as well, and the culture practices and sets of social relationships through which music and songs were produced, disseminated and consumed. Ideas, values, attitudes and what is generally referred to as ideology are taken into account, as are factors such as gender, age, geography and traditions. Nor is our series above the struggle. We do not pretend to have helped produce an objective record. We are, unrepentantly, on the side of the majority, and our main perspective is from 'below', even though the whole musical field needs to be in view. We hope that by clarifying the history of popular musical culture we can help clear the ground for a genuinely democratic musical culture of the future.

Dave Harker and Richard Middleton

Notes on Contributors

J.S. Bratton, is Reader in Theatre and Cultural Studies at Royal Holloway and Bedford New College, University of London. After reading English at Oxford she completed a D. Phil on popular culture, and taught English literature for some years before pursuing the wider study of culture. Her publications include *The Victorian Popular Ballad* and *The Impact of Victorian Children's Fiction.*

Anthony Bennett is Lecturer in Music at the University of Sheffield and co-editor with Paul Smith of *Broadside Song and Ballad in Britain* (forthcoming).

Jane Traies is a theatre historian, author of *Fairbooths and Fit-ups* and co-author of *Astley's Amphitheatre*, and is Headteacher of Swakeleys Comprehensive School Hillingdon.

Peter Bailey teaches history at the University of Manitoba. Author of *Leisure and Class in Victorian England* and several articles on the popular culture of the period, he is preparing a book on the social history of British music hall, and is editor of this volume's companion, *Music Hall: The Business of Pleasure.*

Michael Pickering is Senior Lecturer in Communications Studies at Sunderland Polytechnic. His publications include *Village Song and Culture*, which won the 1983 Katherine Briggs Memorial Award. He is co-editor with Tony Green of *Popular Song and Vernacular Culture* (forthcoming).

Dave Harker teaches at Manchester Polytechnic. His publications include *One for the Money: Politics and Popular Song* and *Fakesong: the Manufacturer of British 'Folksong' 1700 to the Present Day*, and he is General Editor of this series.

Lois Rutherford is taking an MSc in Applied Social Work at Wolfson College, Oxford. She has worked in theatre and light entertainment, and undertook her research into music hall at Girton College, Cambridge.

Introduction

I've just been informed by the manager here
That the reason I'm back at the Empire this year,
Is because it states on my contract quite clear,
I must sing a song with a chorus;
I've found one at last – it's a terrible thing,
But still it must go with a rush and a swing;
So when I've sung it once, for goodness' sake sing,
And bring down the roof that is o'er us.
If the song doesn't go, well I do, that's all,
So here and outside this chorus please bawl:
O, O, Capital O, Why it should be so I really don't know,
O, O; now let it go!
If you don't know the chorus, sing, O, O, O.

(Words and music by J.W. Knowles, sung by Wilkie Bard
[1903].)

A silly song – the second verse says cheerfully, 'The words they are putrid, the metre's all wrong, And it gets a lot worse, too, as we go along – so please leave the Hall if your heart is not strong, it gets on your nerves, does the chorus' – and one which epitomises the curious situation of the music hall in relation to British popular music. The singer and the audience, the management and the song, are described as being locked into a network of relationships that is acknowledged as exploitative and phoney, even as the song is generated and enjoyed. The spontaneous audience participation supposedly at the heart of the music hall's 'popular' status – the chorus-singing on which the cosy togetherness of the Good Old Days' myth is founded – is exposed as a deliberate fabrication written into the contract by the management, which rewards the performer according to his ability to sell his manufactured bonhomie to the audience. But the song is not a bitter denunciation of the system; the response it invites is the same participation at which it scoffs, and the singer would have failed indeed if the audience were not singing heartily by the end. The comic performer is employed by the retailer to convince the consumers, shares with the latter an awareness of their mutual exploitation, and pretends that with their complicity he snatches a victory over the boss:

The manager's tearing his hair at the side,
And saying, "Come off!" but I shalln't move a stride –
By the clause on my contract he'll have to abide:
I'm singing a song with a chorus.
He's bet me a quid I forget the last verse,
But I think that he'll have to dive down in his purse.
The song's bad enough, but singing it's worse, –
I'm stuck! I've forgotten the chorus!
If I don't sing it right, it's a quid off my screw,
So please let it rip, and perhaps I'll pull through.
　　O, O, capital O, etc.

The song works on an extraordinary cross-cutting of levels. The comic stands on the stage singing a song which the audience knows to be a fiction, which some will have heard before, at first house or earlier in the week. He pretends, however, that the events are occurring as he narrates them and the manager is in the wings; they accept that fiction, which has a known place in the conventions of variety performance – normally the bogy-man invoked is the stagehand with the hook whose job is to get failed acts off quickly. Bard describes the manager as distraught at the dreadful song, anticipating a disaster, and delights in his own impunity, protected by the contract. He is singing what he likes, turning the tables upon the manager by means of his own improper clause – improper because it attempted to dictate what the performance should contain, and that is a contract to be made only between the performer and the audience. (Such clauses did of course exist, and caused real friction.) But then the dreadful song is tossed in the air again and the conflict goes in another direction, when Bard asserts that the manager had bet him that he wouldn't remember the last verse – which must mean he had heard it already, so the vision of him tearing his hair is cancelled by the picture of the two betting on it. The invocation of a bet is a good way to the heart of a British audience having a night out, and they are immediately asked to sympathize further with the singer, who is suffering because he has to sing such a bad song. The fun extracted from what he is singing stands apart from the idea of the bad song, which by now exists in some ideal dimension. When he makes the final twist, pretending to have forgotten the words, the bet, part of the ritual of shared leisure, is superseded by a final appeal to take sides: to sing with him against the management and prevent him losing 'a quid off my screw'. With this they launch into the chorus, 'O, O, capital O, etc.', whose mysterious but suggestive phraseology I take, reluctantly, to be nonsense mouth-music, not an oblique attempt to suggest the nature of the economic relations underlying the power of the manager.

　This trivial and forgotten song is only unusual in being more explicit in its self-reference than other late music-hall songs, which were usually just as self-consciously related to a practice and tradition acknowledged by all parties. The complexity that its existence suggests in the transactions between capital, labour and consumers in the entertainment business is the subject of this book;

the analysis of the songs, sketches and other materials of the halls will aim to achieve a more precise understanding of why music hall was popular, and, perhaps, a clearer vision of what is meant by the term 'popular song'.

[Music hall was obviously 'popular' in the sense that it was widespread: an unavoidable experience for any Victorian or Edwardian individual, from the Queen herself to a Dorset farmworker. It gave rise to a dominant form of song in Britain from, say, 1840–1920, flanked on one side by the 'parlour ballad' and on the other by the surviving body of rural and urban workers' songs. Song in the halls had several phases of development, gradually evolving distinctive structures from theatrical, convivial, workers' and street-song sources during the establishment of the institution, up to 1860, then consolidating into recognisable patterns over the next 20 years, always remaining open to influence from, for example, imported American styles. During the 'heyday' of the halls, after 1880, performers, writers and composers worked within an established song tradition of great flexibility and power, before the impact of more aggressive competition began to undermine it, some time during the First World War.]

To determine whether it was a 'popular' tradition in the sense of belonging to the people, or whether, or the contrary, its place in the class struggle was as an organ of social control manipulated by the petit bourgeoisie, incorporating or destroying the workers' song culture, is a question which must be addressed in two ways, both equally important: by an examination of the economic and legal history of the institution, and by a close scrutiny of the transactions which took place within it. The field is huge, and under-researched; few people have so far brought either the stringent specificities of social history or the imaginative discipline of cultural studies to bear upon it. This book and its companion volume *Music Hall: The Business of Pleasure*, edited by Peter Bailey, make a beginning, employing approaches which range over several scholarly disciplines. Together, in Peter Bailey's words, they are 'concerned to reconstruct the wider and deeper patterns of operation and performance within which the great halls and their stars worked, to locate the structure and process of music hall as a dominant form of cultural production in the context of a modernising capitalist society, and to relate such studies to the major interpretative debates of recent scholarship in social history and cultural studies'.

The Introduction to *The Business of Pleasure* offers a summary of the chronological development of the halls to which readers not familiar with that old, old story may refer. It goes on to outline the interpretative preoccupations of the many writers who have so far told the tale: the nostalgic apologists from within 'the Profession', the romantic idealists who claim the music hall for the folk, and the perspectives of the few modern, generally sub-Marxist or cultural-materialist, writers who have challenged these interpretations, but offered only reductive accounts and extrinsic models by which to understand a dynamic and complex discourse. The historical essays then discuss in detail the caterers who created and profited from the first boom of the leisure industry, the developing grandeur of the halls they built, and their confrontations with the licensing authorities, the audiences and the performers. In contrast the present volume seeks to explore and analyse the product on which this structure of capital, labour and consumption rested – music-hall performance.

The analysis of past performance, central in any endeavour to understand cultural history, is so fraught with problems that anyone even half equipped to undertake it might be forgiven for refusing to try. The more we know, the more we realize how unknowable are such experiences at second-hand. But the endeavour is essential, because the external, verifiable information available to us about buildings, billing and business – the determining structure – is meaningful as a signifying practice only when related to the transactions in the auditorium, where the words were sung and spoken. We can only know what music hall is if we know both how it worked and what it meant. It is the business of this volume to begin upon the exploration of that meaning in terms of performance and style.

The analyses offered here are based upon the assumption that such performances do not only reproduce or display ideologies, but contribute to their construction and modification. In the music hall, and in the uses made of music-hall materials outside the theatres themselves, the Victorian and Edwardian social consensus can be seen in the process of creation and modification. The dominant ideology – the generally agreed set of assumptions and values by which those in power are able to maintain their position – rests always upon constant, multitudinous renegotiations about what it is right and sensible to think and to believe. The music hall, a powerful force in nineteenth and early twentieth-century culture, was bound to be an important site of these hegemonic negotiations. Each time an idea about social relatonships and the economic world in which they exist was voiced, reinforced or challenged by a performance, it had some effect upon the view of the world which the audience accepted as real and true. The transaction was not simply that a singer or a comedian said this or that, and the audience believed it. As in the Wilkie Bard song I have quoted, there was a much more complex combination of the fiction the performer created and the audience's responses to it, issuing, perhaps, in a mutual confirmation of assumptions, but quite possibly in some less resolved, ambiguous dissonance of several ideas presented together, all felt to be part of the truth.

These essays also assume that an analysis of these meanings is possible by an examination of the surviving evidence. The method is to take the text, the cultural product, and see how it works by means of its conventions of expression and exchange to produce a reality which is accepted as truth by the participants, and so becomes a 'lived ideology' in itself.[1] This is a far more problematic procedure for students of past performances than it is in the study of narrative, where this formulation originated. Its most elaborate demonstration has been Pierre Macherey's 'Jules Verne: the Faulty Narrative'.[2] He took a single science fiction story, whose circumstances of publication could be precisely located and whose reception could be to some extent reproduced by the analyst, since, of course, the story still exists. A music-hall turn, by contrast, consisted of several elements, uniquely performed on perhaps thousands of occasions. Since humour, particularly parody, is a powerful element in the music-hall style, nothing was fixed or inevitable in any performance or response. Tone, and therefore meaning, would depend not only on the song, the rest of the act, the previous turn and those expected to appear later, but also on the status and customs of the hall, the day of the week, and the mix and mood of each individual audience. Moreover the song would be carried away from the hall and used, perhaps with quite different meanings, by members of the audience singing it at home, in the streets or at other gatherings; and the songs and the singers were used by the professional machinery of management, publishers and press to project yet other meanings.

The transaction within the hall was complex enough. The music hall in the nineteenth century was more like the Restoration playhouse than any performance space we know now: in full light, brighter than that which shone anywhere else, a packed auditorium contained a constantly shifting audience that was not one group but many, the old divisions of box, pit and gallery fragmented into class, sex, money and age-based distinctions between the favoured few at the chairman's table, the celebrating parites in the boxes or at the long tables, the loungers in the bars or on the promenade, and the young chorus-singers in the gallery. As in the seventeenth century, any or all of these groups might be inattentive at any given moment, busy with its own concerns. A song had to command attention. It might appeal to them all together, but equally it might address the boys or the girls in the gallery or the married couples, it might glorify the young gents or scoff at their swagger; or, like the best Restoration prologues, it might speak line and line about to each part of the house, setting them laughing at each other, calling on the powerful emotional force of their rivalries and antagonisms to reinforce a climactic endorsement of the song and the singer himself.

The elements of music-hall performance which one must take into account in any analysis begin with this central dynamic of singer and audiences, but do not end there. The performance would differ considerably in meaning and effect from hall to hall, and outside the playing spaces a flourishing specialist press and a market for published songs refracted and altered the meaning of music hall to suit its own purposes, and in doing so created a myth which fed back into the performance experience with increasing power as years went by. It is no help at all to the would-be analyst that our approach usually has to be made through these already mediated versions of music-hall song. A sharp awareness of the nature of this evidence, its biases and its role in the cultural negotiations under consideration, is part of the discipline required in construing the meaning of the performance.

A less manageable problem for the analyst is the forging of a method with which to approach the evidence; a set of tools which will prevent the falling back upon methods of literary explication which are 'an unholy alliance of technical description and ideologizing impressionism.'[3] There are commentators who would argue that it is not possible, that any attempt to dissect the content of popular culture and draw conclusions about its meaning to its original consumers is bound to fail, that 'these attempts to delve into the meaning of products or the (unconscious) intentions of the creator probably tell us more about the *projective abilities* of the analyst than they do about the nature of the product or the purpose of the producer.'[4] But the alternatives offered, chiefly the sociological process called 'content analysis', which is designed to randomise and atomise into pseudo-scientific objectivity the sampling and description of the material, are inadequate to the task of understanding so complex a discourse, as well as casting a dangerously spurious air of objectivity over what can only be opinion. They tell us nothing worth knowing that is not already obvious. 'Technical description' is required, and 'impressionism' must be avoided as far as possible. We must try to break out of narrow academic specialisation, but also admit our limitations, making what we say open to scrutiny, avoiding jargon, and stating frankly where we stand outselves. Only humility in the face of the inevitable limitations of our access to the past makes possible the distinctive contribution of aesthetic analysis to cultural study, which is, in Raymond Williams' words, the 'sustained and detailed analysis of actual cultural works'.[5] As scholars immersed in the study of these works as part of the culture in which they were created, we must try to arrive, by scrupulous and detailed description of what we see, at truth more valid and comprehensive than anything produced by quantitative, pseudo-scientific analyses.

All the essays in this volume attempt to follow this procedure, bringing various scholarly practices to bear. They cannot be comprehensive, since the body of materials that has survived is so massive and, in the main, so unyielding to investigation: it is difficult to find a way past the kaleidoscopic, self-reflexive, endlessly slippery surfaces of a world thickly polished with comic conventions. For this reason, and because we are interested in what the institution was in its active relations to the culture, the essays do not attempt global explanations of the central meaning of music hall, but approach it instead via its points of transition and connection, the places where the making of music-hall style can be seen working, engaging with other genres or traditions, or with elements which are being absorbed via negotiation or incorporation. Perhaps the most comprehensive essay is by Tony Bennett, which shows the steps by which the comic song of the heyday of the halls evolved musically, adapting or discarding elements of the wider vocabulary of popular song under the particular demands of music-hall performance.

The most specific pieces are Dave Harker's essay on Joe Wilson and my own on Jenny Hill. These essays have only a superficial resemblance to the old style of music-hall memoir, which dealt in cherished biographical fancies. We have both found it necessary to engage critically with the myths created around the stars who made the halls. Dave Harker seeks to show how the modern view of Joe Wilson as a champion of working-class culture in the North East, bearing the banner of the people into the new-style concert halls, is a fabrication partly set up deliberately by his petit-bourgeois patrons and publishers, who found him useful for his willingness to transmit their values and attitudes to the working class by means of his 'local' songs, and partly created unwittingly by the acceptance of Wilson as a local working-class hero by later generations of song publishers and singers. Dave Harker's unpicking of the myth to reveal its financial and cultural roots in Wilson's personal transition to petit-bourgeois status offers an insight into the way the music-hall myth, rather than the performance itself, could be said to have been an active agent in incorporating potentially subversive working-class song culture. He demonstrates in action the workings of a selective tradition, the 'continual selection and re-selection of ancestors' discussed by Williams.[6]

My essay on Jenny Hill does the same job in respect of the incorporation of female talent into what was very obviously a patriarchal structure. The music-hall myth-makers present her career in a way which has transformed success, wealth and independence into a story of suffering and pathos more suitable to her gender, while mediation by reporters and the publishers of sheet music has disguised her performances so effectively that we find it difficult to discover what they contained that so pleased her working-class female admirers. Both essays demonstrate the need for a full-scale study of the apparatus of the myth-making process, the contemporary music-hall press and the huge volume of value-laden writing and self-consciously nostalgic perform-ance by which the idea of the music hall has been created and perpetuated to the present day.

Jane Traies and Peter Bailey approach the interactions between working class and bourgeois values manifested in the halls at a point closer to the core, the actual moment of performance. They each analyse a chosen body of songs, the stereotypes created and negotiated in them, and their reception and performance. Peter Bailey's essay approaches the meanings of the 'swell' persona which was a distinctive element of the music-hall style, and Jane Traies defines and investigates the comic projection of the bourgeoisie, and of the working woman. These three figures were based on fractions of the audience, which had potentially conflicting perceptions and desires, and these essays begin upon the process of understanding the class complexity and awareness of music-hall audiences, and the part played by the entertainment itself in the cultural negotiation and resolution of their tensions.

The two remaining essays focus upon the interface between music hall and other forms of entertainment in the nineteenth century. Lois Rutherford approaches the conflict between the music hall and variety stage and the legitimate theatre, the skirmishes that went with the constant redefinition of the boundary of interests, via the structure and content of the dramatic sketches licensed by the Lord Chamberlain for performance in the theatres and in the halls. Michael Pickering takes another distinctive form of music-hall act, the use of blackface, and explores its meanings in relation to the various milieu in which it could be found. Most bills in most music halls throughout its history included some kind of 'Ethiopian' or 'minstrel' performance, but there were also blackface elements in stage comedy, on the one hand, and in the customary practices of mumming and guising on the other; and there were independent Minstrel shows which evolved in Britain separately from other entertainments. The connections and discontinuities between these, and the meanings assigned to and derived from the black mask upon the white face, offer a richly revealing vein of exploration in the culture of the British Empire.

Much remains to be done. There is still a wealth of surviving song to be dissected, and ways need to be found to analyse the meaning of non-verbal performances, from slapstick clowning to gymnastics. The focus of all these essays is primarily between 1860 and 1900, and they do not attempt to cover the whole life of the halls, which could indeed be argued to continue today, displaced to newer media. We need to understand more about the music hall in the days of its creation and dominance before we can account for its death. Its revenant existence today as a powerful image in the projection of the past for the purposes of cultural definition and manipulation is yet another story, and one which needs to be told in the context of the modern entertainment industry, or perhaps in an examination of the uses of 'popular history'.

More controversial, perhaps, in the context of the study of popular music, is the concentration in this book upon the metropolitan music hall, and with one exception only, on London as the central location and source of music-hall style. The old assumption that London was the centre of the music-hall world has been repeatedly denounced by modern writers who wish to forward the claims to originality of other areas – or rather, to forward the claim of one or two other areas, notably the North East. Dave Harker writes, in this volume as elsewhere, from that perspective. But in the absence of any other evidence or sustained research to demonstrate generative power or a capacity to sustain its own separate culture from any other area, it would seem that the unanimous conviction of performers and managers that they must go to London to find the headquarters and the driving force of music hall must be endorsed by our work. In the companion volume to this, which draws more material from regional studies, Jeremy Crump concludes from his investigation of Leicester that 'music hall, far from being a focus of local and regional popular cultural expression, served as a conduit for the further permeation of national standards of performance and national imagery'. The music hall was, on the whole, metropolitan and proud of it, and so must we be too.

Origins/ myth

1   *Music In The Halls*

ANTHONY BENNETT

Music hall, itself central to late Victorian popular culture, had at its centre an endless procession of songs united above all by a common musical language. It is a paradox that this essentially ephemeral art is known and judged today by those of its products which have passed 'the test of time' – a process of mediation which inevitably distorts our view. This essay seeks to shed light on music-hall song less by reference to 'outstanding' songs or singers than to the evolution of certain common, and eventually dominant, features of style and structure. To this end it concentrates particularly on the 1860s, 70s, and 80s.[1] It also tries to account for the fact that music hall marked a radical break with earlier popular song – the first and arguably most important upheaval in an area where change had hitherto been gradual. I shall therefore spend some time dealing with the roots of music-hall song in the earlier nineteenth century, and focus on three conjunctions which together gave it its unique character: the conjunction of traditional with sophisticated musical culture; of group with solo singing; and of song features with those of the dance.

A definition is needed at the outset. I use the term 'popular' in a social, not a stylistic sense; but it is not, of course, a precise class term. Rather, what virtue it has lies in identifying a characteristic, or an interest, or a culture, as being distinct from that of the ruling class. It follows that the actual social group whose common interest, cultural experience or whatever is to be called 'popular' will vary not only according to historical period, or place, but also according to the phenomenon under consideration. Equally variable will be the relative predominance, either numerically or in terms of hegemony, of any one class or group among those thus associated. A predominant group, in either of these senses, will influence the distinguishing characteristics of any popular culture or repertory – and these characteristics in turn can tell us much about that group. The class composition of music-hall audiences is discussed elsewhere in this volume and its companion: it varied, and some coincidence of working-class and petit-bourgeois musical experience is clearly indicated (extending indeed to other groups in some of the metropolitan halls). But the numerical predominance (at least) of the working class does not seem to be in doubt.[2] I therefore take the appropriate nineteenth-century popular musical repertory within which to consider the phenomenon of music-hall song to be that delimited by working-class musical experience in its manifold varieties and responsive to working-class taste; and use the word 'popular' in cognate senses throughout.

A qualification is also needed. I refer almost exclusively to London – a decision dictated by the evidence available to me in any quantity, and by the belief that limited reference to any other centre or region would do it little service, and tell us nothing about any overall contrast between London and the provinces. It is possible that future research will reveal a significantly different musical style prevailing in provincial halls, but at present it seems unlikely.

The Roots of Music-Hall Song

Song in the first half of the nineteenth century, unrivalled either by literature or by any form of regularly organized entertainment, must have been at least as vital an element of popular culture as it is today. Moreover, it was as heterogeneous as it was lively, the origins of songs current at this time varying as widely as their subject matter and style. If we examine the most representative sources of information available – the countless thousands of halfpenny broadsides and cheap song-books produced all over the country, by which the words (but scarcely ever the music) of these songs were transmitted in print – we see 'traditional' ballads rubbing shoulders with theatrical airs, lyrics of the drawing-room with rough-hewn songs of topical humour, and so forth. Old favourites, traditional or otherwise, persisted beside newly composed texts, but the constant proliferation of the new cannot fail to claim our attention, as presumably it claimed that of contemporaries.

In the music of these songs, however, the importance of the old is immeasurably greater. Late eighteenth-century composers are as well represented in the tune repertory of popular song up to the mid nineteenth century as any contemporary composers, while a topical song might be written to a traditional tune at least a century old, often with the appropriate tune title given above the words. In fact the explosive vitality of this burgeoning song culture was confined almost entirely to its texts. In terms of new music it had virtually no life of its own, and the reasons are not hard to see. While the texts of songs were available in print to the popular market, their tunes had still to be transmitted orally, and the age-old practice of writing new words to existing tunes inevitably continued.

Thus popular song remained caught between two interdependent musical cultures. On the one hand was the oral tradition, now fast dessicating and apparently lacking either the vitality or perhaps more simply the time, in the few decades under consideration, to generate any significantly new material. On the other hand was the now dominant language evolved over centuries by professional composers. Specifically, a long line of English song composers, running from Purcell through such eighteenth-century figures as Leveridge, Hook, Shield and Charles Dibdin, to the composer-cum-arranger William Reeve active around the turn of the nineteenth century, had contributed many tunes to this popular culture. Not that they, nor contemporary composers such as Jonathan Blewitt or Henry Bishop, wrote directly for the popular market, which lacked any way of rewarding them. Their income was derived primarily from the theatre, and their tunes were taken second-hand, with or without the addition of new words, into popular consciousness. But the infiltration of composed music had gone on long and steadily enough to have produced an irreversible shift in the centre of gravity of that consciousness, away from a tradition (the remnants of which were so highly prized by the 'folk song' collectors of our own century) based on purely melodic, modal thinking, towards a reliance on harmonically conceived structures. The harmonies underpinning these structures were limited, and the melodic and rhythmic gestures which they governed had an equally restricted expressive range, largely because English musical theatre had always resisted the deliberately dramatic style of Italian opera in favour of a simple lyricism, and from *The Beggar's Opera* (1728) onwards, had itself been happy to draw on traditional material. The supremacy of this lyrical style is emphasized by the flourishing of essentially comic one-man-shows, given by performers such as Charles Dibdin, John Collins and John Bannister, which filled theatres around 1800: the songs, around which such shows were loosely structured, needed little drama or passion.

While many songs thus originated in the world of the professional solo singer, their place in everyday life was obviously very different – spontaneous, informal and even (when a tune was hummed or whistled for personal pleasure) unconscious. Nevertheless, music has always been essentially a social activity, and had we no other evidence, the existence of a thriving song-publishing industry would suggest that the occasions for singing were not entirely casual. In fact the keyword to describe this whole song culture seems to be 'harmony'. Countless cheap song-books have 'harmony' or 'harmonic' on their title pages. This cannot be taken literally in the musical sense, for there is no evidence to suggest that harmonization was practised at all commonly (glee singing in three or four parts is only marginal to this culture). Rather the expression is a happily combined musical and social one, which we might best render 'convivial singing': it encompasses both unison 'choral' singing and solo singing by one member of a group to the others, while the many songs with choruses obviously combine both modes.

This convival singing seems to have taken place above all in harmonic 'clubs' or 'meetings' in tavern rooms, where each participant entertained his friends in turn (we must assume it was overwhemingly a male activity). Tavern music of this sort has, of course, long been recognized as one of the principal antecedents of the music hall, though in this connection attention has inevitably been concentrated on the best-known West End establishments, such as the song-and-supper rooms catering for the relatively (and sometimes extremely) affluent, where, during the 1830s and 40s, the gradual emergence of the professional or semi-professional popular singer can first be observed. So it is worth stressing both the continuing importance of group singing – music was still largely a participatory experience – and the wide social spectrum of this convivial activity. Thackeray (whose list need not be doubted despite its fictional context) numbered country tradesmen and farmers, in London for their business ... squads of young apprentices and assistants ... rakish young medical students ... university bucks ... handsome young guardsmen, and florid bucks from the St. James's Street Clubs; nay, senators ... and even members of the House of Peers[3]

among those frequenting the 'Fielding's Head', generally reckoned to be based on the fashionable Cyder Cellars in Maiden Lane. The social span of Thackeray's list is large, and yet represents the upper part of the spectrum. Many more establishments catered for working-class customers, those who, as Dickens put it

in the daytime, wear aprons and paper caps ... [and who enjoy] an alternation of music and chat and smoke; they do not pay for the music, but regard it as a kind of bonus – a something given in by the capital landlord.[4]

The evidence of songs printed in London and elsewhere points to a huge central repertory common to all these classes; and if this is true of songs, it must mean that an even greater proportion of tunes was held in common: a national repertory rather than a popular one.

If this outstanding fact about early nineteenth-century popular music – that it simply had no style of its own – can be partly explained, as suggested above, by the prevailing conditions of composition and publication, the complementary explanation is to be found in the conditions under which the songs were sung, heard and thus perceived. The harmonic meeting may have provided a location for the enjoyment of song, but the main function of the singing was to contribute to the convivial atmosphere. The songs themselves, moreover, were not products of the institution but common property, brought in by the participants themselves from outside. When music was provided by the establishments it was merely, to begin with at least, a 'bonus'. Before any feeling could arise that popular song had an identity of its own, requiring and indeed deserving its own musical style, a double differentiation had to take place: song itself had to be perceived as a distinct area of popular culture, and that culture as a whole had to be differentiated in a positive and even exclusive way within the national culture. Only gradually did the new relationship between singer, song and audience brought about by the rise of the professional popular singer, together with the focusing of that relationship within the self-contained and self-conscious milieu of the music hall, enable each of these conditions to be met.

It is not surprising therefore that the repertory of the first generation of music-hall singers – or rather the generation of singers who span the development from tavern and song-and-supper rooms to music hall proper in the mid century – continues this reliance on pre-existing melodies. The songs of W. G. Ross, Sam Cowell, J. W. Sharp and their contemporaries in fact use old tunes in four different ways.

Firstly, these men simply continued to sing old songs. Thus, for example, Sam Cowell could still sing in the 1850s (and as an adult song) *A Frog he would a Wooing go*,[5] originally popularized by the clowns Grimaldi and Liston in the first decade of the century. Secondly, they continued to set new words to old tunes: for example, the much-used tune of *A Frog he would a Wooing go* carried another of Cowell's songs *Widow Glib and Sir Steeple*, with words by George Daniel.[6] The process was cumulative. Cowell's repertory included a comic version of the Hamlet story, beginning 'A Hero's Life I sing', originally written at the beginning of the century by Theodore Hook and sung by such comedians as John Fawcett and John Bannister.[7] The tune to which Hook's song was set was *Bobbing Joan* or *The Rakes of Stony Batter*,[8] which had been popular in the eighteenth century and continued under a bewildering variety of names to carry songs which were current alongside Hook's, some even as late as Cowell's singing of it. Cowell's tune, incidentally, substitutes (or perhaps restores) duple in place of Bannister's triple time, and by doing so dispenses with the many pauses necessary in Bannister's version.

Thirdly (continuing an established nineteenth-century practice), a number of existing tunes might be strung together as a medley, carrying a more-or-less continuous narrative. Thus Cowell's comic version of the 'Gothic' ballad *Alonzo the Brave and the Fair Imogine*[9] calls for 11 tunes drawn from varied sources, including Italian opera (Bellini's *La Sonnambula*), blackface minstrel songs (*Lucy Long*), and tradition, both English and Irish. The traditional Irish tune well known through Thomas Moore's song *Believe me if all those Endearing Young Charms* serves as an introduction to the medley, and recurs halfway through. There are declamatory passages (marked 'recitative') at the 'dramatic' moments, as when Alonzo's ghost arrives to claim his unfaithful lover at her wedding, which emphasize the structural similarities between a song of this type (despite its reliance on borrowed material) and the contemporary melodramatic songs ('sung monologues' would be a more accurate term) ultimately inspired by the operatic *scena* and sung with great success to middle-class audiences by Henry Russell. *Alonzo* is, in part at least, a parody of such melodramatic songs. But even as a vehicle for parody the Russell-type monologue never took root in the music hall, and the Cowell medley (despite the opportunities for humour it offered not only in the telling of the narrative, but in references to words and phrases associated with the tunes being used) marked the end of a tradition rather than the starting point of a music-hall genre.

Alonzo is interesting, however, since it illustrates also the fourth method of relating new songs to old – comic reworking, which in the mid century took on a particular, though short-lived, importance. Not only is the *Alonzo* tale as a whole reworked, but the song *Billy Taylor*, which provides the final tune in the medley, was itself a comic version, popularized by J. W. Sharp and by Cowell himself, of the traditional ballad *William Taylor*. It functions here, therefore, as a sort of signature tune, to which Cowell can sing a typically comic 'moral' and conclude with a 'Tiddy iddy tol lol lol' refrain.

Leaving aside the unique case of *Villikins and his Dinah* (originally a theatrical parody of street song taken up by Cowell and others), the most celebrated example of reworking is W. G. Ross's *Sam Hall*, which he sang at the Cyder Cellars and elsewhere in the 1840s and 50s. The origins of the traditional ballad

Jack Hall on which Ross based his song, and which belongs to the long-established and grizzly genre of the hanging ballad, have been traced back as far as the beginning of the eighteenth century (it is not possible to say which, if any, of the surviving tunes associated with the ballad Ross used).[10] The novelty of his version came from the harshness of the language and delivery, in particular of his 'Damn yer eyes' refrain. This refrain bears thinking about. It is written specifically for theatrical delivery, indeed for shock effect. Popular songs had frequently had a short refrain, but its function was quite different. Structurally it gave a sense of balance; and beyond that – since it was normally associated with the tune rather than with a particular set of words – a sense of stability. Its effect was for the singer at least as much as for any listeners, and significantly it was very often nonsense, though nonsense with a distinctive rhythm: 'Derry down, down, down derry down' or 'Rumpti iddity ido'. To the extent that the function of the professional singer changed from sharing a song with an audience to delivering it in character, as Ross did, and as new tunes replaced the old, the nonsense refrain disappeared. Music-hall songs rarely have them, although there may be a nonsense element in the ubiquitous chorus.

Sam Cowell's importance during this transitional period is attested by the collection already cited, *120 Comic Songs sung by Sam Cowell*, which shows also the breadth of his repertory[11] – overwhelmingly made up of songs which pre-date his singing of them and use old, even eighteenth-century, tunes. Even in the minority of tunes which are new, such as Cowell's own for *The Ratcatcher's Daughter*, no new style is evident. The important thing (for contemporary buyers as well as for our understanding of the emergence of music-hall song) is that they were all associated to some extent with Cowell: it was around individual singers and their acts that the music-hall song, with its new and distinctive style, was finally to crystallize. The fact that the collection could be reprinted in 1876, however, is a reminder that even as late as this the new type of song had achieved no monopoly on taste.[12]

Orchestras and Composers

Before the new style could finally take root, music hall had to meet two further conditions: it had to support orchestras which could act both as accompaniment and foil to the solo voice; and it had to support song writers, specifically composers, who would produce the new material in sufficient quantity.

Accompaniment in the earliest halls was by piano, as it had been in the taverns which 'supplied' music and in the song-and-supper rooms (although at least one of the latter, Evans's, had a harmonium too, a feature found also in the Canterbury Hall).[13] Dickens reports in fact that 'the first attempt to introduce a piano at Evans's created quite a revolution among the old habitués' accustomed to unaccompanied singing, and implies that it was the lower-class taverns which first introduced accompaniments.[14] If he is right in stating further that these earliest pianists, 'broken-down music masters … blind or nearly blind' played only by ear, there was another barrier to the adoption of new music. In time, more competent pianists appeared. (An interesting aspect of this development is that, as even the smaller halls grew in respectability, it became common to employ women pianists – perhaps failures, in the eyes of comtemporaries, in the marriage market for which they had been groomed, but able to sight-read music.) With sight-reading a skill that could be reckoned on, the way was cleared for new music.

At the same time, more and more halls built up an orchestra around the nucleus of the piano, with the pianist, or the first violinist, acting as musical director and perhaps arranger. Inevitably these orchestras (whose members might earn about 25 shillings per week) varied considerably in size. By the late 1870s at least, a large and flourishing hall, whether in London or the provinces, might have a band of about 25 members.[15] At the other extreme (and far more commonly), a visiting singer could probably reckon on a band of five to play his or her accompaniments. (Singers, incidentally, would take the band parts of their songs around with them: the songs were literally as well as legally their property.)

From 'musicians wanted' adverts in trade journals such as *The Era*, it is clear that versatility was at a premium, and that in the smallest halls, as in touring companies, the same person might even be called upon both to play and sing. From these adverts as well as from a handful of articles and published letters, it is possible to deduce that the 'basic' combination of instruments consisted of two violins, flute, cornet and double bass, plus a piano which could fill out the harmony. A letter in *The Era* (28 September 1879) giving practical advice on the scoring of songs shows how this basic texture could be elaborated by the addition of colouristic or decorative parts according to available resources. The 'lowest style', says the writer,

> is perhaps that ... in which, with seven or eight nominal "parts" there are really only three (two trebles and a bass), the rest being *unison*.[16]

Thus the flute doubles the first violin, the cornet the second violin, the clarinet the cornet, etc. While scorning this method, the writer cautions that in more imaginative scoring, all 'cues' should be put in the first violin copy:

> the leader will no doubt play as required those notes, whether for oboe, clarionet, corno-Inglese or what not. In scoring for music hall, however, it is best to write real-parts for only two violins, flute, cornet and bass, with supplemental parts for clarionet and trombone. Side-drum and triangle may be added, if wanted, and the piano score should supply chords. All such effects as *obbligato* parts for viola or violoncello should be avoided.

This letter was one of a revealing series dealing with the problems experienced by both singers and composers at the hands of music-hall orchestras. In another (5 October 1879) a composer writing from Wigan complains:

> Not long ago I went into a large music hall in an adjoining city to hear a lady sing some pretty songs of my scoring. She was down for the first turn after a grand operatic selection, in which the orchestra numbered about twenty-five. The

selection finished, the gentlemen gradually disappeared until only five were left. The parts I had so carefully written for cello, clarionet, second cornet, trombone, etc. were unplayed. On my way round to the stage-door ... I met one or two of the orchestra just rolling into a public-house, while the remainder evidently found more entertainment in a game of "Nap" in the bandroom than in doing their business.

Other letters stress that singers should always carry a complete set of at least 10 parts – even though players will not always be available:

Many singers have only five parts, and at ... large halls the gentlemen of the orchestra will kindly "vamp" for them; but it cannot be expected that the music will then sound so well ...[17]

From these and other sources we can deduce several things besides the (variable) constitution of the bands: that discipline was often lax; that some degree of improvisation, from the pianist or other players, could be expected when necessary; that some music-hall composers at least had a commitment to their works beyond a merely financial one; and that relatively sophisticated music – like the 'grand operatic selection' mentioned above – had its place in the halls. The last point is worth emphasizing, since we risk thinking of music-hall singing purely in terms of comic songs especially written for the halls. A review in *The Era* of an evening at the Canterbury Hall in 1890 includes a reminder that this is only part of the picture:

Miss Lydia Yeaman's ballads are accompanied on the grand pianoforte by Mr. Frederick J. Titus, and it is pleasant to hear the enthusiastic reception accorded to this cultivated vocalist by an audience generally supposed to be impatient of sentimental singers.

'Sentimental' and 'serio-comic' vocalists had their place beside purely comic turns, as did 'refined' quartet singing, sometimes by family groups.

Nevertheless, from the outset it was the comic singers who epitomized music hall, and essential to their acts was the projection of an assumed character, or range of characters. Every singer, aspiring or established, therefore needed a body of songs recognizably their own. At the same time the stereotyping of these assumed roles – swell, coster or whatever – and of the situations depicted in the songs, precluded the need for any great differentiation of individual songs either by subject matter or style. As music hall became established as the new and dominant mode of popular entertainment, what mattered more, as argued above, was *overall* novelty of style.

A minority of singers wrote their own lyrics, and a handful – most notable among them Harry Clifton – their own tunes as well; but the majority depended on a new breed of lyricists and composers which arose to meet the demand. These men generally lacked a formal musical training. Felix McGlennon, for example, a Scot who came to London via Manchester, where he maintained a publishing business issuing penny song-books, taught himself to compose:

I used to hum a tune and then strum it on a child's dulcimer, painfully seeking out the names of the notes. Then ... find a piece of music that ran to the same metre, and with that for my model ... divide my 'composition' into bars. Gradually I acquired a rudimentary knowledge of music, and substituted the piano for the dulcimer ... I can with its aid commit my melodies to paper, and that is all I need.[18]

Joseph Tabrar, while of working-class origin, had the advantage of having been a choirboy, singing at Evans's as well as at the Italian church in Hatton Garden. Later, teaching himself to play any instrument he could lay hands on, he worked his way through various music-hall jobs, on and off-stage, to become a musical director and, eventually, a freelance song writer and arranger.

Both Tabrar and McGlennon (like G. W. Hunt, the first to make a name as a song writer for the halls in the 1860s and 70s) wrote lyrics as well as tunes, but more commonly a song was the result of a partnership, and in many cases such as McGlennon's, where the composer had little or no musical training, the song would then be arranged by a third hand. A bargain might be struck directly with a publisher, but in most cases the song would be offered to a singer (the chances of eventual publication with royalties then depending on the song's success on stage). In this case it was rare for the writer or composer to be able to dictate the terms of the bargain: around 1880 the average rate for a song was one guinea, and far lower sums were common. An attempt in the 1880s to improve the position of lyricists and composers by unionization was only partially successful, and it remained necessary, if a song writer was to survive, to produce and sell songs in prodigious numbers. Thus the economics of song writing demanded a technique of mass production just at the time when the stereotyping of songs and the emphasis on a recognizable music-hall style permitted it.

The numbers of songs produced by some writers were indeed staggering. G. W. Hunt claimed, when interviewed by *The Era* in 1894, to have written over 7,000 songs during the previous 30 years. Felix McGlennon claimed in the same series of interviews to have written at least 4,000, and Joseph Tabrar no less than 17,000 – words, music and band parts:

no – let's be accurate, not [band parts] for the whole 17,000. Here are 24 manuscript books, 300 songs in each ... but ... in my old days I have sat in the York for a whole day and written 30 songs. I have sold a song for as little as a shilling ...[19]

It is clear that originality was of little consequence. Tabrar adds, with some irony:

Think of a catchy refrain. Think of the d——d silliest words that will rhyme anyhow. Think of a haunting pretty melody — and there you are. The fortune of your publisher is made ...

McGlennon explained that his aim had always been to match the taste of the moment, and went so far as to call his own songs rubbish:

> the main thing is catchiness. I will sacrifice everything – rhyme, reason, sense, sentiment, to catchiness. There is, let me tell you, a great art in making rubbish acceptable.

> ... But as to mere imitation, why, one must give and take. If a rowdy song takes the ear of the public, and rowdy songs set in, why, I must needs write them. [The] music hall songs of all time run in clear grooves – drinking songs, flirting songs, mother-in-law songs and so forth ...[20]

The approach to song writing which emerges from these interviews is clearly geared to mass production—the assembling of recognized formulae to meet the known needs of a given genre and to produce effects both predictable and easily assimilated. And this applies not only to the lyrics, which had been written in much the same way by the old broadside writers in the first attempt to mass-produce popular song, but now to the music also. Because popular music today is so firmly tied to these techniques of mass production it is something of a shock to realize that the popular was in fact the last area of musical composition to which they were applied. (The throwing together of eighteenth-century operas, with their highly stylized numbers, is perhaps the clearest example of the earlier application of these techniques in 'art' music.) Inevitably such techniques act first as a unifying, and subsequently as a conservative factor in the development of a style. It remains to pinpoint the principal features of the style which emerged in the 1860s and 70s, coalesced in the 1880s, and without fundamental change continued dominant into the present century.

The Development of the Style

The most obvious models, for a style which would be distinct both from earlier popular song and contemporary 'serious' ballads, lay in dance music. Not only did its essential gaiety match the mood of the halls, but it was familiar and, being the most rigidly patterned of all genres, it was simple to reproduce. The two main dances of the later nineteenth century, the waltz and the polka, provided the basis for countless songs, and even when the *tempo* demanded by the words makes these models unsuitable, the regularity and simplicity of rhythm characteristic of dance music is still present. The chorus of G. W. Hunt's *The Custom of the Country*, with its dotted rhythms in the second half of the bar and its use of syncopation, provides a typical example of polka rhythm (Ex. 1).[21]

Ex 1: The Custom of the Country [1876]

It's a cus-tom of the country, A cus-tom of the country

Reproduced by permission of Ascherberg, Hopwood and Crew Ltd.

It is common for the chorus to emphasize the dance elements in this way, or to bring them into the song even if they have not previously appeared in it, as one means of differentiating itself from the solo stanza. Ultimately this distinction, and the relative importance of the chorus which it both reflects and heightens, became the most pervading characteristic of music-hall song. In the 1860s and 70s the distinction can be seen emerging to varying degrees, and brought about in various ways. At one extreme are choruses which merely repeat the music of the stanza, or a section of it, as in Hunt's *Did You Ever Go to Hampstead in a Van?* [1876]. The only significant difference between the 16–bar chorus and the first 16 bars of the stanza is that the chorus is sung twice in a row, the second time *fortissimo*; since the stanza has only one contrasting (16–bar) section, the resulting *ABAA* structure runs a high risk of tedium over the song's five stanzas, especially since the brief orchestral interlude is a close variant of the *A* section. A song from the fringes of the music-hall tradition, Harry Clifton's *Polly Perkins of Paddington Green* [1864] shows even less concern for variety. The chorus simply reproduces the second 8 bars of the stanza, giving, since it is itself repeated, an *ABBB* form. Luckily the tune is a very good one, which still survives today, though not at its original mock-tragic *tempo* 'Maestoso Pomposo'.

In some songs, like Hunt's *The German Band* [1865], the chorus is given its own tune but keeps the rhythmic characteristics and general melodic style of the stanza. In others there is a change of metre for the chorus, often, as mentioned above, to a polka or waltz, but not always: *Up in a Balloon*, one of the many songs written by Hunt for George Leybourne, has a swinging quality throughout, gentle in the anecdotal 6/8 stanza, and sharpened into a dotted rhythm as the audience joins in with the gleeful 2/4 chorus (Ex. 2).[22]

Ex 2: Up in a Balloon [1868]

There is no mistaking the effect: the audience's entry is, musically, the high point of the song. Incidentally this song, like many of Hunt's, spawned not only a female version, sung by Nellie Power, but at least one broadside parody, *Up in a Back Room:* at this transitional stage for popular song it was, ironically, the new material coming out of the halls which fed '... the old school of burlesque writers, who found it very handy to annex ... [Hunt's] melodies and refrains, of course by way of making game of them – a very cheap and effective kind of humour.'[23] Some songs which do not change metre for the refrain nevertheless change the predominant rhythmic pattern, and may call also for a change of *tempo*. This may be explicit (as in Hunt's *Gone to Smash* [1876], in 3/8 throughout but marked 'Not too slow' for the stanza and '*tempo di valse*' for the chorus) or simply implicit in the rhythmic patterns used: Leybourne's celebrated *Champagne Charlie* (composed not by Hunt but by Alfred Lee) seems to require a reduction in *tempo* to preserve its swagger through the fanfare-like triads of the chorus (Ex. 3).[24]

Ex 3: Champagne Charlie [1867]

The fecundity of the early music-hall composers extended only to their melodic writing: their harmonic language was rudimentary and bears no comparison with that of, say, the contemporary 'parlour' ballad. Even such a fluid tune as Clifton's for *The Railway Belle* [1865] is based on only three chords. Tonal range is correspondingly narrow. Some songs, like *Polly Perkins*, never leave the tonic key. Most, however, modulate briefly in the second part of the stanza, usually to the dominant. This happens, for example, in *Did You Ever Go to Hampstead in a Van?* where the *B* section provides the only tonal relief from G major: the change of key is secured by some straightforward chromaticism (this functional use of chromaticism is typical of Hunt who rarely uses chromaticism decoratively), but even so the final D major chord sounds like nothing other than a dominant preparation for the chorus. This is of course what Hunt intends, giving an increase in tension at this point which is enhanced as usual by a pause. In such cases, when the chord preceding the chorus is a dominant, it is also the bar where a chromatic cliché such as that in *Champagne Charlie* is liable to intrude on an otherwise diatonic melody. Even in the early 1880s, however, the final chord of the stanza is more often a tonic. Only in the middle of the decade is there a decisive shift towards these expectant dominant lead-ins to the chorus, which pull the song's centre of gravity to the moment when the audience joins in, re-asserting once and for all the claim on music hall of communal singing. We may pause to regret in passing, however, that, the winning formula found, such imaginative transitions from stanza to chorus as that in *I'm Getting a Big Boy Now* – perfectly attuned to the misplaced maternal solicitude which is the starting point of this song sung by the decidedly large Herbert Campbell – were virtually precluded (Ex. 4).[25]

A gradual increase in chromaticism, both harmonic and melodic, seems to go hand-in-hand with this leaning towards and dominant preparation for the cadence, so that as the decade progresses a dwindling minority of conservative songs stands out, lacking both features. Allied in turn to the greater use of chromatic harmony is an expansion of tonal range, helping to create variety in stanzas

Ex 4: *I'm Getting a Big Boy Now* [1880]

I'm Getting a Big Boy Now by Henry Nicholls & Oscar Barrett, © 1880 Francis Day & Hunter Ltd., reproduced by permission of EMI.

which tend to be considerably longer than those of earlier popular songs. Excursions to related minor keys become as important as those to the dominant, and are likely to occur briefly in the chorus as well as in the stanza.[26] All this adds up to the assimilation by music-hall composers of the language of the contemporary sentimental 'parlour' ballad, which was in its turn derived from harmonic techniques found earlier in the century in 'art' music such as Italian opera and German lied.

That sentimental ballad and music-hall song now shared so many of the same techniques, and even some of the same formulae, in fact makes it easier to see the essential differences between them, both in structure and intent. The best examples of the sentimental ballad (and we should remember that it too was a mass-produced genre) aim to express their texts with the maximum emotional impact: to this end each phrase is invested with its own expressive weight, and repetition of phrases tends to be avoided. (There may well be, on the other hand, repetition of words within a phrase, and likewise prolongation of syllables, aimed in some cases at disturbing the short-term symmetry.) Thematic construction tends to be loose, rhythm deliberately varied, and expressive gestures prodigally squandered. In a word, the form is discursive. The typical music-hall song, by contrast, makes no such attempt to present a series of differentiated moments. Its balanced phrases are built on regular rhythms, and often a single short motif will characterize the entire stanza. The song unfolds at a rate approximating to that of normal speech, and repetition of words is uncommon. It is normal, however, for at least one musical phrase (most often the first) to recur at least once. Its form is thus economical and, to borrow Brecht's and Weill's term, gestic—the *gestus* or essential attitude of the music being perceived on the level of the stanza as a whole (the chorus may or may not present a contrast) rather than that of the individual lines or phrases.

This very different approach arises partly from the heavy influence of dance music with its regular, repetitive patterns, but equally it stems from the comic function of the songs. When an overtly sentimental mood is introduced we know it will soon be punctured; and revealingly, it is the gestures of the parlour ballad which are drawn upon to inflate the mood in the first place. Thus, encouraged to 'forgive and forget' in J. H. Lester's song of that name, the audience joins in a chorus which duly combines syrupy chromaticism with some sanctimonious diatonic progressions (Ex. 5: note particularly the use of the subdominant in bar 4). Subsequent stanzas make the motto seem less and less appropriate.

Ex 5: Forgive and Forget [1887]

Forgive and Forget by J. H. Lester & Sam Torr, © 1887 Francis Day & Hunter Ltd., reproduced by permission of EMI.

Joseph Tabrar, likewise responsible for both words and music in his *Goodbye, Goodbye, Goodbye*, pulls out all the stops to give a full-scale parody of sentimental song (Ex. 6). Here the deflation comes at what should be the high points of the stanza, with the redundant repetition which extends the first phrase into a ninth and tenth bar, and at the bathetic final cadence; the orchestra, rushing through *For He's a Jolly Good Fellow* immediately afterwards, simply reinforces the absurdity.

In adopting Brecht's and Weill's term 'gestic', I take 'essential attitude' (attitude in both its English senses, of body and mind) to be the sense running most consistently through the various uses each made of the word *gestus*.[27]

Ex 6: Goodbye, Goodbye, Goodbye [1887]

hear her   say, "Good - bye, my boy, good - bye",   I   fan   -   cy I   can

hear her   say, "Tra, la,   la,   Bon soir,   By - by!"_____

(There are obvious parallels with an earlier attempt to theorize the relation of music and words in the theatre, the eighteenth-century concept of *affekt* in opera.) If we are to seek 'meaning' in the music of the halls, then such an approach, rooted in the performing arts, would seem more promising than an attempt to adapt, say, semiotic techniques from linguistic and literary theory. But whereas in Western drama the primary relationship within which attitudes are to be displayed is that between characters on stage, in music hall it was between performer and audience, with the 'character' in a pivotal position. Music was one means of articulating the attitude, but, of course, only one. In any attempt to identify gestic elements within the music of a song (as I shall now do with examples from a single category, the swell song), we must bear in mind that the printed, or even recorded, music represents only a fraction of the whole; and that no analysis can presume to bridge the gap between the perceptions of a twentieth-century observer and those of a nineteenth-century audience – let alone the intentions of a nineteenth-century composer (it may be noted that Tabrar for example, in his prescription for a successful song quoted above, does not bother to mention suiting the music to the words).

The swell song, perhaps the one really new type of song pioneered in the halls, naturally requires a degree of swagger, even aggression. Duple time is an obvious response from a composer, as in *Champagne Charlie*, where the strutting stanza and march-like chorus ideally capture the arrogance of the character. But the same characteristics can be imposed on waltz time. Leybourne also sang, for example, Tabrar's *I Say Cabby* (Ex. 7) where the arrogance comes from a combination of repeated notes, stepwise (sometimes chromatic) movement, and falling intervals emphasized by a short-long rhythm – a favourite music-hall device.

The Marquis of Camberwell Green (Ex. 8), a butcher's assistant who contrives to act the swell by night, was one of T. W. Barrett's characters. The tune by E. R.

Ex 7: I Say Cabby [1882]

Shrosberry runs on similar lines to *I Say Cabby*, but instead of repeated notes, it emphasizes smooth, self-assured lines which plough downwards to the cadences; and where Tabrar goes into a (slightly faster?) 6/8 for his chorus, Shrosberry keeps to waltz time, making good use of swinging, across-the-bar syncopations which the dance allows.

Ex 8: The Marquis of Camberwell [1884]

The Marquis of Camberwell Green by H. Boden & Ed. R. Shrosberry, © 1884 Francis Day & Hunter Ltd., reproduced by permission of EMI.

The true swell, even if like the Marquis his means were slender, was invulnerable, a quality captured in these smooth, confident lines which also allow the singer to produce a full-bodied *legato* tone. But a host of related figures – broken-down, ageing or adolescent 'swells' and the like – invited some degree of mockery. G. W. Hunter took on such a role as *The Bald Headed Swell* [1888], whose sweetheart is 'mashed on' (infatuated with) a rival from real life, Tommy Barrett in fact. The melodic line gets an injection of pathos from chromatic inflections and leaps of up to a sixth, while a 'slow waltz' takes the place of a

Ex 9: The Masher King [1884]

Reproduced by permission of Ascherberg, Hopwood and Crew Ltd.

normal swinging waltz in the chorus. Edward Jonghmans' tune for *The Masher King* (Ex. 9)[28] is in a slightly faster triple time, smooth in rhythm but incorporating a series of wide leaps.

Historically this disjunct style is not vocal at all but instrumental; it makes almost inevitable a *non-legato* delivery from the singer which here distinguishes the preposterous young dandy from the all-conquering heavy swell. Puffed-up youngsters are more severely pilloried in *The Boy about Town* (Ex. 10), where W. G. Eaton's chorus moves from waltz time into 4/4, and emphasizes the jumps in the melody by jerky dotted rhythms.

Ex 10: The Boy about Town [1885]

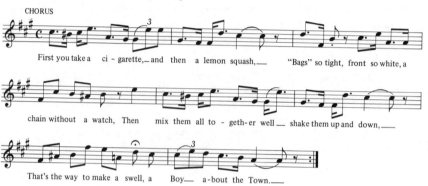

The Boy about Town by W. Eaton & E. V. Page, © 1885 Francis Day & Hunter Ltd., reproduced by permission of EMI.

Such dotted rhythms will subvert any attempt at elegance, but they may simultaneously convey more. In *No More up at Covent Garden Market*, a song which combines the coster and swell genres (Ex. 11),[29] they smack of jaunty triumph: the newly rich coster may lack the style of the true swell, but never mind, the money will do:

Ex 11: No More up at Covent Garden Market [1894]

It would be wrong to suppose that every song sought to depict character or situation in this way. For one thing, the old parody technique still had its uses, seen for example in *The Broken Down Masher*, which re-uses the tune of *The Masher King* note for note. But the devices were available. They could even perform a double function, as in *Knocked 'Em in the Old Kent Road* where the singer tells how he and his wife, in a burlesque of the coster-into-swell situation, drove out in their newly inherited donkey cart, entertaining the neighbours if not impressing them. The tune, written under the pseudonym Charles Ingle by Auguste Chevalier, brother of the song's author and singer Albert Chevalier, alternates jerky dotted rhythms like those of Ex. 11 with almost static bars of minims (Ex. 12),[30] capturing both the infectious hilarity of the scene and its ridiculousness; at the same time it captures graphically the stop-go progress of the cart. An orchestral link between stanzas to allow for comic 'business' manages to condense this stop-go motion into four notes, with an early use of tango rhythm.

Ex 12: Wotcher (Knocked 'Em in the Old Kent Road) [1891]

Wotcher (Knocked 'Em in the Old Kent Road) by Charles Ingle & Albert Chevalier, © 1891 Reynolds Music, reproduced by permission of EMI.

Clearly there is no hint of local colour in this tango rhythm (the only dance used in that way was the jig, which, perhaps in a minor key and with the suggestion of a drone, characterized 'Irish' songs). When borrowed metres other than the staple polka and waltz made an occasional contribution it was rather to stamp the mood. When Rosie Heath sang *She's the Only Girl I Love* [1886] it was to a tune marked *Tempo di Gavotte* – not a true gavotte but with an appropriate quaint poise. Similarly, Florrie Robina sang *Prince Tiptoe* [1886] to a borrowed tune, Celian Kottaun's *Beatrice Gavotte*, which turns out to be a schottische, or kind of slow polka. In both cases, but particularly in Heath's song, the *tempo*, slow enough to avoid the 'swing' of polka or waltz, suggests a rather gentler male impersonation than we generally expect from that genre. A more typical 'manly vigour' is found in the march rhythm of songs like Jonghmans' *Shoulder to Shoulder* [1882] – a straight piece of jingoism sung by Bessie Bonehill.

A march pattern divorced from any military context supplies the framework for Felix McGlennons's *The Bachelors' Club* (Ex. 13).[31] It is clear from the irregular metric pattern of the lyrics that they were written after the tune, or at least with the rhythm of a model fixed in McGlennon's mind – a compositional process which he came close to describing in his interview with *The Era*.

Boys, to a club I belong
And it's delightful, so delightful.
Round goes the wine and the song
And it's delightful, boys!

And as the liquors disappear
The ruby wine each heart will cheer.
We smoke and drink till dawn is near
This is our toast –

CHORUS

Tinkle, tinkle! let your glasses chink!
Bright and sparkling ruby we will drink,
Tinkle, tinkle, up my lads and bawl
Hip hip hurrah! and jolly good luck to us all!

The words are utterly trivial (although of some interest in showing that the harmonic club did not die with the coming of the halls), but thanks to the tensions skilfully built up and released in the music, the song goes off like a rocket. The slow rate of harmonic change characteristic of marches contributes to the effect, but most of all it comes from the way in which McGlennon draws out certain words (crucially the opening word of the first and third lines) over the bar-line, and follows them with a rush of monosyllables to the next point of *stasis*.

Ex 13: The Bachelors' Club [1895]

Reproduced by permission of Ascherberg, Hopwood and Crew Ltd.

This technique would be unthinkable without the continuing rum-ti-tum from the orchestra during the held notes. Whereas in pre-music-hall songs the voice itself had to supply a more or less regular beat, the presence of the orchestra to take over this function freed composers to explore more varied schemes. In particular, the band could echo the singer, setting up a rudimentary dialogue and allowing the voice to end phrases on a weak beat rather than a strong one (Ex. 14) or to bunch up words into short, snappy units (Ex. 15).

Also, in a formula which we now take for granted, the orchestra could provide introductions to songs, and links between stanzas (as in *Knocked 'Em in the Old Kent Road*) which set the stage 'business' within, or rather against, a framework of measured, musical time – a sure way of building up expectation.

I have concentrated on songs of the 1880s and earlier because the last decade of the century, while bringing perhaps the finest songs – and certainly those best known today – saw a confirmation and extension of the characteristics which

Ex 14: What a Blessing [1895]

What a Blessing by John Cooke, © 1885 Francis Day & Hunter Ltd., reproduced by permission of EMI.

Ex 15: Money [1885]

Money by A. West, © 1885 Francis Day & Hunter Ltd., reproduced by permission of EMI.

have been noted, rather than any new departures. This is most evident in the extension of chromaticism which, losing any specific structural or 'expressive' function, becomes a standard colouring of the melodic style. A second tendency is towards an increase in disjunct melodic lines, whose wide leaps likewise lose any specific significance. (These processes, which have parallels in 'art' music, can be considered inflationary ones, fuelled by the need to keep lines colourful and lively.) Both characteristics can be seen clearly in *If it Wasn't for the 'Ouses in Between*, with a tune by George Le Brunn, one of the most productive and successful composers of the 1890s (Ex. 16).[32]

Ex 16: If it Wasn't for the 'Ouses in Between [1894]

If it Wasn't for the 'Ouses in Between by George Le Brunn & Edgar Bateman, © 1894 Francis Day & Hunter Ltd., reproduced by permission of EMI.

Recordings exist which give some idea of how these songs of the 1890s were sung – or rather how the soloists sang them: audiences were not recorded. Gus Elen for example, who sang the above song,[33] had a knack of snatching a moment of falsetto before certain notes, thus increasing the jerkiness of the tune. This was a personal characteristic (which conceivably influenced Le Brunn's shaping of the melody): it is a style of rudimentary ornamentation familiar to us from the singing of some 'traditional' singers, and related to the sort of 'mordent' figure which finds notated expression both in grace-notes and as a triplet in Albert Chevalier's *The Future Mrs. 'Awkins* (Ex. 17).[34] It is significant that Chevalier not only wrote and sang this song, but composed it to suit his own manner of performance.

Recordings show too that, by the 1890s at least, the prevailing style of delivery was an informal, narrative one. With a basic rate of delivery approximately that

Ex 17: The Future Mrs. 'Awkins [1892]

of normal speech, singers could, by adopting a relaxed, flexible approach to rhythm (and in some cases, such as Elen's, to the pitches as well) virtually speak their way through the songs. This flexibility does not extend to the chorus, which tends to be sung rather faster, although this may simply result from the need to accommodate the recording process. It seems likely that this informal style of communication is related to a perceptible shift in the subject matter of the songs, away from the 'here come I' character piece towards a comedy of situation in which the character of the singer is, like the social context, taken for granted. Certainly this shift is accompanied by a decline in the use of polka rhythm with its insistent stress pattern; conversely the more relaxed waltz maintains or even extends its popularity.

While a genre which could still give rise to the concentrated if informal power of *My Old Man Said Follow the Van* on the one hand and the melodic fertility of *Lily of Laguna* on the other was clearly far from exhausted, the late music-hall song was in fact living on its capital. British popular song, having adapted early and successfully to the demands of music hall, was trapped within that institution's need to reproduce continually the established relationship between audience and solo performer. Thus the need to maintain the chorus as an integral part of songs prevented a development towards a genuinely popular blend of music and drama such as the Henry Russell type of monologue might have sparked off. That had to wait until the advent of cinema. And while dance music supplied formulae for countless songs (and while there might be some dancing on the stage), there was no question of *social* dancing in the halls. There was nothing, in fact, to force composers in the early years of this century to look beyond the style which had served them so well. When dance-based music from America swept the country around the time of the First World War, the style was quickly left isolated and antiquated. And as music hall itself finally crumbled under the impact of cinema, it could find no support in a musical language which was essentially Victorian.

2   Jones and the Working Girl: Class Marginality in Music-Hall Song 1860 – 1900

JANE TRAIES

The presence of the middle classes in music-hall audiences from an early date is now generally accepted.[1] Some halls, such as the Alhambra, had 'mixed' audiences as early as the 1860s.[2] Dagmar Höher has found evidence that audiences in several major cities contained 'the working class and those sections of the lower middle class (artisans, tradesmen and shopkeepers, as well as their assistants and clerks) who continued to share a common cultural context with them.'[3] [The geographical and economic separation of the new middle classes from the working class was a comparatively late phenomenon; in the 1890s mixed-class districts such as Islington and Clerkenwell in London were well provided with local halls catering for the demands of both working-class and lower-middle-class patrons.[4] The growth of the lower-middle-class music-hall audience has been seen as a reflection of a licensing policy which was pushing the halls in the direction of respectability.[5] It also reflects, quite simply, a demographic trend: the rapid increase in numbers of clerks and administrators from about 1870, many of whom, incidentally, came from working-class families.]

These modifications to the idea of music hall as a uniquely working-class entertainment must in turn challenge our assumptions about music-hall song. Höher refers to the 'long established stereotypes' which have distorted our perceptions of audience composition and behaviour. A similar set of distortions, which Vic Gammon has called the 'simple-minded notion' of Victorian song,[6] have conditioned our ideas about what was sung in the halls. In the model described by Gammon, the song-type 'music hall' equates only with the social group 'urban working class'. As well as masking (as he points out) the complex interrelatedness of music-hall song and other types such as 'parlour ballad' and 'folk song', this notion has also limited our idea of what is 'typical' in the content and attitudes of music-hall song. Hundreds, perhaps thousands of music-hall songs have survived, a few on record and many more in the form of song books and sheet music; yet there is a marked tendency to draw repeatedly on the same small handful of well-known songs. Thus early music hall is regularly characterised by reference to *Sam Hall* and *Villikins*, while *A Little of What You Fancy* is recognised as 'the keynote of music hall entertainment at the turn of the century'.[7] The Jingo song is invariably quoted in discussion of politics and propaganda; love and marriage are often dealt with by reference to *Trinity Church*. Probably the most thoroughly explored aspect of music hall has been as an expression of working-class culture, and so 'coster' songs are slightly better represented in the literature: *My Old Dutch* and *My Old Man Said Follow the Van* are closely followed by *Costermonger Joe* and *The 'Ouses In Between*. Obviously the songs which were most widely known in their own time and remain well known today are significant, and are likely to be typical, but there are always dangers inherent in a small sample, and one which tends to be late in date. More importantly, the concentration on a limited number of songs, particularly where they are not subjected to any detailed textual or structural analysis, tends to support rather than challenge prevailing notions about music hall's cultural place, and to simplify our ideas about it.

I recognise of course that the use of songs as historical evidence is fraught with controversy and that recent scholarship has, rightly, sought other kinds of source material for the formation of theory about the culture, politics and class attitudes of the halls. In renewing the claim of the songs themselves as evidence, I do not wish to sidestep the problematic nature of interpreting such material. Martin and Francis have identified this problem in relation to the photography of the Victorian period:

> each of its pictures offers us a unique record. At the same time they share one important quality with the graphic artist's work, for every one is the consequence of a deliberate act. A photograph is a document, and the historian's first business is to ask of it, as he would of any other record, who made it, to whom it was addressed, and what it was meant to convey.[8]

All these questions must be asked of the music-hall song: the record they offer may be coloured by the deliberate, selective art not only of the writer and the composer, but of the performer (where that evidence survives) and even of the graphic artist who made the song cover, and whose emphasis may be different again. To the mediation of these contemporary makers must be added the selective bias of the historian's own cultural position and intention. Nonetheless, if we are to progress beyond the myth which sees the class attitudes of music hall simply in terms of self-congratulatory coster songs and antagonistic satire on toffs and swells, a much wider examination of the available song texts is required. Where the lower-middle-class section of the audience and their preoccupations reflected in the music-hall songs?[9] If so, in what ways? As the butt of working-class satire, or as the vehicle for the imposition of middle-class values on the working-class audience? Or is there evidence to suggest that the songs had a role in expressing and exploring sympathetically the concerns and worries of this element of the audience in a way with which they could identify?

These are the questions which I address in this essay. In order to do so I have tried to identify songs which deal specifically with middle-class (and particularly lower-middle-class) characters, lifestyles or social situations, and which were performed by music-hall artists. It goes without saying that the initial – and rather arbitrary – selection of such material is made, independently of the researcher, by chance (what has happened to survive) and then by the idiosyncrasies of the storage and retrieval systems in different collections. I have used three main sources: the entirely random offerings of second-hand bookshops and dealers, the theatre collection at Harvard University, where printed songs are catalogued under the name of the performer, and the British Library, where all music is catalogued by composer and title. Within these constraints I have attempted, first, to lay hands on all music-hall songs available. So far I have studied about 500 comic songs (i.e., those narrative, situational or character songs performed by comic and serio-comic vocalists). Of these, about 70 conform to the criteria of 'middle-classness' described above, and the descriptive analysis of these forms the basis for this chapter. My method has been intentionally descriptive as well as analytical, because one of my purposes is to make them familiar to the reader, and because it is in the details that the cultural significance of these songs often lies. The voice of the clerks and the shop assistants is one of the voices of music-hall culture.

As I worked, a second set of questions began to emerge. The songs I was using had all achieved the double life of performance before an audience in the music hall and sale in printed form for the drawing-room market. (This must partly explain the rather large proportion of 'middle-class' songs in my sample.) There was, of course, some overlap between the two audiences, but there would also have been a considerable number of people who did not attend the halls but who played, sang or listened to the songs at home. What can the songs in their printed form (almost always, in the case of comic songs, with the addition of an illustrated cover) suggest about the reactions of the two different audiences? What aspects of the song, for instance, are emphasised by the illustrator? Are there discrepancies between the messages conveyed in the words and the pictures?

Many of the songs when examined in this way prove semiotically complex. A good example is *Tuner's Oppor-tuner-ty*:[10] a comic song, written and performed in the late 1870s by Fred Coyne, a minor Lion Comique and comic vocalist of steady if not phenomenal popularity. The song was published by Howard and Co. in 1879, and has a pictorial front by Alfred Concanen, which suggests that it was aimed, like many printed music-hall songs, at the home music market as well as at public performance. The cover gives the lyric writer as Harry Adams; but the most superficial examination of the words shows that they are little more than a variant of a familiar broadside type. The simple story is told by 'Fred', and concerns Miss Crotchety Quaver, whom he admires. She is 'sweet sixteen' and a 'player of excellent skill' who likes to 'play' all day and all evening too:

And to keep her Piano in tune she would have
A good tuner constantly there,
And he'd pull up the instrument three times a week,
Just to keep it in proper repair.

The chorus describes the work of this piano tuner, making the most of the metaphor which is (in the tradition of the bawdy ballad) the song's main *raison d'être*:

> And first he'd tune it gently, then he'd tune it strong,
> Then he'd touch a short note, then he'd run along,
> Then he'd go with vengeance, enough to break the key,
> At last he tun'd whene'er he got an op-por-tu-ni-ty.

Matters come to a head when the tuner's services are being called on 'once ev'ry day', causing Fred to remonstrate with the young lady. He receives short shrift from her, and is kicked out of the house, 'a foot, (his or hers) in my back'. However, the last verse finds his self-respect restored, since he has learned from his experience:

> I got over my folly, I courted again,
> A bewitching but sensible maid,
> But I went in for tuning, and in less than a month,
> I was quite an adept at the trade.
> Now we're married, and all my doubts and my fears
> Are for evermore laid on the shelf,
> For if ever her instrument gets out of tune,
> I am able to tune it myself.

The appeal of this song is obviously a basic one, and its only claim to originality is that the writer has provided, with the idea of the piano, an up-to-date variant of the song type which already included drummers, flute-players and organ-grinders. The interesting point about the use of the piano as a metaphor is not just that it gives the required contemporary twist to the traditional theme, but that it is, intentionally or not, distinctly class-specific.

The invention of the upright piano in the early years of the nineteenth century and of the technology which made it both more robust and cheaper to produce had, by 1880, made the piano a feature of every middle-class drawing-room,[11] and a status symbol in every lower-middle-class and artisan household which could afford it. For upper-class girls musical accomplishment was an essential element in their education; for the daughters of the aspiring middle classes it was both a desirable status symbol and an insurance policy in case a girl had eventually to support herself by teaching. Thus young ladies and aspiring young ladies all over England spent hours a day at the keyboard, preparing for the social demonstration of their accomplishments.

Girls played; men sang, or listened, or turned the pages. This convention provided a socially acceptable opportunity for physical proximity, for a tête-à-tête in the corner of the drawing-room away from the gathering round the fire or the card table; and quite quickly the piano gained a second symbolism besides that of class status. The image of the girl at the piano and the young man hovering behind her or sitting at her side became a potent symbol in Victorian and Edwardian art and literature for budding romance (Amelia and George in *Vanity Fair*), the growth of sexual awareness (Maggie and Stephen in

The Mill on the Floss) and seduction (Holman Hunt's *The Awakened Conscience*, and many popular magazine illustrations of the period.)[12]

Alfred Concanen's picture for *Tuner's Oppor-tuner-ty* (fig. 2.1) which is typical of his vivacious, economical use of detail, uses all the connotations of this popular image and a range of other visual clues and conventions to present the purchaser with an immediate grasp of the song's central situation. The young man who has just pushed open the parlour door expresses his shock (like an actor) with his eyes and backward-leaning stance, and, courtesy of a popular illustrator's convention, by his falling hat. He is otherwise unruffled, and his hair and clothes suggest the respectable middle-class man, while his hat, stick and gloves have already told us that he has just arrived in the house. He has presumably let himself in, suggesting his familiarity with the household (or a lack of servants), and with some eagerness, since he has not left his hat and cane in the hall.

The couple he has surprised are established with the same economy: the piano tuner is signalled by his hair and whiskers as an artist and a foreigner; moreover, he still has his instrument in his hand. With the other hand he embraces the girl, though not in such a way as to conceal from us any of her significant features: the exaggeratedly small waist, well-rounded bosom and the swelling bustle accentuated by a huge bow, situated at the exact centre of the cover's design. Beyond these physical charms she is not characterised in any detail, except that she appears the least perturbed of the three.

The background detail of the picture turns the trappings of middle-class domesticity to ironical use. The pictures over the piano ('Cupid and Psyche' and 'Apollo Exalted') are perhaps a comment on the ideal and the reality of love and music, as well as on the pretensions of bourgeois taste; the barometer in the hall reads 'Stormy'. There is nothing grand or affluent about this house: the upright piano and the tiny hall belong to a suburban villa, a lower-middle-class home at the end of the omnibus route from the City.

Together, the words and the picture seem to raise perplexing questions about the intended audience for this (and other similar) songs, whether performed or printed. The existence of songs about the 'blackcoated salariat of commerce, administration and the distributive trades', the 'pretentious clerk',[13] is generally known; they are most frequently accounted for as working-class ridicule of the effeminate non-manual worker,[14] an instance of class antagonism. This fits with Stedman Jones's definition of music hall (as distinct from its West End variation) as an expression of working-class culture;[15] but it does not fit with many of the songs themselves, including this one. The tone is quite clearly not hostile to 'Fred' who tells us the tale: partly because of its role as bawdy – the audience stand beside the first-person narrator as voyeurs – but also because of his last verse success, in which we share his change of status to one who can himself perform the desired act. As the audience swung into the final chorus after the performer sang the verse quoted above, they would clearly be describing, with relish, his sexual virtuosity rather than that of his rival, giving voice to a paean of praise for Fred.

A similar manipulation of audience reaction from tolerant, amused sympathy

Figure 2.1   Harry Adams, Tuner's Oppor-tuner-ty, *photo British Library, reproduction by permission (H. 1783.c. (24)).*

to laughing admiration is found in many songs, for instance Arthur Lloyd's *All Through Obliging A Lady*, discussed below. Thus it is misleading to discuss the appeal of the song in narrowly class-specific terms; its subject matter would appeal to men of all classes. But under what circumstances? Thirty or forty years before it was written, a natural audience existed in the all-male clientele of the song-and-supper room; but by the late 1870s the audience at most music halls would contain not only working men, but their wives and girlfriends; not only 'a few fast clerks and midshipmen' but respectable family parties.[16] Did they all enjoy a song like this?

This quetion leads to a consideration of who might buy the song. The presentation of the printed music, with full coloured cover, suggests the 'drawing-room' market: the illustration sends out middle-class messages, with only veiled hints as to the style of the song. At sixpence, *Tuner's Oppor-tuner-ty* is unusually cheap, perhaps suggesting an expectation of buyers younger or poorer than usual, but there are many songs rich in potential sexual innuendo (such as *A Raspberry Tart with a Little Poke Bonnet* and *He Taught Her to Sing Tra-la-la*) which fall into the two-and-sixpence to four-shilling category. They sit oddly with the accepted picture of the audience for sheet music – the middle-class family and their guests round the drawing-room piano. It is a picture reinforced (if not created) by numerous paintings and novels of the period reflecting affluent middle and upper-middle-class homes. The tendency of many Victorian writers and artists to suggest that people were all like this, unless they were picturesquely poor, ragged but cherry-cheeked and cheerful, has not been entirely avoided by even the more radical of twentieth-century historians. Obviously there was a great deal going on between these social extremes, and it was reflected in the matter of home entertainments as well as everything else. The surban drawing-room was not necessarily sacred ground:

> In the evening Carrie and I went round to Mr and Mrs Cummings' to spend a quiet evening with them. Gowing was there, also Mr Stillbrook. It was quiet but pleasant. Mrs Cummings sang five or six songs, 'No, Sir', and 'The Garden of Sleep', being best in my humble judgement; but what pleased me most was the duet she sang with Carrie – classical duet, too. I think it is called, 'I would that my love!' It was beautiful ... I never liked Mr Stillbrook ... but I must say he sings comic songs well. His song: 'We don't want the old men now', made us shriek with laughter, especially the verse referring to Mr Gladstone; but there was one verse I think he might have omitted, and I said so, but Gowing thought it was the best of the lot.[17]

Some glimpses of music at home can be gained from music-hall songs themselves. There is *Jones's Musical Party*[18] by Harry Clifton, which belongs to the 'song of songs' convention, where humour derives from the matching of singer and song: at Jones's party a lady sings a song in which she wishes she were a bird, a smart young swell sings a coster song about Jerusalem the coster-monger's donkey, and all sing *When Johnny Comes Marching Home*. It is a simple, topical song of direct appeal, neatly summarising the range of popular song in the 1860s, and incidentally demonstrating the considerable overlap between what was being sung in the halls and in the drawing-rooms. The cover picture, drawn by H C Maguire, features the singer in evening dress, in a well-appointed drawing-room with grand piano. The excruciating singing and playing of the lady at the piano is rather crudely satirised; the other people present have expressions of polite suffering. Once again it would be difficult to claim this song solely for the working-class audience's ridicule of polite society; it could just as easily be read – and presumably performed – as a joke shared with those who have experienced such a party.

The turn-of-the-century song *Jones's Parlour Floor*[19] describes a party of less pretension and considerably more vigour:

> I live in a quiet suburban street
> And every Saturday neighbours all meet
> To have just a party and ball on their own,
> At old Tommy Jones's a man that's well known.
> Chorus:
>   ... there you'll find the boys, and the girls about a score,
>   Dancing to the music on Jones's parlour floor.

The song's message is that although

> The ballroom of Jones's is not polished oak
> And the ladies don't mind if their partners smoke

the participants are respectable, and love music:

> We're none of us vulgar we're all trim and neat
> On Saturday in our suburban retreat.

The social status of the friends and neighbours of this second Jones is defined with some care. They are not 'vulgar', but they are obviously not genteel either; they live in a 'suburban retreat' from their work, and enjoy themselves on Saturday night in a boisterous but non-criminal way:

> We're just a bit noisy but do nothing wrong
> The week through we're working and earning the brass,
> But when Saturday comes, why we try to be class.

Jones stands at the boundary where the lower end of the middle class shades off into (or, more exactly, tries its hardest to distinguish itself from) the 'improved' working class; he is separated by his means from the affluent middle class, and by his aspirations as well as his means from the successful butcher or baker with a gold watch and chain and daughters away at school. Jones himself is perhaps a clerk in the City, but he might be a superior shop assistant or a commercial traveller; he earns a salary that allows him (just) to make a swell appearance when he's young and single, but makes respectable family life in the suburbs with parlour piano and maidservant a serious struggle.[20] His origins are difficult to guess: he might be the youngest son of a respectable *Daily Telegraph* reader, 'the Young Man of the Day',[21] or burdened by a widowed mother in ungenteel poverty, like Mr Guppy in *Bleak House*. His position is difficult to define because it is marginal, but also because it is potentially mobile. However true for the majority that 'class is a life sentence',[22] mass education and industrial and commercial expansion had, by the 1870s and 80s, produced in Jones aspirations to upward social mobility.

A word about his name. When Victorian novelists, songwriters or journalists needed a name for any representative Briton who fell between the social extremes of Champagne Charlie and 'Arry 'Awkins, they frequently turned to Jones. (His friends and workmates are always, of course, Brown, Green and Robinson.) As the two songs quoted above illustrate, the name had as many different overtones as there were gradations of the British middle classes, and might be used for a businessman dining at his club,[23] a publican,[24] or the man everyone knows who always turns up at the wrong moment,[25] just as easily as for the marginal character whom I am describing: its ambiguities make it a good choice for him. The name is often associated with social mobility: the Great Vance's satirical song *Fitz-Jones the MP*[26] discloses that the 'old man' of this newly elected member was 'plain Billy Jones', who 'made his money out of bones, And likewise out of soap'. Most of the Joneses never achieved this apotheosis, of course, but I make no apologies for adopting the name as a generic term for the purposes of this discussion.

The only aspect of Jones's character which has received any critical attention is that of the 'fake swell', usually (but not always) appearing in songs sun by male impersonators, such as Nellie Power (*La Di Da, Such a Mash, Oh I Say*) and later Vesta Tilley (*Seaside Sultan, By the Sad Sea Waves*). There is a proper distinction, not always drawn, between the fake swell who is actually an impoverished gentleman desperately trying to keep up appearances, and the young man of limited income who scrimps and saves in order to 'do the heavy' or 'the la-di-da' in his time off. Both of them were likely to receive similar deflationary treatment in the songs. However, it is interesting in this context to note Willson Disher's description of Vesta Tilley performing *By the Sad Sea Waves*. He notes that, while she usually mocked 'the masher she mimicked', she could produce a quite different effect when she sang about the City Toff:

> She picked on the poor little London 'chappie,' earning fifteen shillings a week and spending every penny he could spare on haberdashery for a week at Brighton, where he hoped to pass muster on the promenade as a real masher. Again the story goes against the hero of the song. Back at business, he found that the beauty he met at Brighton was the girl in the cook-shop. No doubt the song-writer had a little mockery in mind. In performance, however, this was magically translated. What we felt when Vesta Tilley showed him to us was not derision but pathos. She felt for him and with him, and her tenderness over that little scrap of humanity was evident in all the portraits she painted from that time onwards.[27]

57730

The repertoire of the male comic singers from the 1860s onwards reveals a much fuller picture of the life of the young man of the petit bourgeoisie. Comic singers were amongst the most versatile artistes, protean in the range of personae they might adopt in one performance. A performer who came on as a swell and sang about Champagne Charlie might work through several comic and nonsense songs on, say, the problems of money, marriage and parenthood before finishing with a coster number in crew cut wig and thick dialect.[28] It is among the songs in the middle of this list (and the middle of the range of class gradations it represents) that Jones is to be discovered. The prolific songwriter and performer Harry Clifton (remembered for *Shabby Genteel* and *Pretty Polly Perkins*) frequently explored the social vulnerability of those on the class margins. Just as often, though, his songs are a celebration of Jones and his world. *The Commercial Man*[29] tells a story about Tommy Brown, a traveller in fancy goods, who though young and much teased by the older travellers in the commercial hotel, proves more than able to take care of himself. When a swell tries to make a fool of him, he offers to buy the man's nose – to be collected when dead. The swell falls for the trick; and when Brown calls in the waiter with hot tongs to brand his property, 'the tables are turned'. The terrifed bully breaks off the bargain and has to pay theforfeit of champagne all round. Thus the song offers not only the familiar appeal of seeing the underdog win, but a specific chance for vicarious triumph for all the Tommy Browns in the audience.

The all-male milieu of the Commercial Hotel is beautifully caught in the Concanen, Lee and Siebe lithograph for the cover (fig. 2.2), which shows Tommy Brown as it were centre stage, with his back to the fire. In this case he is not a portrait of Clifton (who was stout, mature-looking man even when young), but the smart young sprig of the song. On the fire behind him is a kettle for mixing drinks, and on the mantelpiece, with its large mirror, are vases of spills for lighting cigars. The tables, like those in a public house or music hall, have wrought iron legs; under one is a spittoon. Sitting and standing in the room are other men of various ages, the younger ones noticeably 'flash' with velvet lapels to their coats. There is, however, one significant discrepancy between the song and the picture. The aggressor is specifically described in the song as a 'swell'; whether this indicates a real toff or (more probably) one putting on airs, it signals someone against whom the sympathies of both working-class and petit-bourgeois elements of the music-hall audience can easily be recruited. The cover picture, however, shows a rough-looking individual with a red nose and short, upbrushed hair reminiscent of the stage coster. The picture is drawn for a bourgeois audience (those who would buy and play the song) and gives a different and crudely class-oriented view of what the 'enemy' looks like. The appeal is still the triumph of the young commercial traveller, but apparently against the jeers of a working man.

The Commercial Man is unusual in offering a glimpse of Jones at work, a less common theme than Jones at play, probably because the social situation holds so many more pitfalls, and therefore opportunities for comedy, than the workplace. Harry Liston, (who was a commercial traveller himself before becoming a music-hall singer) sang a song called *Blindman's Buff*[30] which

Figure 2.2 Harry Clifton, The Commercial Man, *photo British Library,
reproduced by permission (H. 1264 (6))*.

describes the fun and the hazards of this party game; he prefers it, he says, to charades or forfeits, even though there is a danger of catching old and snuffy Miss Porter, or of getting your foot caught in the coal scuttle. The cover, by Concanen, shows a hectic game in progress in the drawing-room, with overturned chairs and prostrate figures. More formal occasions offered the possibility of more serious gaffes. J W Cherry's *I'm a Timid Nervous Man*,[31] sung by W. Randall, tells the story of a Ball at which the singer says inane things; accidentally sits on an old lady's lap; leaps up and knocks another one over; bows and upsets a waiter's tray. Introduced (by Brown) to Miss Jemima Green, he asks her to dance, treads on her dress, getting the trimming round his legs, and finally brings six people to the floor. Overcome with embarrassment he flees, but in his haste takes the servant's hat and coat instead of his own; when he returns he hears them all laughing at him. It is a song which captures, even though it exaggerates, the terrors of the social scene for a socially insecure young man; perhaps the most telling embarrassment is that of mixing himself up with a servant. Only the performer, sensitive to the composition of audience, could decide exactly on the balance between ridicule and sympathy for the agonised hero of this song; it would be difficult, however, given the combination of inanity and first-person narrative, not to evoke both to some degree.

Even when not plagued with excessive shyness, Jones came low down the scale of eligible wooers for the daughters of the bourgeoisie. His promotion prospects were thin, and the 'big screw' which would enable him to keep a 'good wife at home to cheer me on my road' was a distant prospect. His inability to compete socially in the marriage market[32] is reflected in the comic songs by a host of tales in which he is exposed to rejection (as in *The Calico Printer's Clerk*) or physical humiliations such as being discovered climbing garden walls by policemen, accidentally raising the household by falling in a water butt while climbing to 'her' window, or being seen off by her father and a bulldog (see *Angelina Florentina, Oh! Sophia*, etc). In real life, as in the songs, Jones was doomed to long bachelorhood.[33]

The fantasy solution was, of course, to marry money, like Marie Lloyd's 'drapery kidderty married a widderty' in *Brand New Millionaire*[34]. In comic songs the figure of the young widow, who is not only sexually experienced (and traditionally eager) but left comfortably off by her late husband, often embodies the sum of a young man's ambition. 'Fred Jones, hatter of Leicester Square', who is quite a swell ('You may guess, when he is dressed, he knows a girl or two'), is pursuing this dream in W B Fair's hit *Tommy, Make Room for your Uncle*,[35] The young widow whose little Tommy is so jealously protective of her represents the hope of a financial as well as a physical prize; the final point of the song is not just that the child has thwarted Fred's attempts to lay hands on his mother, but that her assets are revealed in the last verse as taking the form of a pie shop in Seven Dials ('Oh Bloomsbury! do you keep a *pieshop?*') – no upward social mobility there!

In some ways the realistic solution was to woo a working girl. Financially, of course, such a marriage was a daunting prospect: George Leybourne's *Pretty Little Sarah*[36] is worth quoting in full at this point. Like *Tuner's Oppor-tuner-ty*, it reveals the lyric-writer's debt to the broadsides, in this case to a particular ballad. The version of *Pretty Little Sarah* preserved in the Bodleian's collection[37] is a lovesong in the pastoral/idyllic mode and in eighteenth-century poetic diction. It has been used by Leybourne as the vehicle for a concise summary of Jones's dilemma:

> My heart is like a pumpkin, swollen with love,
> For the fairest of the fair girls in creation,
> She is too good for me, tho' a trifle I'm above
> The drudgery and ill-pay of my station.
> Her father keeps a farm-yard in the Mile End Road,
> And for this little damsel of love I have a load,
> I'd spend a fortune on her, but why do thus I speak?
> For what a fortune can I have on eighteen shillings a week?

> Chorus: Oh! pretty little Sarah, with lovely golden hair
> Her beauty jealous maidens may be scorning
> She ought to be an angel, but if rich I were,
> I'd marry her so early in the morning

> The first time I met her, 'twas in the pouring rain,
> I proffered her my arm and umbrella,
> She accepted with a smile, so I said I'd see her home,
> She thanked me with a voice so low and mellow;
> When we arrived at home, she said she'd ask me in,
> But her parents they were poor, said I, "Poverty's no sin,"
> She saw I was a swell and of course I didn't speak
> For I was doing the heavy on my eighteen shillings a week.

> She's got a little ankle, and such a little foot,
> And pretty little fingers running taper;
> Her waist is round and small, her mouth is best of all,
> With ruby lips not twice as thick as paper;
> She's always dress'd in silks, her notions are so high,
> And though her stature's short, she gazes in the sky,
> When she belongs to me, 'tis not for me to speak,
> But lots of silks she'll get from me, on eighteen shillings a week!

> Her parents they are poor, and she's a milliner
> And earns a pound a week in the City;
> A crown she gives her mother, for her keep and board,
> The rest she spends in clothes to make her pretty.
> She never saves a penny, but tells me that she will,
> To pay the wedding fees – it shows she loves me still,
> But should we have a family (too soon I mustn't speak)
> A wife and fourteen children, on eighteen shillings a week.

Roughly speaking, the first half of each verse follows the broadside version, and the second half is exclusively Leybourne's: part of the charm of the song derives from the contrast between the high-flown diction of the first and the prosaic detail and vernacular expression of the second. Occasionally a detail from the broadside takes on a new life; the umbrella was by the 1870s a 'badge' of the city clerk. Only the last verse departs completely from the broadside version and offers a different kind of contrast, between the girl's present finances (she is better off than her wooer) and the gloomy married future of trying to keep a family on his earnings only.

The lithograph for the cover of *Pretty Little Sarah* is not a full illustration, but the more common 'star portrait': it shows Leybourne at his most attractive, in evening dress and whiskers which are impeccably stylish without toppling over into parody. He is pointing to the sky: the artist would appear to be recording Leybourne in performance of the song ('she ought to be an angel'). If so, the performance must have offered Jones in the audience a piquant combination of the effortless elegance to which he aspired, with a clearsighted analysis of his real prospects. The drawing-room performer, on the other hand, safely beyond the situation described in the song, may simply have become for a moment the successful Leybourne singing a catchy topical song and laughing at, rather than with, its protagonist.

Pretty Little Sarah also gives us a portrait of another character whose ambiguous social position is explored in comic songs of the period: the new working girl. Like Jones, she inhabits a class-marginal world. Like him, she is a reflection of part of the music-hall audience. She comes from a working-class home, but she may work in a shop in the West End, or as a sewing machinist for a smart milliner: at the end of the century she is often found serving behind a fashionable bar.[38] She differs from her sisters in domestic service in several ways. She has a measure of financial independence, and can afford to dress well; she also has a new social freedom. Between home, travel and work she meets and deals with men of all classes from the swell to the coster. The swells are often of the genuine as well as the fake variety. Fred Coyne sang the praises of Julia, the girl in *The Luncheon Bar*[39] in Piccadilly, the prettiest anywhere. The song describes her host of admirers (of every class) and the cover shows them all ogling her. The singer anticipates the universal admiration which will attend the man who finally wins her. Many such songs lay emphasis on the fact that although she may flirt outrageously with her customers, she is by no means easy to seduce; and although she will spend the evening with a young man ('at six o'clock she leaves off work, At seven she's finished her tea: At eight she's drest all in her best, And comes for a walk with me')[40], she is more than likely to marry someone else, probably of her own class.

This is certainly the case with Arabella, the heroine of the song *The Nice Looking Girl*,[41] who flirts shamelessly with the 'dundrearies' taking lunch or enjoying a cherry brandy and an iced pastry in the confectioner's shop where she works. One day when she is playfully boxing the ears of one of these swells, her faithful sailor lover, Harry, returns unexpectedly from sea. He bursts into the shop, throws the gentleman into the street and half-wrecks the premises in the

Figure 2.3   G. W. Hunt, The Nice Looking Girl, *photo British Library, reproduced by permission (H. 1257 (7)).*

process. At this, 'Bell' gives notice and marries her sailor, leaving the dangerous ambiguities of her working role for virtuous fidelity and her proper station.

The song cover (by Hamerton – fig. 2.3) for *The Nice Looking Girl* is interesting, partly for the incidental details of the shop, andalso for its presentation of the girl. Both have an elegance which is not fully supported by the text. The shop appears to be papered like a drawing-room, with drapes and elaborate gas lights, as a setting for the cakes, ginger beer and other refreshments on offer. The customers in the background taking their lunch look ordinary-enough gents, but those at the counter are swells, the 'moustache-twisters' and 'dundrearies' mentioned in the song. 'Bell' herself is in every point a conventional beauty of the day: with her glossy black ringlets, rosebud mouth, small waist and improbably small hands and feet (revealed by a handy gap in the counter), she is reminiscent of the fashion plate in a women's magazine or the idealised heorine of a novel. Certainly she has more to do with the ideal woman of the drawing-room singer who bought the sheet music than with Bell's real-life counterpart in the music-hall audience. Did anyone ever wear a full crinoline to work behind a shop counter?

At first view this song cover has obvious similarities to that for *Millie's Cigar Divan* (page 43) but a buyer who expected the same kind of saucy innuendo would be disappointed. *The Nice Looking Girl* is a deeply respectable moral song. The writer is (unusually) a woman, Mrs Harriet Bowmer, who is also given as the performer of the song. The style of the lyric, with its double rhymes and complex sentences, has the ring of the drawing-room ballad:

> The gent's courage forsook him, like a baby Hal shook him
> Such an object he looked with his hair out of curl ...

At one or two points the writer's moral intention breaks in:

> But as they've done her sisters, these moustache twisters
> Soon brought her to grief as you shortly shall learn.

There is a distinct feeling here of the missionary use of popular forms for godly ends: the song writer's equivalent of moral tracts got up as penny dreadfuls. The story obviously has popular appeal – the 'stage sailor' appearance of the hero on the cover is not the only feature of the song reminiscent of domestic melodrama – but on closer inspection the triumph of the strong young working man over the effete gent and the rescue of the heroine from dishonour smack of the mediation of middle-class morality. I have not been able to trace a history of performance of *The Nice Looking Girl*, but I would hazard a guess that unlike the other songs I have mentioned, its impulse was from the drawing-room to the halls, rather than the other way round.

Generally speaking, songs for women singers (such as Annie Adams' *English Girls* and Nellie L'estrange's *No You Don't*) celebrate and defend the independence of the girl who could look after herself, knew her own mind and had her own latch key, and was too worldly wise to be taken advantage of or 'got round'.

Her ability to exercise choice, to defend her virtue against all comers (*No You Don't*) and to outwit men by a combination of sexual attractiveness and cunning (Leybourne's *Bloomsbury Square* and *Dark Girl Dressed in Blue*, page 40) are reminiscent of the active heroines of Child ballads. Perhaps this is why songs performed by male singers display such an ambiguous attitude towards her. I have argued that Jones is often presented sympathetically, as it were from the inside, in music-hall songs; this is not generally true of the working girl, who poses a potential threat to the self-possession of men of all classes. On the whole, songs about her address the difficulties of the men who meet her rather than any conflict in her own position.

Harry Clifton explored the problem in a series of songs in the 1860s. One of the most widely distributed, to judge from the number of copies and versions still extant, was *Isabella and Her Gingham Umbrella*.[42] The singer/hero of the song is a Jones, 'engaged in the City from 10 to 3': he was presumably going home from work

> On a Monday afternoon in the latter part of June,
> From Waterloo I started for a ride to Battersea

when the Citizens' Boat stopped at Hungerford Pier, and a beautiful girl stepped on board. She was 'bosen of a bonnet-shop in Battersea' and daughter of an Islington barber. The hero idolises her, but disillusion sets in when he sees her doing 'double shuffles' with a 'ginger-whiskered fellow' at a 'sixpenny hop' in Islington. Physical (and sartorial) humiliation is added to Jones's sufferings when she hits him over the head with the gingham umbrella, smashing his 'new six-and-six'.

Jemima Brown, or the queen of the sewing machine[43] is another example. The cover picture shows Jemima behind the counter of a linen draper's shop, exquisitely dressed in blue and white with puff sleeves and a crinoline, her fair hair in ringlets and a demure expression on her face, while her admirer, seated on the shop stool, gazes ardently at her and not at the collars he is pretending to buy. In the background a bevy of other pretty girls are working sewing machines. The song tells the story of their relationship, which begins when he meets her on a railway station, 'on the Brighton line', and learns her name from the label on her travelling box. He takes her out, but she leaves him and he next sees her in a 'baby-linen builders in the Burlington Arcade'. He is rendered ludicrous by his infatuation:

> She look'd the Queen of a Sewing Machine,
> I spent many a crown,
> In collars and straps and babies' caps
> To gaze at Jemima Brown.

This time he has to seek an introduction in order to ask her out. They meet at eight that very evening and go to Cremorne, where they take tea and shrimps and bitter beer, and waltz together. Soon after this he sees her with another man who she says is 'her brother Bill'; a little later she prevails on our hero to lend her £50 because her 'father had a loss', and then disappears for good. Years later he catches sight of her in a shop in Camden Town:

> She was weighing out potatoes, throwing coppers in the till,
> Three lovely children by her side, the image of brother Bill.

The possibility of being conned by a pretty girl is a recurring theme in songs throughout the period. Clifton's *Dark Girl Dressed in Blue*[44] (sung by Leybourne) is probably the longest surviving and best known. Several versions survive, including at least two contemporary American ones. Fred French sang a song called *The Destitute Orphans*[45] in which he loses money and a diamond ring to a pretty confidence trickster; the gent in G W Hunt's *Bloomsbury Square*[46] (sung by Leybourne) lends £10 to a young 'lady' who says she has left her purse on the piano at home in Bloomsbury Square – but of course doesn't really live there. The idea of the working girl often merges and overlaps with this idea of the female deceiver; obviously the working girl poses a threat, or at least a problem, for the middle-class man because she is so elusive of social definition. Her fashionable dress and confident behaviour transmit messages which are ambiguous not only in class terms but in sexual ones as well. If, like Jemima Brown, she is going to take emotional and financial advantage of her admirer, and then go off with a greengrocer, the admirer suffers the double rejection of his person and of his lifestyle and values. In *The Afternoon Parade*,[47] one of Vesta Tilley's many songs set at the seaside, the besotted hero is conned out of £20 by a barmaid who finally marries a pot-boy. Again, Harry Clifton offers an early insight into this painful situation: *The Railway Bell(e)*[48] is the story of a commercial traveller in the pickling-vinegar trade whose own struggle to rise above the vulgar is revealed in the language of the song: he loves a girl 'who serv'd behind the First Class bar on the Chatham and Dover Line... Refreshment room, I ought to say'. She has numerous beaux, from dustmen to swells, but finally chooses the Railway Guard, to the comical heartbreak of our hero ('the memory will almost *break* this *tender* heart of mine') who feels 'as silly as a farmyard goose'. The cover picture (figure 2.4) picks up and exaggerates the reason for her choice: the puny traveller stands no chance against the physical attractions of the tall, handsome working-class man:

> 'Appearance' was against me dead,
> 'Twas 'ten to one on the Guard',
> For without doubt I'm getting stout,
> At least I'm far from slim,
> I'm five feet six, he's six feet five,
> All polished neat and trim.

T W Lee (who collaborated for a while with Concanen) has elaborated the discrepancy between the two men, by ignoring the reference to Clifton's stout build, and making the rejected suitor a puny weakling. He is a 'gent' with sparse straggly whiskers and mean features; his umbrella (always a visual barometer of a character's stylishness and/or virility) is ridiculous; he is

Figure 2.4   Harry Clifton, The Railway Bell(e), *photo British Library, reproduced by permission (H. 1264 (10)).*

encumbered with luggage; his amazement and his posture are ludicrous. The Guard is large, with luxurious manly whiskers, impeccable uniform, flashing eyes, and 'an elegant foot in a Wellington Boot'. No wonder the lovely Fanny looks so pleased to be stepping into the compartment marked 'Engaged'. Although the story, as usual, is told in the first person by the rejected suitor, this one offers little consolation to him, illustrating as it does the humiliating vulnerability of a young man whose position lays him open to rejection from his social inferiors as well as from those he aspires to imitate. The picture, as well as the words, clearly indicates that the laughter evoked by this song in all types of audience would be at the expense of the little man; but how unmixed that ridicule was would doubtless be determined by how closely each man identified with which character.

For the middle-class male there is another element of uncertainty about the working girl, and that is the question of her sexual availability. She is usually selling something, but is she prepared to sell herself? These doubts about her moral status continued into the twentieth century; Marie Lloyd's song about *The Barmaid*[49] captures neatly the spectrum of responses (from 'awfully jolly girl' to 'brazen hussy') which she elicits from her customers, male and female. One of the best examples of this nexus of ambiguities is found in John Cooke Jnr's song for the great Macdermott, *Milly's Cigar Divan*.[50] The song celebrates the cosy cigar divan in Piccadilly and its fascinating proprietress Milly:

> She says her name is Millicent, and that she comes from France,
> But well I know she comes from Bow – they used to call her Nance,
> She started her cigar shop on ths strength of her good looks,
> And now I'm told she's patronised by marquises and 'Dooks'.

Milly is reputed to make a thousand pounds a year, and in the third verse we are given some idea of how she does it (one cannot help feeling that this verse, and the whole song, would gain a great deal in performance)

> Now fascinating Milly has a novel scale of charge
> To all but very wealthy men her prices would seem large
> For instance – an 'Havanna Smoke' would cost you 'one and four'
> But if Milly bit the end off she would charge a shilling more.

The Concanen cover for 'Milly' (fig. 2.5) is a perfect complement to the song. Seen from inside the shop, a crowded omnibus goes along Piccadilly; in the doorway hover a group of hopeful 'mashers' about to seek for Milly's attention; at the centre the current 'swell' customer is being served by Milly, enjoying her company while smoking his cigar. Milly stands among her cigar boxes in a red and white pinstripe dress which is smart but not flashy; Concanen has managed without unduly distorting either her or the picture's perspective to draw her in a way which allows us to appreciate both her face and her bustle, visible somehow over the counter. The picture is full of the sharp observations which make Concanen's work so enjoyable: the ludicrously identical appearance of the mashers; the advertisements for 'Mashers Cigarettes' and 'Ugly Cut Tobacco'

Figure 2.5 John Cooke, Milly's Cigar Divan, *photo British Library, reproduced by permission (H. 1260.b. (38)).*

(jokes, but also suggesting the social range of Millie's customers?). The 'divan' as pictured here does not seem very different from an ordinary shop; but the red velvet stool in the foreground draws the mind toward the undisclosed inner parts of the premises – a mere visual suggestion to echo the suggestion of the words. The last lines of the song give a final touch to Milly's portrait. Many men want to marry her, for her money,

> But Milly's up to snuff and won't be tied to any man
> She'd rather keep her freedom and her own cigar divan

The tone is admiring: Milly seems to have gained the respect of her customers. Most working girls could not carry their independence to such lengths: for many of them, as for Jones, life in fine clothes and the company of swells would end at marriage.

Marriage and married life are, of course, a staple of comic song; for Jones as well as 'Arry the idea at least was joyful, and the wedding itself an excuse for a party and a drunken spree, like one so joyfully described in *La-Didily-idily, Umti-umti-ay!*, or, Jones's Wedding.[51] The kind of social and physical embarrassments which dogged Jones as wooer were not, however, magically removed by marriage: in fact the wedding night itself could be fraught with the indignity and embarrassment which constantly threaten those whose class status is insecure. *Tom Richard's Wedding*[52] tells a farcical tale of a couple who arrive at the country town where they hope to spend their honeymoon. They have been forestalled by 'excursionists' and the hotel is completely full. Eventually they are put up in a bathroom, and go to bed in the bath. The bride intending to ring for a maid, pulls 'the rope that fills the bath', and drenches them both. Unable to find the door or a light, Tom finally pulls another rope and they are deluged a second time, by hot water.

> Assitance soon arrived, and when the door was batter'd down,
> They found the water nearly deep enough the pair to drown,
> Poor Richard's Bride, in sorry plight, and wringing wet good lack!
> Was like a Monkey perch'd upon the top of Richard's back;
> She grasp'd the hair upon his head, and held it precious tight,
> While he was fumbling for the door in vain without a light:
> They both were rescued, and I hope their future may be bright,
> And make up for the troubles of poor Richard's Wedding Night.

As a married man, Jones becomes far less noticeable in the songs: partly, perhaps, because he could no longer afford to attend the halls so frequently; but more probably because his preoccupations were no longer class differentiated – nagging wives, too many children and shortage of money not being restricted to the petit bourgeois. Nonetheless, a proportion of songs about the married state do have a clearly middle-class ambience, either in their subject matter or setting: *We Won't go Home till Morning*[53] describes a 'nice select harmonic club, We're called the convivial chums', which is socially just a step or two higher than Chevalier's *Our 'Armonic Club*.[54] It is an escape for the married man where he can drink and stay out late, though he will have to 'face the music' when he does go home. The wife's role in these songs is either to try to prevent him enjoying himself, or to exhibit a nagging curiosity about what he's been up to: the wife in Arthur Lloyd's *Tell Me the Sign, John*[55] drives her newly initiated freemason husband into the spare bedroom by her persistent enquiry. The songs also deal with the fantasy of escape to the freedoms of bachelor days, though showing very clearly to the young married couples in the audience[56] that this is fantasy only: the erring husbands always get caught. Fred French's song *Angelina Brown*[57] is about a young married man who goes on a spree to Ramsgate. His flirtation with Angelina ends prematurely when they are cut off by the tide and discovered by his wife. Vesta Tilley's *For the Weekend*[58] has a similar moral, and uses the archetypal story of the man who courts a girl only to find she is his own wife.

The appeal of these songs is of course the central appeal of all comedy: the exploration in a safe form of the audience's potantially anti-social (in this case adulterous) desires. In the songs the desires can be both expressed and controlled; the would-be adulterer is made ridiculous, so that laughter at his expense relieves the tension of all. In being caught out he is also being saved from the destructive results of his desires, the 'wife as mother' acting as the agent of control through which the social and moral order remains inviolate. This moral function would render songs such as these acceptable to the drawing-room market as well as to the middle-class members of the music-hall audience, and both of these, I would argue, are important targets for these songs. I do not mean to suggest that they were not also enjoyed by working-class members of the music-hall audience, and thus arguably involved in the production of the cultural hegemony; on the contrary, it is just this kind of complexity of appeal and response which I wish to emphasise.

The pervading message of the songs about marriage is of course that Jones, like other men, must eventually settle down and accept his fate. The presence of a home and family can even be a support and a comfort, an idea nicely captured by Harry Clifton's *The Family Man*,[59] which contrasts the life he has lost with the married state, but concludes it is better to be happily married. Even the children can be a joy as well as a worry: Leybourne's *Don't make a Noise or Else You'll Wake the Baby*[60] balances the new father's wild joy with his frustration at constantly being told to be quiet because it's sleeping. For a final glimpse of Jones married, Arthur Lloyd's *All Through Obliging a Lady*[61] (fig. 2.6) will do very well. The owner of the piano stool in which the four-shilling printed song might rest would at once recognise the comfortable room, with the patterned carpet and wallpaper, cheerful fire, and kettle on the hob, which is depicted on the cover. On the wall is a tasteful picture of a Dutch windmill in the snow, on the fringed mantel piece a clock under a glass dome and china ornaments. On closer inspection we see that this is a bedroom: the brass bedstead lurks discreetly in a far corner. In the centre of the picture sits a man in a blue velvet dressing gown, his head wrapped in a scarf; he is obviously suffering from a bad cold. His feet are in a hot mustard bath (the mustard is on the little table by him, together with his gruel and his bedroom candlestick). That he has been

Figure 2.6 Arthur Lloyd, All Through Obliging a Lady, *photo British Library, reproduced by permission (H. 1260.g. (1)).*

treated to various patent remedies is evidenced by the nitre paper on the table and the wrapper for Allcocks Patent Plaster on the floor.

The song reveals the origin of this affliction; its humour derives largely from the fact that it was performed as if with a cold in the head, and the words are printed in such a way as to help the amateur performer achieve the same effect:

> The Bus was full idside,
> There wasn't roob for ady bore
> But! the codductor startled us
> By opedig the door
> SPOKEN: And saying will any gentleman oblige a lady, Well I've always been noted for gallantry to the fair sex, so I jump'd up and said I will, where is she? brig her id, You'll have to get outside first said the codductor

What he is actually being asked to do, of course, is to give up his seat to the lady. He does, and catches cold by sitting outside in the rain for the rest of his journey. He is ill for a fortnight afterwards, 'all through obliging a lady'. His wife puts him to bed, nurses him, and (perhaps in order to make something more of a rather thin song) in the last verse suddenly presents him with twins:

> I'm proud to be a father, but I didn't expect that *bore* trouble, ad
> Chorus: All through obliging a lady...

Much of this song (and all of its innuendo) is contained in the patter, which would presumably give the best opportunity for exploiting the 'cold in the nose' delivery, but which is also capable of subtle variation to suit the audience: the printed version only represents the song as sold. In some ways themes which can be found in songs about the young man Jones are echoed here: but the excursion into attempted gallantry and its physically uncomfortable consequences are softened by having a home and a loving wife to return to. The twins are a comic cliché, a problem that can at least be shared with other husbands through the conventions of comic song. There is no real pain in this song, because it is about (and for) a man who no longer needs to struggle: he has found his place and accepted it. The 'culture of consolation'[62], if it existed, was not a working-class prerogative.

While beginning to provide answers to the questions with which I began, the songs continue to raise others. It is clear, I think, that the voice of the lower middle classes in the music-hall audience can be heard in a significant number of the songs sung there. The clerks, shop assistants and commercial travellers who appear in the songs are not simply the butts of satire, but are represented with sympathy and with understanding of their preoccupations and insecurities. Of course the exact balance of response would depend on the performance and the composition of the audience. I do not wish to deny there was also opportunity for the transmission of middle-class values to the working-class audience through this kind of song, and there is no doubt that the response to Jones by different sections of the audience would vary considerably and would represent differing kinds of cultural negotiation. I would suggest, however, that these differences were not clear-cut. The experience of the struggling clerk would in fact have been fairly close to home for many working-class families, not only because they shared a cultural context but because many of these clerks were the sons of working-class families, first generation products of mass elementary education. The class tensions which the songs about Jones exploited and sought to negotiate were felt within families, as well as between social groups, and the response of a working-class member of a music-hall audience might, for instance, combine class contempt with family affection.

The figure of the working girl offered the music-hall audience a similar variety of levels of response. Women could enjoy her cleverness, vivacity and independence; men of all classes had the consolation of a problem or humiliation aired and shared. At the same time the songs could act in a greater or less degree as vehicles of cultural change and manipulation, embodying messages about class and gender roles.

That there was a drawing-room market for this type of comic song is evident from the large numbers which were printed for sale, and from their range of prices (up to four shillings). I have suggested here that the style of their presentation, particularly in terms of the cover illustrations, can help us to an understanding of the ways in which these songs appealed to the middle-class family audience. In some cases, such as *The Commercial Man*, the difference of response in two audiences is clearly signalled by the graphic artist's emphasis.

These conclusions, arrived at by close attention to the surviving materials, offer no final solution to the puzzles of class and cultural definition in the music halls. Rather, they blur the clear-cut picture presented by some earlier commentators – a desirable effect, if it prompts further study of an almost inexhaustible resource.

3   *Champagne Charlie: Performance and Ideology in the Music Hall Swell Song*

PETER BAILEY

In his commentary on Gustave Doré's famous pictures of life in London in 1872, Blanchard Jerrold reports with distaste his sightings of 'grotesque imitations of that general enemy known as "swell"'.[1] Some 20 years later, the performers who had become the first big music-hall stars by celebrating this social type in song were looked back on with revulsion. These 'Lions comiques', in one recollection, 'were the most vulgar and objectionable creatures that ever faced the public ... Champagne Charlie and the rest of them became the rage and turned the music halls into veritable sinks.'[2] Some modern writers have not liked the swell songs and their performers any better, seeing them as a reactionary diversion from the development of an authentic and combative working-class culture.[3] Clearly here is a phenomenon which made a powerful impact upon polite and popular consciousness. This essay tries to understand why this was so. It concentrates on the making of the swell song as a performance type that constituted its own ideology in the sense of a shifting yet coherent cluster of meanings, constructed and contested in action, both within the music hall and the larger social and cultural world of which it was part.

I

The swell song remained in the repertoire in several variants throughout the history of the halls, but it was at its most vigorous and eruptive in the 1860s and 70s. Typically, the swell was a lordly figure of resplendent dress and confident air, whose exploits centred on drink and women; time, work and money scarcely intrude as the swell struts his way across town in the company of other 'jolly dogs'. The swell song was a major feature in the repertoire of a new generation of comic singers who rose to fame in the mid 1860s. Young men in their early twenties, they were the darlings of the first music-hall boom, while the professional finish of their performances provided a new standard of comic realism. The two most notable in the contest for popular favour were George Leybourne and Alfred Vance, who made their metropolitan debuts within a few months of each other in 1864–5.

Of the two, Leybourne has left the more vivid impression.[4] He dominated the music-hall stage for most of his lifetime, and his classic hit *Champagne Charlie* both defined his own life and provided one of the more durable images of the era. Often said to hail from Wolverhampton, Leybourne was in fact born in Gateshead in the North-East in 1842, the son of a currier and part-time theatre musician. His early life remains obscure, but he worked first as an engine-fitter, then as an entertainer in the North and Midlands under the stage name of Joe Saunders. There are differing accounts of what or who first brought him to London, but he seems initially to have carried on his trade as an engineer while playing the smaller halls and penny gaffs of the East End.[5] His debut in the big halls came in early 1865, when he was noticed at the Metropolitan, Edgeware Road, doing a mechanical donkey act, an obvious transplant of his craft training; the following year he appeared dancing on stilts as Chang, the Chinese Giant. Though a Geordie and devotee of Ned Corvan, Leybourne never seems to have drawn on his home culture for his act – several commentators thought him a cockney – yet it is plain that throughout his career he was a performer of considerable versatility. Among other talents he was a fine ballad singer, but his comic singing brought him his greatest success and it was *Champagne Charlie* in 1866 that first made him a star and won the 'volcanic appreciation' of music-hall audiences.[6]

In 1868, in one of the legendary moments of music-hall history, George Leybourne, 'The Original Champagne Charlie' (fig. 3.1), was signed to an exclusive 12-months engagement at the Canterbury by William 'Billy' Holland, the flamboyant 'People's Caterer', who placarded London with details of the

THE ORIGINAL "CHAMPAGNE CHARLIE."

Figure 3.1 George Leybourne, the original 'Champagne Charlie'. Cartoon form Entr'acte, *24 August 1872. Photo by permission of the British Library.*

terms. Among the duties that were to earn him £1,500 for the year, the contract stated that 'George Leybourne shall every day, and at all reasonable times and places when required so to do, appear in a carriage, drawn by four horses, driven by two postillions, and attended by his gooms'. Thus every evening Leybourne left his home in Islington to be driven down to Lambeth by barouche. He was to be the swell off as well as on stage, bedecked in fur-collared coat and diamond solitaire, and plying his public with champagne provided by wine shippers eager for publicity. Leybourne was 'bound in heavy pains and penalties not to appear at any other Music Hall or place of amusement without the express permission of Wm. Holland'.[7] He did, however, play several other London halls concurrently, no doubt under a farming agreement between Holland and Charles Roberts, his agent, who also promoted him in concerts at the more respectable venue of St James's Hall and despatched him on a tour of provincial music halls in 1869. Heavily booked for as many as six London halls in a night, 'Leybourne the pluralist' had to plead with enthusiastic audiences to release him so that he could meet his schedules across town. He repeated his success in the North and the Midlands, similarly parading himself in carriage and four, and commanding big salaries. Combined nightly appearances at Leeds and Bradford were said to have made him a weekly salary of £100 upwards. Provincial proprietors exulted at his popularity: 'Simply announce Leybourne, and in spite of the weather, the doors are besieged; open them and in half an hour's time, the hall is packed and money refused.'[8]

Tall and handsome, genial and unaffected in manner, and with what Jenny Hill recalled as 'a curious faculty of filling a stage',[9] Leybourne sustained his star status into the next decade, though he paid dearly for his success. He was acclaimed in Paris, appeared before the Prince of Wales, and acquired a country estate. The trade press censured him for his vulgarity, some of his fellow artists thought him guilty of sharp practice, and proprietors became uneasy about his unpunctuality, but his public loved him. According to an oft-repeated story, Leybourne in private despaired of the emptiness of his success and the absence of true friendship amid the milling crowds. Yet he remained the good fellow of his most successful stage role. Notably generous with hand-outs as well as the drink, he was dubbed 'honorary high almoner to the profession'. Eager to enlarge on any irony that confers a tidy pathos on the life of a star, some have seen a metaphor for the decline of Leybourne's career in the setting of one of his later songs, where the erstwhile swell sang the praises of life in a teashop – 'Ting a ling' rather than 'Slap Bang'.[10] Quite apart from the likelihood that the song was more an effective parody than a dying fall, the evidence is that despite collapses in health and some fall from favour Leybourne sustained the vigour of his stage characterisations to the end. The true pathos of his career needs no invention. Reports of his several indispositions attributed them to consumption, but his death certificate records exhaustion and abscess (cirrhosis?) of the liver. He died penniless, at the age of forty-two.

A less engaging character than Leybourne, Alfred Peck Stevens, the Great Vance, was his biggest rival.[11] Born in London in 1839, he started work as a solicitor's clerk, then played a variety of roles in the theatre before transferring to music hall in a blackfaced double act with his brother. By 1864 he was drawing big crowds as a solo comedian, notably at the Metropolitan. Like Leybourne, Vance was a versatile performer; he enjoyed much success as a stage cockney and was a master of the vernacular 'celler flap' dance, but he won most acclaim with his swell songs.

Hired by Charles Morton for the Oxford in 1866 as a counter-attraction to Leybourne, Vance challenged his rival with his own hymn to champagne, *Clicquot, Clicquot! That's The Wine For Me.* The two then worked their way in competitive antiphony down the wine list. A less aggressive and more mannered performer than the other lions comiques, Vance also established a considerable reputation as a popular concert artist, appearing before more select audiences in London and conducting annual tours of the provinces with his own concert party.[12] He hardly seems to have modified his repertoire for his respectable clientele and still played his swell and his cockney – 'the dainty exquisite and the rugged vulgarian' – back to back, though the reviews applauded him more as an actor than a vocalist.

Like his rival, Vance was an accomplished showman with a talent for self-advertisement – he drove to his engagements behind a pair of cream-coloured ponies with smartly liveried boy grooms.[13] Unlike Leybourne, Vance managed his own career and seems to have taken himself more seriously. Although he also was indicted for vulgarity, his general persona was less roguish than Leybourne's. The minister at this funeral revealed how as an aspirant performer himself he had been deterred from seeking a professional career after a lecture by Vance on its moral hazards, suggesting the latter's caution in negotiating his own path to success. In the 1870s his absences from the halls grew longer; on his more frequent returns inthe 1880s the reviews were still complimentary, and his latter-day success seems to have been more durable than Leybourne's. He died from a heart attack in the wings of the Sun music hall in Knightsbridge in 1888. Though still said to command a high salary, he left a total estate of £39.7s.5d.

A number of other performers were billed as lions comiques and included swell songs in their repertoire. Of these G H. MacDermott enjoyed comparable notoriety, though his greater speciality was the topical song. Arthur Lloyd was noted for the accuracy of his impressions based on exhaustive scrutiny of everyday life, and was an early success with his hit about the cockney swell *Immensikoff, the Shorditch Toff.* Harry Rickards made his name in the late 1860s as a parodist of Champagne Charlie, and pioneered a notable variation on the type in his portrayal of the military toff, *Captain Jinks of the Horse Marines.* Other contemporary comic stars were Jolly John Nash, Tom Maclagen, Harry Liston and Ned Hammond. Also important were a number of women performers who specialised in male impersonations and are discussed below.[14]

II

This brief review of the emergence of the lions comiques accords at several points with a conventionalised picture of modern showbusiness as a voraciously commercialised institution. We see leading entrepreneurs competing for novel attractions as they slug it out in a trade war for control of the big London houses. The comic singer is slicked up, hit songs are delivered by professional writers, and the new package is advertised in sensational fashion. Agents exploit their charges, and sponsors promote their product by identification with the star and new images of conspicuous consumption. And yes, amid the money and the success and the hype, the star is confronted with the emptiness of it all, knows alienation, and dies an exhausted commodity, himself no better than a spent champagne bottle. However crude and one-sided the picture is, we need to acknowledge the powerful role of the forces of production in the making of the swell song and their singers.

Music-hall promotion in London in the boom years of the 1860s was a highly personalised and competitive business dominated by a feisty cadre of proprietorial grandees.[15] When Weston of Weston's Music Hall in Holborn contested Morton's opening of the Oxford in Oxford Street in 1861, the clash was represented in the prints as a prize fight for the West Central Stakes. There was talk that Weston and other managers had tried to suborn the magistracy in order to deny Morton a licence.[16] Undoubtedly there was a seamy side to the trade war but the bid to capture and hold audiences relied on the more public tactics of out-shining and out-shouting your rivals. Here the proprietor traded upon his own expansive presence, playing host and servant to the crowd, publicising himself, his amenities and his entertainments at lavish dinners and benefits where he himself was the star.

Morton essayed a more temperate personal style, but his contemporaries had little regard for restraint. Ned Weston, who was seen by some as the more dominant figure of the early 1860s, provided champagne on the house and invited the public to his large suburban estate in Kentish Town. Extravagance and over-speculation contributed to his decline, and he was forced to sell his Holborn hall in 1866 to William Holland. The most flamboyant of all the London caterers, Billy Holland specialised in taking on fading establishments, undertaking expensive renovations and mounting bold new programmes; in his time, he sought to galvanise the London public with Blondin, bull-fighting and barmaid competitions. Arguably, in buying up the 'exclusive' services of George Leybourne in 1868 to revive the depressed fortunes of the Canterbury, Holland was doing more than seeking just another publicity coup; he was promoting a style and image that pointed up the grand manner of the caterer, flattering the big man and his public alike, suggesting a community of bluff and carefree revellers. In promoting Champagne Charlie, Holland was promoting himself and the general business of pleasure.

Though far from being puppets, it seems obvious enough that the performers were ready accomplices in the manufacture and marketing of the swell. The swell, as already noted, was not the only role in their repertoire, but it was the one which gave them their sharpest identity with their public and, crucially, within their own profession. The more successful performers were sharing, often in quite spectacular fashion, in the music-hall boom, but it was still a fiercely competitive and insecure way to make a living. With the proliferation of halls in

London and the provinces, the profession increased in number and mobility, and in this ever-widening and over-populated world, the artist too had to shout louder to be heard.[17] It became essential to advertise, to be known to be in circulation. Not to advertise could 'kill' an artist, generating rumours of sickness, retirement or death; Leybourne more than once returned from the dead to read his obituaries with relish. Advertising was a matter of posters and placards, of column inches in the trade press, coloured portraits on sheet music, and the distribution of cartes de visite (introduced in 1859) bearing the artist's photograph. Even so, the star of the 1860s was far from relying on the mere reproduction of himself, because much of the necessary advertisement had to be done by personal presence.

If earnings and opportunities at the top grew in pace with the expansion of the industry, the monitoring and construction of professional success lay with a relatively small and still physically knowable nexus of interests in London, an inner world of top proprietors, agents, pressmen and fellow and sister artists.

Two mutually reinforcing innovations of the period did much to institution-alise this world. In 1870 the Oxford under Morris Syer began its regular Saturday matinees for professionals. It was an occasion for the audition of new talent, and 'reunion' among established members of the profession; all those in the business were admitted free. The year before had seen the publication of a new trade paper, the *London Entr'acte*, unique among a cluster of similar productions in the 1860s for its durability. It did not displace the *Era* but its reporting concerned itself much more with personalities and gossip than its staider contemporary. Much of the *Entr'acte's* colourful copy came from the Oxford matinees.[18] For those in the know its allusions and innuendoes recorded the making, bending and breaking of innumerable deals and reputations. The atmosphere at the Oxford was one of feverish glamour and display as the performers, proprietors, chairmen and agents disported themselves in their best finery and put away much food and drink. The mix of big names, supplicant new talent and an admiring public also provided an ideal setting for conspicuous treating and other generosities. Here the grand style of the swell was the definitive style. Thus to master it on stage as well as with the company at the Oxford bars gave the performer as it were a double presence in his professional community.

But the swell was not just a vehicle devised to gratify the self-images of the music-hall world – he was derived from life, and already had a long history. Partridge dates the term from the early years of the century when it denoted a fashionably dressed man or woman of the upper classes, and though subsequent usage broadened its meaning considerably it always retained some sense of derivation from a genteel or aristocratic archetype. Beyond that it is possible to give the type some further specificity under three counts. The swell was defined in terms of dress, and where this was a meticulous and obsessive preoccupation which marked him off from the common herd we may talk of the swell firstly as dandy (or 'dandizette', though the term was increasingly reserved for men). The languid upper-class swell of this type had long been played as the effete fop of English stage comedy, and was a frequent comic target in pantomime in the early century,[19] but he achieved apotheosis in 1861 with E A Sothern's great popular success as Lord Dundreary in Taylor's *Our American Cousin*. His make-up and wardrobe were widely imitated, and Dundreary's centre parting and side whiskers were adopted by the lions comiques.[20]

In a second variant, as rake or man about town, the swell was considerably more boisterous and obtrusive. Here he stands in line with the drinking songs of the eighteenth century and the exploits of Corinthian Tom in Pierce Egan's tales of the 1820s as the lordling hell-bent on the good time.[21] There is much horse-play, drinking and laughing and a good deal of noise in general. An actual site for these forays into low life in the 1830s and 40s were the song-and-supper rooms around the Strand, important if minor antecedents of the music hall and an all-male Bohemia for those who wished to escape convention. The collection of bawdy songs that made up the programme for one of these notorious establishments, the Coal Hole, was subtitled *The Swell's Album*. Another leading room, Evans's, later became a principal rendezvous for upper-class hooligans in the ritual excesses of boat-race night. This type was met with early in the music hall; thus Morton when he opened the Oxford was confronted by the swell who would sweep the board of crockery and glasses that he might pay for the damage and exclaim 'Damn the expense!'[22]

Lastly we come to the swell as counterfeit. Though located originally among the *ton*, the term swell carried an early suggestion of the bogus, particularly in the appellation 'swell mob', denoting a class of pickpockets who dressed in style to escape detection as they mingled with their fashionable victims.[23] But the sham swell was more commonly registered as a social rather than a criminal menace. He appeared in great numbers on London streets in the 1830s and 40s as the much despised 'gent'. As Ellen Moers puts it, 'this was a label pasted on young men on the bottom of the respectable class, the scrubby clerks, apprentices and medical students who scraped along on less than £50 a year, calling themselves (hopefully) gents, and their betters (admiringly) swells.' Albert Smith in his *History of the Gent* of 1847 pilloried the type for a spurious gentility of dress and manner, and a *Punch* cartoon registered the phenomenon as 'A Most Alarming Swelling'.[24] But the upstart clerk and his kind would not go away, for they already constituted a sizable, self-conscious consumer group with its own emergent sub-culture.[25] Certainly these gents and would-be swells found a haven in the early music halls and singing saloons. *The Town* in 1838 noted the proliferation of 'Cockney swells' – mostly linen-drapers' assistants and shop men – at the Castle in Regent Street. J Ewing Ritchie, an early music-hall hater, recorded 'juvenile swells' at the Eagle Tavern in 1857 and again at a hall in Hungerford Market where he noted 'one or two awful young swells with excruciating all-rounders' (a type of collar).[26] A programme from the Victoria Saloon in Old Street in 1843 announces the appearance of a comic singer as 'The Modern Slap Up Swell' and several titles show that the swell was the subject of popular song before the arrival of the lions comiques.[27]

In his several guises the swell was well known in life and literature by the 1860s, suggesting in a single word both an ideal and its debasement. Inside and outside the halls the lion comique and the swell song had some interesting cultural stock to exploit and play off.

III

An obvious entrée to the songs themselves is *Champagne Charlie*, written by
Leybourne with music by Alfred Lee, published in late 1866, and remaining a
popular item in Leybourne's repertoire till his death.[28]

I've seen a deal of gaiety
   Throughout my noisy life,
With all my grand accomplishments
   I never could get a wife.
The thing I most excell in is
   The P.R.F.G. game,
A noise all night, in bed all day,
   And swimming in Champagne.

CHORUS:
For Champagne Charlie is my name,
Champagne Charlie is my game,
Good for any game at night, my boys,
Good for any game at night, my boys,
For Champagne Charlie is my name,
Champagne Charlie is my game,
Good for any game at night, my boys,
Who'll come an join me in a spree?

The way I gained my title's
   By a hobby which I've got
Of never letting others pay
   However long the shot;
Whoever drinks at my expense
   Are treated all the same,
From Dukes and lords, to cabmen down,
   I make them drink Champagne.

From Coffee and from Supper Rooms,
   From Poplar to Pall Mall,
The girls, on seeing me, exclaim
   "Oh, what a Champagne Swell!"
The notion 'tis of everyone
   If 'twere not for my name,
And causing so much to be drunk,
   They'd never make Champagne.

Some epicures like Burgundy,
   Hock, Claret, and Mosell,
But Moet's vintage only
   Satisfies this Champagne swell.
What matter if to bed I go
   Dull head and muddled thick,
A bottle in the morning
   Sets me right then very quick.

Perhaps you fancy what I say
   Is nothing else but chaff,
And only done, like other songs
   To merely raise a laugh.
To prove that I am not in jest,
   Each man a bottle of Cham.
I'll stand fizz round, yes that I will,
   And stand it like a lamb.

It seems a simple enough text, with the exception of the obscure cabalistic reference to the 'P.R.F.G. game' (a good bottle for the reader with the most convincing gloss!) It is a tale of heroic consumption in which our champion keeps the champagne industry afloat virtually singlethroatedly – by his own prowess (he swims in it), and by his generosity in treating others. As the new and unrivalled elixir of the drinking man, champagne despatches hangovers and brings instant renewal. Appropriately befuelled, men may conquer the night and obliterate the day. Under Charlie's leadership (note the chummy and disarming diminutive) the invitation is open to all, though the nature of nocturnal exploit is vague: it is certainly noisy, may well be daring and will generally put the 'boys' on their mettle. It will impress the girls. There is no great literary artifice here – no 'beaded bubbles winking at the brim' – no narrative development, and the music is a simple and repetitive march tune. Its popularity was nonetheless, in the puffery of the day, 'immense', and it received its ultimate accolade form the Salvation Army who appropriated it for a hymn tune.

How are we to explain the remarkable success of this unremarkable song? My method here has been to relate it to others of its type, to understand their range of connotation or web of associated meanings within a particular social and historical context, to reconstruct the dynamics of their performance, reception and use, and to extend this exercise to define the swell song as a genre, as well as register the specifics of its most notable hit.[29]

Like many others of its type, *Champagne Charlie* was most obviously a song of release and action. The release is from the almost literally unspeakable purgatory of the daytime; for Charlie it is merely a recuperative interlude, though for most it must have implied work. The action is that of the boys on the spree, 'good for any game at night'. In Vance's *Slap Bang, Here We Are Again*, which celebrated 'our British Gentlemen', the action was more specific, for 'They play cricket, box and torture cocks' before repairing to the Opera, then Evans's. Together with the zest for traditional manly sports goes the role of the swell as man about town combining the fashionable with the fashionably disreputable. The ritual delinquencies that went with the latter role are suggested in the song sheet cover of another Vance hit, *Jolly Dogs Galop*, where the jolly dogs are shown in retreat from the police; *The Swell*, published in Birmingham in 1867, also recounts a brush with the law after the boys refuse to pay a cabman.[30] The action (over a wide if predictable territory) also involves a great deal of noise. Champagne Charlie makes a noise all night, Vance's

Howling Swell announces himself with 'Crash, smash!' (no doubt as a follow up to 'Slap bang!') and J H Milburn sang *Come Along Boys, Let's Make a Noise*.

But above all else in these songs of license, action meant drinking. Here champagne was king. Other drinks were celebrated, but it was champagne that was installed as the sovereign cordial of the good time and the only tipple for the real swell. Leybourne, whose repertoire included anti-temperance as well as drinking songs, drank the stuff by the pint tankard, and we may recall Ned Weston the proprietor treating his customers to champagne on the house. Waiters placed bottles on all the tables in every part of the house, reported the *Era* under the title 'Champagne for the Million', adding that it was a gesture 'which seemed utterly incomprehensible to the visitors'.[31] Within a few years there could have been few music-hall goers who were not familiar with the idea and image of champagne – if not with its consumption.

Champagne had a long-established reputation as a fashionable drink. Charles Townshend, the eighteenth-century wit and politico, had previously enjoyed the title of 'Champagne Charley'. It had been a favourite of the marcaronis and dandies (Beau Brummell had reputedly cleaned his boots with it); it was sold at Vauxhall, prescribed at the spas, and later celebrated by Byron. Only the best people could afford it. A drop in prices in the 1840s and 50s doubled its consumption, but the great breakthrough came after 1861 when Gladstone reduced the tarrif, bringing champagne within reach of the middle classes (Gladstone himself took a quart with his dinner).[32] Sales grew dramatically and were duly recorded in the *Era* together with warnings of cheap imitations made from gooseberries or rhubarb. Whatever its provenance, champagne was on regular sale at music halls by the mid 1860s from 6 to 10 shillings a bottle. In 1864, for example, it was to be had not only in the famous Canterbury music hall in Lambeth, but also in the Canterbury music hall in Sheffield, where a certain W Revill was advertised singing *The Glorious Vintage of Champagne* to the cutlers and grinders who comprised the 300-capacity crowd of this modest establishment.[33]

The consumption of champagne among working people either inside or outside the music halls cannot have been extensive, whatever the promotion stunts of the wine shippers and the endorsements by music-hall celebrities, but its myth was democratised. Some working men lived the myth briefly during the wages boom of the early 1870s when there were indignant reports of miners indulging in 'sealskin jackets and bottles of champagne', and champagne did appear on the shelves of some co-operative stores by the 1880s.[34]

The majority no doubt took their ease with less exalted drinks, yet even here significant changes in taste complemented the language of the champagne shippers who stressed its properties of lightness and purity – the *Era* extolled champagne as 'a great restorative' whose 'intoxicating effects were rapid but transient'. Changes in brewing and the cheaper production of glass were already producing a new emphasis on 'drinking by the eye' and a growing preference for sparkling, lighter-bodied beers over traditional heavy-bodied brews. The champagne of the new beers was Bass Pale Ale introduced nationally in the late 1860s and commended in glowing terms by that otherwise sober journal of improvement and reform, the *Beehive*. The 'light, sparkling, exhilarating beer', proclaimed an editorial in the working-class paper, 'satisfied thirst, refreshes the spirits and suits the stomach', suggesting further that 'it induces habits of temperance and moderation.' Champagne and beer alike were thus represented in the rhetoric of an emergent mass consumerism with its emphasis on lightness and brightness and the benign and easeful experience of consumption.[35] Champagne, of course, was made to promise this and more. In the years of the first great music-hall boom, 'fizz' symbolised glamour and high success – 'Will it fizz?' meaning, will it go, was the expression music-hall people used of any new venture throughout the rest of the century.

The reactions of one working-class audience to a comic singer's invitation to drink champagne was noted by Walter Tomlinson in a Manchester hall in the 1880s:

> The exquisite fitness of this query to such an audience seems to tickle the fancy of the ladies, and one near us observes to her companion with good-humoured sarcasm, 'Oh yes! of course we has champagne for supper every night reglar!'[36]

It is the good humour that counts. If they could not share directly in its bounties, songs about champagne flattered them by its invocation of high life, and its invitation to vicarious participation.

Being a swell or lion comique required more than making appropriate noises and drinking appropriate drinks – as Charles Norman sang in 1868 (in the Star at Bermondsey), *So Much Depends Upon The Style In Which Its Done*. Dress and bearing were of central importance. The stage swell paraded all the apparatus of genteel apparel, though variation and distortion were common where the object was parody. Thus Arthur Lloyd often performed in bizarre dress and make-up, sporting a coat with exaggerated lapels, an outlandish silk choker and 'a forty Cardigan power moustache'. In his song *The Dancing Swell*, Harry Liston was reported as wearing 'a pair of unmentionables (trousers) which no one outside of Hanwell (a lunatic asylum) would think of putting on'.[37] Clothes were of course among the fundamental properties of stage comedy and trousers were inherently comic, particularly where their incumbent suffered for fashion's sake. 'How did you get those trousers on and did it hurt you much? sang George Leybourne in his *Comet of the West* (End), and the same question might have been asked of the gaudy striped pants he wears in the song cover to *Champagne Charlie*. Presumably a direct rendering of his stage costume for the song, it depicts Leybourne in collar and tie, waistcoat and cutaway jacket, sporting a set of Dundreary whiskers, a cigar, a cane, and the cut-down top hat with the curly brim that became known popularly as a champagne charlie hat.

Here it seems that Leybourne was to some extent sending up the swell style, but in other similar roles he could be irreproachably genteel, and was most frequently recollected for his studied portrayal of the society gentleman. 'George', recalled Percy Fitzgerald in the 1890s, 'was never seen out of a dress suit', adding that there was a common belief that he took part in the brilliant scene enacted on stage. This enduring image derives no doubt from Holland's successful promotion of Leybourne off as well as on stage, but the dress suit and the appropriate manner of its wearing was as much a necessary accomplishment for the lions comiques as for the parodies they wrought upon it. Vance wore formal evening dress for several of his songs and was recalled as 'the best groomed comic singer ever to grace the halls' (though his feet were said to be distinctly bigger than the fashionably Lilliputian size of his song-cover portraits). Jolly John Nash later claimed to have been one of the first vocal comdeians to adopt society's evening dress, so we may accept that it was something of an innovation in music-hall stage costume.[38]

The appropriation of gentility could be suggested by association as well as emulation. Several of the most popular swell songs were set in the specific territory of fashionable society. Vance had a great hit in *Walking in the Zoo*, at a time when London's zoological gardens were the preserve of an exclusive private society –'zoo' was the lyricist's vulgar contraction, said to be a term offensive to the ears of its select membership. Vance also went *Lounging in the Aq*(uarium), a favourite haunt of fashionable men about town, and Rickards sang of *Doing the Academy* and *Strolling in the Burlington* (Arcade).

Just as this transcription of fashionable life could in part be actualised with a glass of cheap champagne, so too was its approximation democratised through the new availability of cheap tailoring. The market leaders were Elias Moses and Son. Since the 1840s they had been servicing the 'gent' from their several emporia in central London, offering ready-made menswear which aped the fashionable line and drew the fire of the satirists for its ill-bred affectations.[39] By the 1860s there were several large firms in the market and their advertisements appeared regularly in the *Era*, the *Entr'acte* and the working-class *Beehive*. The theatres and music halls provided them with a prime showcase for their products and the stars were eagerly wooed for their endorsements. Sothern's dressing room was crowded with salesmen as tailors and haberdashers sought to create a fashion through some new addition to Dundreary's wardrobe.[40] Moses' ads claimed the patronage of a number of stars, and Vance got free suits in return for plugs for his tailor, Edward Groves, who had shops next door to the Canterbury and Metropolitan halls. Arthur Lloyd hymned two other firms in *Immensikoff*, his hit about the Shoreditch toff, and Jenny Hill's similar hit, *'Arry*, spelt out costs: 2 guineas for a suit, 13/– for 'bags'. The halls were particularly sensible to the claims of fashion, its provisioners and prices.

The range and exuberance of the popular wardrobe grew in other ways. The introduction of aniline dyes in the 1860s affected the dress of all classes, but it contributed mightily to the profusion of boldly coloured cravats, waistcoats and trousers so beloved of the swell on and off stage (and now vividly reproduced on song covers through the parallel innovation of colour lithography). The new technology of electroplating brought cheap 'Birmingham' jewellery to the masses, providing a new element of display in popular dress. Another vital accesory came within easier reach in the 1860s, when Gladstone took two-thirds off the duty of manufactured tobacco and gave the nation a cheap cigar.

We may note also a new attention to self-presentation. The spread of photography no doubt encouraged this – photographers were already reaching downmarket in the 1850s and 60s through fairground booths – but the music hall in particular intensified the interest, for it was in one respect quite literally the mirror of fashion. From its early days the music hall had made extensive use of mirror glass, a feature inherited from the gin palace. As well as provided a greater illusion of space and comfort, the mirrors made for an increased self-consciousness of bearing and appearance. 'All round the hall', remarked a review of the refurbished Middlesex in 1872, 'handsome mirrors reflect the glittering lights, and offer abundant opportunities for self-admiration.'[41] As the lion comique paraded his fashionable self on stage, members of his audience could with a sidelong glance decide how their own image matched up to that of their hero.

For the performer, boldness and singularity of dress were useful in making immediate impact upon an audience subject to a range of distractions within the hall, while it also gave opportunity for several forms of stage business. Vance made great play with large handkerchiefs which he pulled from his waistcoat. Hats, canes and monocles could be variously adjusted, twirled or manipulated, and gloves (lavender) – their putting on and taking off – were frequently noted as part of the stage business of the swell. Leybourne was complimented for 'the majestic sweep of his handplay'.[42] The significance of all this is elusive. Mastery of the genteel wardrobe and its accessories was an accomplishment that would add to the authenticity of the stage portrayal of the swell; it would also be prime territory of comic parody. But dress and its manipulation had its own code on the halls, though clues for its deciphering are few. One critic reprimanded Vance for the vulgarity of his handkerchief play – littering the stage with them, he said, 'suggested a state of undress'. Was this the intended message, commonly understood, or the reaction of a singular, over-heated imagination? There was also suggestive business with the cane; the performer might extend the knob of his cane across the footlights as a surrogate handshake to members of the audience. Such sartorial-cum-gestural innuendoes were likely important features in the performance of swell as well as other comic songs.[43]

The full manner of performance is of course difficult if not impossible to reconstruct. We have the text and the music and some indicatiors of vocal style in the surviving conventions of music-hall type performances. But we have no record of what Barthes calls the particular 'grain' or materiality of the voice, and only occasional printed and presumably bowdlerised snatches of the 'spoken' or patter which the comique would have slipped in between verses (Leybourne was particularly notorious for his interpolations and spontaneous exchanges with the audience). Yet it seems plain enough that swell songs were delivered robustly, even aggressively. The previously noted emphasis on noise-making in the songs certainly suggests this, though this may have been a functional as well as stylistic device, as performers strove to cut through the din of a self-absorbed audience and noisy environment. Certain lyrics and song covers suggest a languid style of delivery as in Leybourne's *Cool Burgundy Ben* and Vance's *Lord Swoon*, but the more obviously bacchanalian songs were vocally and physically more assertive, sometimes with direct audience encouragement – thus it became common for the crowd to interject a shouted 'Yes!' at the end of each line in the chorus to *Champagne Charlie.*

Swell songs came with a distinctive body language. An interesting guide to comic singing from 1869, for those who wished to reproduce the music-hall style in the drawing-room, considered Vance the prime exemplar of 'Gentleman comedy' – significantly Leybourne is absent from th list of appropriate models – and noted 'a kind of pliability of body' in the former.[44] For most performers on the halls this would have been an understatement. Jerrold remarked of the swell in the penny gaff that the song came 'with a jerk at the beginning of each line, in true street style', a style readily reproduced on the halls to judge from the periodical *Fun* (7 October 1871) which noted 'The staring, flaring, glaring, swearing popular Lion Comique'. We may take it that the swell postured and strutted on stage, very much the male peacock.

Plainly the swell songs offered a particular construction of gender and sexuality. The novelist, William Pett Ridge, looking back on them, declared that they 'gloried in sex' as well as drink.[45] On the face of it, the swell is the rogue male, playing the field and resisting entrapment by marriage — 'With all my grand accomplishments,' sings Champagne Charlie in inverted parody of the spinster's lament, 'I never could get a wife.'[46] Undoubtedly the nature of the swell's sexual exploits were amplified by innuendo, patter and gesture, but the record here is sparse and elliptical with little more than the occasional report suggesting the miming of a conquest, as in the arm encircling the waist of some accommodating barmaid.

On the evidence of the text, however, partial though it may be, the swell's relations with women are far from predatory. 'The girls on seeing me, exclaim / "Oh, what a Champagne Swell"' — to be acclaimed or adored by women seems enough. The swell — and the built-in tumescence of the label can hardly have gone unexploited in the patter of the comique dealing with an audience well schooled in bawdy and scattered with prostitutes — the swell was cocksure but unconsummating. His was the sexuality of display, perhaps of provocation, but not obviously of engagement. Is this sex for those who don't want it, or sex for those who can't get it, or sex for those who couldn't handle it if they did? There is some correspondence here with the predicament of the young clerk in the city as revealed in the letters to the *Daily Telegraph* in the late 1860s on the Young Man of the Day.[47] Often a newcomer to London, he found contact with females of his own station restricted by tight parental control, while marriage was being longer deferred by rising financial requirements. If it is likely that he was also deterred by the formalities of respectable dalliance, it may well be that he was too wary, too impecunious, or too inhibited to avail himself of a prostitute's services. In his involuntary abstinence he may have salvaged some masculine pride from identifying with the assertive but disengaged sexuality of the lion comique. The stage swell conducted a drama of masculine display, a form of collective narcissism — that of men showing off to other men.

Is there further meaning to be squeezed out of the swell song as songtext-cum-performance type? Current critical practice emphasises the polysemic properties of the most obvious of cultural forms, demonstrating how these can be made to reveal deeper structures of complementary and oppositional relationships within wider systems of signification and text/context interdependency. Such analysis demands attention not only to the author/ performer, but to the reader/receiver as crucial agent in the construction of meaning. Before turning to consider the music-hall audience in this role, I should perhaps step outside the cautious practice of the historian with his nose pressed up close against the sources, and offer some bolder interpretive scheme in the spirit of the structuralist disciple who urges that such analysis should possess 'surprise value'.[48] What does strike me in larger symbolic terms about the swell song is the inherent tension between images of indulgence and constraint. On the one hand there is the licence of champagne-induced pleasure and the way in which it is literally bodied forth in performance, on the other hand is the constrictive nature of the dress in which the authentic good time is pursued — the formality and corset-like line of evening dress and the grip of the collar, the 'excruciating all-rounder' of Ritchie's report. This could be read as expressive of a deeper tension within capitalism itself on the admissability of pleasure and consumption in a work-centred culture. No great surprise in this, perhaps, but I turn for that to gorgeous George himself, who concluded *Champagne Charlie* by brandishing a bottle fitted with a device that exploded the cork to order, a final ejaculatory flourish whose *signifiance* I leave to the critical imagination of the reader.[49]

IV

Thus the swell song engaged with its audience through a wealth of social, material and stylistic connotations, encapsulated within the part realistic, part idealised, part parodied, but instantly recognisable persona of the lion comique. Leybourne and company reflected and produced a particular definition of a contemporary social type, showing how it might be lived out through a specific repertoire of behaviour, appearance and manner, and exalting its particular masculinity to an admiring bachelor sub-culture within the halls. Yet the swell songs also engaged the attention of other constituencies in the audience, while within their more obvious target groups their meaning was often shifting and ambiguous.

To understand the further reach of the swell song and its ambiguities it is necessary to emphasise how endemic was the element of parody in music-hall song and performance. Any popular style or hit was immediately vulnerable — *Champagne Charlie* was instantly parodied on stage, and Leybourne's carriage and four was mocked by Walter Laburnum who drove a cart and a pair of donkeys in its wake. We have seen too, in passing, how the swell songs and their performance might carry an element of self-parody. In some of the songs, however, the thrust of parody was much more scathing and direct, while in performance a number of them allowed a mixed interpretation in which the role was offered for applause or derision simultaneously, according to the varying discriminations of a composite audience.

Like its more vengeful brother satire, parody operated in two basic directions, neatly rendered in our contemporary usage as to send up or to put down. Thus it might exaggerate pretension to the point of absurdity, or it might choose the alternative tactic of reducing what was represented as extraordinary to the commonplace (as with Laburnum's donkeys and trap). Songs like Vance's *Lord Swoon* operated through hyperbole to parody the swell at his most effete, but a commoner sub-type was the deflationary song which exploited what we may recall as one of the long-standing historical-cum-literary categories in which the swell was known — that of the counterfeit.

The swell as sham, the gent as fraud — as we have seen, these had been ready targets for attack from outside, but they drew a good deal of fire from inside the halls too. Swell songs, commented the *Era* (20 August 1865), 'frequently draw forth satirical remarks and odious comparisons between the real and the ideal'. The stratagems and sacrifices to which those of modest means were forced to resort in pursuit of the ideal provided obvious humorous capital. *How Does He Do It?*, sang G.H. Macdermott of a certain son and heir to two pie shops in Surrey who paraded as a toff in the West End: 'His name is Jones, but he asserts / 'Tis Henri Montmorency.' Maintaining appearances on a slender or non-existent budget was a common theme: as Walter Laburnum's *Fashionable Fred* proclaimed, 'I have a decent coat / Though I haven't got a groat.' But the note of indulgence, and even applause for these small-scale social heroics, was seldom more than a hairline away from a mockery that could be quite devastating. Parody became particularly explosive in the acts of the female swells, the male impersonators who aped the lions comique. Their acts were in themselves parodies, but their specific impact came in the way they pressed home their mockery of the swell as counterfeit, charging not only that he was less than the real thing in terms of dress and manner, but that crucially he was less than a man.

Male impersonation was an integral part of the English theatrical tradition, and its particular embodiment on the halls in the form of the fashionable young man was to become one of the major performance types in nineteenth and twentieth-century variety. In this and its variants it is a complex phenomenon that deserves much fuller treatment than can be accommodated here. But it does seem that the female as gent was a more disturbing characterisation in the 1860s and 70s than in its later apotheosis in such as Vesta Tilley. On one level, of course, we may take it that the role flattered the men in the audience. What could be more admirable than that a woman should want to take on the attributes of the superior sex (with the saving clause that this was an episode at play rather than a real social challenge)? Casting a woman as 'one of the chaps' also served to reduce distance and the difficulties of formal address between the sexes, suggesting that she might be manageable on male terms rather than as an unpredictable female. But as might be expected in this role there were considerable ambiguities and, in the particular context we are dealing with, the honorary chap might turn round and savage those presumed to be 'his' pals.

This comes across strongly in the songs of Nellie Power, whose career as one of the earliest female stars on the halls derived largely from her swell impersonations. (Others noted in playing the role were Kate Harley, Jenny

Stanley, Fannie Leslie, Louie Sherrington, Annie Hindle and Ellie Wesner.) Nellie Power made her name originally in the late 1860s doing imitations of George Leybourne, and in 1872 she had her first independent hit with *Tiddy fol Lol* which celebrated the doings of a real swell:'He's got ten thousand a year, tiddy fol lol / Drinks champagne at the bars / Smokes Intimidad cigars ...' The anonymous hero of the song was the son of a tailor called Brown, but in other matters his credentials were impeccable. He is also acquitted on the implicit charge of doubtful masculinity: 'Though he looks and dresses well / He's no lardy dardy swell.' It was to this latter theme that Power returned in her next and biggest hit, *The City Toff or The Crutch* (stick) *and Toothpick*. This pilloried the imitation swell both for his paltry style and his effeminancy:

And he wears a penny flower in his coat, lah di dah!
And a penny paper collar round his throat, lah di dah!
In his hand a penny stick,
In his mouth a penny pick,
And a penny in his pocket, lah di dah!

The song remained a hit for two years, selling a thousand copies a day acording to its author, E.V. Page, who pocketed £500 in royalties. The song certainly hit home with the subject of its caricature, for on one occasion a young man in the audience was so incensed that he hurled a soda water syphon at Nelly Power.[50]

Though this seems an exceptional incident, it is plain that the swell song exploited the tensions generated by the ambiguities and oppositions of class, status, gender and generation. Circumstantially at least, it seems that the oppositions lay not just between performer and his target group but between sections of the audience. Most songs were less openly provocative than Nelly Power's, but in large mixed urban audiences they could be read in ways that excited a variety of cross-cutting responses. To working-class spectators, a man like Leybourne could demonstrate the triumph of the natural gentleman in his convincing portrayal of upper-class manners, while remaining one of them — according to Chance Newton he often reverted to his 'mechanic manner'. At the same time, as we have seen, Champagne Charlie was a compelling role-model for the young clerks in the audience. But if the swell song exemplified and validated a certain style, it also drew attention to those like the young clerks who might fall pathetically short of the ideal. If Leybourne might have appealed to workers as an example of what one working-class commentator, Thomas Wright, the Journeyman Engineer, called a 'genuine swell ... a being to be admired', his performance might also have confirmed them in their distaste for what Wright called 'the cheap imitation swell (who was) fit only to be kicked'.[51] In this Wright was also attacking the youth of his own class for such affectations, adding a generational tension to the mix. One of the earliest notices of Nelly Power's success with *The Crutch and Toothpick* was from the Cambridge music hall in the East End, where Leybourne had been a great hit as Champagne Charlie. It was a hall with a strong working-class following, but with a good number of clerks in its audience too.[52] We can perhaps now understand why such halls gave the swell songs their popular momentum.

Perhaps too it was in such halls that clerks got their own back for any aspersions on their social skills, by enjoying themselves at the expense of another variant in the genre, the coster swell. Again, this is an important type in itself, and at this point was a more vigorous representation than the sentimentalised cockney of the late century. It was commonly played back to back with the society swell as in Vance's 'dainty exquisite and rugged vulgarian'. Another notable coster swell act of the period was Lloyd's *Immensikoff, the Shoreditch Toff* from 1873 (at the peak of the wages boom). Most of the song proclaims the superior style of his wardrobe, and was clearly the stuff of parody — thus the song cover shows him in all the conventional apparatus of the swell, but he carries a club in place of a cane. One writer, reviewing another song of the type, *Spicey Bill*, noted the singer's extensive patter which included much attention to his 'toggery … the while wiping his nose on his sleeve'.[53] One can almost hear the sniggers from the clerks.

But again, parody might march hand in hand with validation, further exploiting sectional antipathies within the audience. Jenny Hill enjoyed nationwide success with a coster song (also the result of meticulous observation) called *'Arry* (E.V. Page again), introduced in the early 80s but no doubt inspired by the series of comic stories written by A.J. Milliken in *Punch* in the 1870s; their hero, also an 'Arry, became established in the language as a shorthand for the stereotype cockney swell, and indeed in general for the working man as lout on the spree.[54] One reviewer clearly read Hill's song on these terms: 'We should like all the 'Arrys in London to see her in character and to learn how ridiculous they are.'[55] However, though some might see the song as a put-down, it contained within it a jaunty defence of its hero:

> The Upper Ten may jeer and say
> What cads the 'Arries are,
> But the 'Arries *work* and *pay their way*
> While doing the lah-di-dah.

Did hearty proletarian cheers then drown the sniggers of the counter jumpers? Certainly the coster swell was not an automatic figure of fun among his cockney fellows. The costermonger was not in fact strictly a proletarian, but a penny capitalist with a necessary streak of competitive individualism. His trade demanded a certain style and self-advertisement of which the swell might be a natural projection, and the surge of casual migrants into London in this period may have added a further note of defensive pride. Thus what from outside might be seen as a caricature may well have appeared within its own culture as the celebration of an authentic indigenous type. From this angle, the cockney swell was neither a lout nor a buffoon, but the small man writ large.

V

In the swell song, music hall began to establish its own distinctive voice. Together with other modes within the broad field of comic song it marked a shift away from the leisurely narrative of the ballad tradition to a more episodic or situational representation.[56] The song was no longer that of a traditional air but one commercially produced by a professional song writer, the words by a professional performer or lyricist. The text was now less literary or poetic, and comes poorly from off the page, relying as it did on performance *and* reception to detonate the charges that lie in the compressions and ellipses of its otherwise unremarkable language. (Singers were frequently taken by surprise at the way the audiences would 'manufacture' meanings unsuspected by the performer.) The swell songs exploited a range of cues that drew the audience into active recognition of its own various social selves, and directly exploited the sympathies and distances within and between them. As a genre, its form can only be satisfactorily defined in terms of performance and use.

In content, the swell song is one of male exploit and display; in both, its historic and contemporary models are aristocratic or upper class though the style is never merely imitative, but rather an appropriation. In its actions there is a sense of licence, particularly where they echo the traditional exploits of lordlings about town, thumbing their nose at authority and tasting the forbidden pleasures of low life. But the licence of the swell song seems less hell-bent and destructive (either of self or others), and more a matter of the indulgences of a self-regarding and mock-heroic male freemasonry, excused, if excuse were necessary, in the disarming and egalitarian language of the 'boys' on the spree. In display, the songs celebrate the new availability and consumption of the externals of fashionable life, demonstrating how they were to be mastered while wryly acknowledging the difficulties of this exercise. In the arch and knowing manner of the halls, the songs and their singers provided a style manual for those who sought status and identity in appearances.

In all, the genre projected a potent if slippery ideology of pleasure and social identity, which fused a traditional utopianism with the wakening yet uncertain expectations of a modern industrial society. The swell was a product of a larger system of liberal capitalism that was now affording its subordinates a greater share of its economic surplus, while offering a fuller sense of membership through the extension of the franchise (1867) and various middle-class schemes of cultural association or 'social citizenship'.[57] Although a rogue and arrivist branch of the system, the music-hall industry echoed the mainstream discourse of consensual liberalism, but in a language and symbolism shorn of the latter's moralising gradualism. Thus within the ancient conceit of the common man as king for the day — or lord for the night — the swell song transcended the short-run gratifications of the traditional good time and offered its own sensational vision of a more permanent world of progress and plenty. It is a measure of the plausibility of such a vision that the swell was so hugely indulged. At the same time, the music-hall public withheld full faith in such a promise, just as working people generally withheld full faith in a liberal society whose rhetoric of meliorist incorporation could not disguise the continuing inequities and deprivations of their class experience. Parody safely deflated the swell's more extravagant promises, and one retort to *Champagne Charlie* challenged him directly as a cruel delusion:

To hear them praise the sparkling wine
It makes a man severe
When they know they cannot raise the price
Of half a pint of beer.[58]

If music hall found its own voice in the swell song there were many who disliked what it had to say. Leybourne was said to 'spurt filth from his mouth', and the lions comiques were generally vilified for their glorification of sex and drink.[59] But the more revealing charges against the halls of this period were those that recognised a more insidious malaise. A writer in *Tinsley's Magazine* of April 1869, who seemed well acquainted with the halls, thought music hall more dangerous now that it had replaced 'vulgarity of the coarsest kind' with 'vulgarity gilded'. He deplored 'its levelling-up theory of democracy ... and that sham gentility which has become so abnormally prominent among the striplings of the uneducated classes.' Under the tutelage of the stage swell, the 'gent' was becoming a yet more numerous and intrusive discomfiture to polite society.

Business collapses and a flattening out of profit levels disturbed bourgeois confidence in these years, while the extension of the franchise and increases in wages announced a newly advantaged lower class. The democratisation of leisure seemed to threaten social as well as political and economic differentials, as another contemporary noted:

From being machines, fit only for
machine work or inert quiescence, the
masses are given the liberty of being
men — gentlemen indeed, if in that
term be applied the possession of
leisure, the power of being 'at large' —
a coveted attribute of gentility.[60]

The swell, the gent, and 'Arry (*Tinsley's* lumped them all together) now threatened gentility along a wide front. Add to this the charge of effeminancy and the fear that he was an endemic product of the degenerate modern city, and we can appreciate why the swell was castigated as 'that general enemy', to recall Jerrold's phrase, that could not be simply laughed away.[61]

The full resonance of the swell song in popular life during its heyday in the 1860s and 70s remains elusive. Certainly it captured a wide audience, clearly registering as a hit with the working classes as well as with the young counter-jumpers; it also won its following in the provinces as well as the metropolis. Indeed it has been seen as marking a distinct change in the class consciousness of popular culture, a change away from an anti-aristocratic and populist tone attended by a fall in the intellectual level. Vance and Leybourne are represented as aberrations from an authentic working-class voice, glamorising the aristocracy and blunting class animosities.[62] The schema of which these interpretations form part command respect but inevitably they oversimplify. Stuart Hall has reminded us that all popular forms combine the bogus and the authentic[63] — in the swell songs the combination is less an amalgam than a dialectic. The swell song was certainly not hostile to the aristocracy, but neither was it an exercise in slavish adulation. As we have seen, it was a knowing vulgarisation, with an ironic and self-conscious regard for the absurdities as well as the plausibilities of the exercise. As a text the swell song is intellectually banal, but as a performance type its levels of engagement are complex and various, at once idealised and realistic, normative and satirical.

If it departs from the true path of class conflict, the swell song nonetheless confronted approved values. A form of bohemianism, it automatically offended the bourgeois, setting play against work, heroic consumption against exemplary abstinence. In a similarly carnivalesque yet less abrupt way that was characteristic of music hall, it played with the prescribed categories of rank and gender. In historical terms, the swell song suggests a half-fantasised, half-actualised search for a style appropriate to an era of popular advance, when occupational sub-cultures were losing their primacy in working-class life, and the more homogenized culture of the late century had yet to cohere. In the lion comique's appropriation of the new formal dress there is a significant displacement of older traditions of holiday colour and display, but the suit is not yet the body's gaoler nor (with the flat cap) the fuliginous and hegemonic uniform of a regimented proletariat.[64]

Though the swell might be a powerful projection of energy, confidence and some defiance, I have suggested the counterpull of a certain folk-wariness, and there are other qualifications to be made if this re-evaluation is not to become too enamoured of Champagne Charlie and what one contemporary called his 'magnificent cheek'. It must be emphasised that the swell triumphalised a form of male behaviour in which women were merely accessories like the cane and the bottle. Moreover, his egalitarian generosity may often have been realised at the direct expense of women, as one victim from the Black country testified:

> I married a swell I did ... when I married him in the morning he had a smart gold watch and chain, and a smart dickey (shirt). But when we came to go to bed at night I'm blessed if he had even a shirt on; and ever since then I've had to keep him by working in the brickyard, and not only keep him, but find him money to drink.[65]

If he could avoid such destructive consequences for himself as well as others, the common man might enjoy himself richly through identification with the music-hall swell. In 1869–70, the Nine Hours movement laid claim to greater leisure time, and its working-class leaders couched their demands in the sober official language of improvement. But the enthusiastic reception afforded George Leybourne on his appearance at benefits in support of the cause bespeaks other projections of popular betterment among the rank and file.[66] Thus it can be argued that amid all the counterfeit trappings of the swell and the showbiz manipulation of the music-hall industry, Champagne Charlie spoke with the authentic voice of his class.

4   *White Skin, Black Masks: 'Nigger' Minstrelsy in Victorian England*

MICHAEL PICKERING

It is often thought, so far as popular song and dance is concerned, that the widespread influence of exported forms from America began around World War One. This common perspective ignores the whole phenomenon of 'nigger' or blackface minstrelsy. Dating from the second quarter of the nineteenth century, it essentially involved the impersonation of blacks by white performers who were offering white audiences a selective and stereotypical depiction of Afro-American character and culture. Quickly taken up in England after its introduction in London in 1836, 'nigger' minstrelsy became one of the most prominent forms of popular entertainment in the nineteenth century, both inside and outside the music hall. Why this immense appeal? Wherein lay its lasting success across the whole social spectrum of white audiences in Britain?

Blackface minstrelsy was intended from the first as commercial popular entertainment, and it remained as commercial entertainment to the end. But it was not only that, and regardless of its scale, the success of minstrelsy in Victorian England cannot be explained without reference to its use and aesthetic values for the broad mass of the population. These values were centrally lodged in the clowning of minstrelsy. Everybody loves a clown. Clowns speak to us of joy and sorrow, wisdom and folly: the inseparability of opposite attributes. Among other things, clowns flatter us by making fun of us; they affirm our good sense of ourselves by displaying that sense in an inverted image. But as a form of clowning, 'nigger' minstrelsy was at the same time socially and historically specific. There were, of course, many antecedents in England for the use of burnt cork: in poaching, in social protest and in popular custom. The functions and meanings of blackface masking in these activities were determined by the context of its use. If clowning is commonly a form of socially inverted behaviour, and dependent on disguise, then many of the features of minstrelsy were shared by customary dramatic and processional practices in eighteenth- and nineteenth-century English popular culture, particularly in relation to blacking-up. What distinguished minstrelsy in England from mumming in the vernacular arts and from other kinds of clowning

Fig. 4.1

Fig. 4.2

Fig. 4.3

Fig. 4.1 The 'Jim Crow' caricature. This version is taken from the cover of a forty-four verse New York edition of the Jim Crow song. The print combines the two stereotypes of male blacks predominant at the time: the tatter-demalion plantation hand and the urban dandy. (Author's collection).

Fig. 4.2 The foppish vanity of a swell 'coon' as portrayed on the cover of an 1843 edition of *Dandy Jim from Carolina*. Photo Bodleian Library, reproduced by permission (Harding Collection, Box 171).

Fig. 4.3 An 1871 edition of Will S. Hays' *The Little Old Cabin in the Lane*. Photo Bodleian Library, reproduced by permission (Harding Collection, Box 176).

in pantomime, music hall and circus entertainments was that it worked predominantly through the impersonation of black people by men of white skin.[1] As a form of mediation such impersonation popularized and amplified the historically limited knowledge of the 'negro' and in so doing helped to crystallize particular characterizations and stereotypical recognitions of black character.

In accepting this, we must at the same time beware of the dangers it may entail. Perhaps the greatest impediment to developing a historical cultural analysis of blackface minstrelsy is the restriction of attention to what we, in a changed historical context, define and rightly condemn as racist. The tendency of presentism, or 'chronocentrism' as Banton has called it, is 'to interpret other historical periods in terms of the concepts, values, and understanding of the present time'.[2] Signalling this danger is not a way of allowing backdoor entrance to a defence of empiricism in historical practice. 'The serious historian', as Carr has commented, 'is the one who recognizes the historically conditioned character of all values, not the one who claims for his own values an objectivity beyond history'.[3] Historical enquiry requires a reciprocal process of interaction between the historian in a given present and his or her evidence from the past, and between ideas and concepts and the inevitably contradictory manifestations of historical phenomena. We are today more sensitized to the presence of racism in our social midst than were our Victorian predecessors. This is, of course, to be welcomed, but a chronocentric emphasis upon the racist elements of 'nigger' minstrelsy, for the purposes of ideological censure, may nevertheless blinker our vision of its other important aspects. This may well reduce the possibility of moving towards a comprehensive account of minstrelsy's abiding appeal and success, and may well impede our understanding of the efficacy of the blackface code in facilitating a range of artistic acts.

Without wishing to minimise the contribution of 'nigger' minstrelsy to a developing English racism during the Victorian period, I shall argue that the significance of minstrelsy has to be understood in terms of a complex and variable relationship between three coordinates: theatrical convention, symbolic meanings and historical process. The symbolic meanings associated with minstrelsy were manifold and contradictory, and moved in an oscillating process between the two other coordinates, so that we have now to attempt to understand the dynamic of that movement if we are to explain the meanings it generated. To begin this attempt, in what is here an intentionally provisional way, it is necessary to give an account of how blackface minstrelsy developed in Britain. In some ways this was paralleled by its American development, which has been amply chronicled.[4] I shall therefore confine my own account to a brief resumé, concentrating particularly on its specifically English evolution during the Victorian period.

As a form of popular drama and music, the history of blackface minstrelsy in England falls roughly into three main phases. It would be folly to give these any rigid definition, since there was considerable overlap between them; they are nevertheless in certain ways distinctive. In the first phase, from 1836 to the mid 1840s, minstrelsy evolved from an initial solo type of performance within a routine theatrical package towards an autonomous institution with established conventions, a specific style of performance, and sufficient magnetism and repute soon to warrent the staging of an entire show in separate halls or theatres. During its first decade in England, minstrelsy also began to shift in tone from an earthy robustness and frenzied excitement towards an appeal in refinement and sentimentalism. Also detected during this phase is an incipient process of adaptation to the traditions and characteristics of English popular culture, and the early signs of a growth of distinctively English features. These shifts of tone, content and form were continued in the second phase, which lasted until the end of the nineteenth century.

This period saw the maturation of the minstrel show, particularly between 1850 and 1870, when minstrelsy was in its hey-day. Its basic structure as a form of entertainment was quite rapidly developed; individual parts within the show became specialized and certain roles precisely delineated. In contrast to the early music hall, the minstrel show quickly established a reputation for respectability and propriety that was long maintained. Accompanying this process, connections with Afro-American culture became increasingly exiguous, and minstrel troupes — a development occurring towards the end of the first phase — gradually grew larger, leading to the formation of companies along conventional business lines, and a general shift in the shows themselves towards diversity, grandeur and lavishness. As competitive pressure grew in the later nineteenth century, commercial tactics and gimmickry were cultivated more and more as a way of promoting custom and countering opponents; standardisation set in; ownership of companies became increasingly concentrated in the hands of fewer people; and a diversification of entrepreneurial interests began in order to secure greater control of the entertainment market and to protect companies against rival concerns or shifts in taste in one particular sector of the market. One such shift affected minstrelsy itself, during the 1890s and 1900s.

The third phase, from 1900 onwards, is a story of slow decline. Attempts at revival were occasionally made, with varying degrees of success. For new generations there was a novelty attraction in minstrelsy, while for those who could recall the grand days of the Mohawks or Sam Hague's Minstrels, nostalgia was a great source of appeal. To a considerable extent minstrelsy's decline was wrapped up in the decay of the music hall as a major cultural institution, though as with the music hall its acts and conventions showed a resilient propensity towards adaptations in other media and forms. The legacy of blackface acts can be traced in film, television, vaudeville, the enormous production of 'coon' songs by Tin Pan Alley, ragtime, early jazz and popular dance, and its potential continued to be successfully exploited in such acts as those developed by Al Jolson, Eddie Cantor, Amos n' Andy, Scott and Whaley, and BBC radio's 1930s Kentucky Minstrels. The Black and White Minstrel Show was the last vestigial, yet long-enduring flowering in Britain of the whole minstrelsy tradition.

While there were, both in England and America, various precedents for an impersonation of blacks on stage, and for the singing of 'negro' songs by whites, before the advent of minstrelsy itself, T. 'Daddy' Rice's negro impersonations had an immediate and explosive effect. The origin of his *Jump Jim Crow* song and dance is shrouded in legend, or rather embattled in conflicting documentation. The only certainty is that Rice copied it from a deformed black stableman, though how authentically black it is in origin is now impossible to tell. Yet the song, with its famous burden

> Wheel about and turn about
> An' do jis so,
> An' eb'ry time I wheel about
> I jump Jim Crow

and its comical dance, met with tremendous success in this country, following Rice's first appearance on the metropolitan stage, at the Surrey and the Adelphi, in 1836. (Fig. 4.1) Rice's singing and dancing were the centre-piece of a burletta written by him, entitled *Bone Squash Diabolo*, and this was succeeded over the next two years by similar 'Ethiopian operas', as Rice styled them.[5] Jim Crow became a pervasive presence, and not only on stage; spin-offs, such as Jim Crow hats and cigars, were marketed, and a mock autobiography quickly rushed into print.[6] Apart from being the major hit of the time, the song and dance of the 'lame old nig' were quite literally seminal in the development of nineteenth-century popular culture, because they inaugurated a whole new and long-durable form of entertainment. With them, as Charles Mackay put it in 1887, the 'nigger mania broke out with a virulence that has never since wholly subsided'.[7]

Though Rice only made one further visit to England, in 1842, he had set the trail of minstrelsy ablaze. John Dunn, styled the 'English Jim Crow', and J. A. Cave were among the first successful imitators of Rice in this country, but there were soon many others. In 1843 two other American minstrels visited – Ned Harper, famous for his burlesques of 'negro' character, and Joe Sweeney, who introduced the modern form of the banjo to England.[8] More significantly in the same year were the performances in London and the provinces of the celebrated Dan Emmett and his Virginia Minstrels. This was the first minstrel troupe to appear in England, though the Buckleys, an English family who had emigrated to America in 1839, also started up as a minstrel quartet in 1843 and were very successful, both in the States and in England, which they visited in 1846 and again in 1860.[9]

The emergence of the minstrel band occurred primarily for commercial reasons, a way of attracting audiences in a year when business was bad for New York theatres and popular entertainment seemed to have gone stale. But as Nathan has shown, the new combination was influenced also by a trend in 'negro' minstrelsy towards ensembles of two or three performers, and by the success in Europe and America of vocal quartets such as the Tyrolese Family Rainer.[10] That said, due acknowledgement should go to Emmett and his troupe for being the first 'nigger' minstrel band as such (despite claims to the contrary, particularly by E. P. Christy). In England as in America, it was Emmett's troupe who first popularised the classic minstrel combination of banjo, fiddle, tambourine and bone castanets, and while these instruments were later added to, they remained at the core of minstrel performance. The Virginia Minstrels also initiated the minstrel show as a separate entertainment form rather than as interval songs and entr'actes, and their success in this was quickly capitalised on by numerous other combinations, such as the Ethiopian Serenaders, the Sable Harmonists and E. P. Christy's troupe, with its host of plagiarists in the 1840s and 50s (Reynolds refers to a veritable epidemic of Christy minstrels in England[11]). By 1860 minstrelsy was firmly established as a stable form of entertainment, and the following decade witnessed an even greater acceleration of its growth.

The considerable dynamism and flexibility of minstrelsy as a cultural form were manifest in, among other things, the innovative format for the minstrel show, which developed during the 1840s and early 50s. Although never completely uniform, the constitutive structure of the minstrel show was basically the same in America and England, and provided a stable and recognisable framework for both touring companies and those staged by native troupes.[12] At the same time the minstrel show format proved sufficiently wieldy for an enormous variation of content to be accommodated within it, including on this side of the Atlantic features which were specifically English.

Shows generally fell into the three or possibly four sections: the first part, the olio, the after-piece and the walkaround. In the first part a single row of minstrels sat around in a semi-circle, with a figure known as the interlocutor in the centre, and at either side the two corner men, Tambo and Bones (in America, the corner men were known as end men). Mr Interlocutor introduced the performance with the standard phrase: 'Gentlemen, be seated. We will commence with the overture.' Following the overture there was a comic question-and-answer routine involving the corner men and interlocutor. The function of Tambo and Bones here seems, at least originally, to have been to undercut the pretension and gravitas of the interlocutor, but more generally the interlocutor served as the straight man to the corner-men's comic gags, puns and conundrums. The innovative framework of their interrelationship was essentially a rapid-fire, cross-talk exchange between diametrically opposed types; comic duos have been developing its potential ever since. The corner men also engaged in madcap antics and buffoonery in the venerable tradition of the Fool, while the interlocutor functioned in addition as a crucial guiding spirit, orchestrating the progress of the whole show. Music as well as repartee characterised the first part. A medley of plantation songs or an operatic selection was used to round off, the end of the section sometimes being marked by a preliminary walkaround that would feature each performer centrestage in his own particular speciality.[13] The olio, as the name suggests, consisted of variety entertainment, and could include such turns as acrobatic displays, clog dancing, 'wench' numbers, stump speeches, sketch acting, musical novelty acts, instrumental solos, glees, renditions of sentimental ballads, mimicry topical skits, illusions and full-scale concerted song performances. This second section proved extremely elastic in form and function, and as a type of variety entertainment prefigured the vaudeville show of the early twentieth century.[14] The after-piece was, in the main, originally intended to burlesque 'high' cultural entertainment such as Italian opera and Shakespearean drama, and basically consisted of forms of slapstick and farce. Stump speeches – mock lectures on current questions or affairs – could also be included in this section. One of the favourite pieces of James Francis of the Mohawks was a skit on temperance oratory, and is typical of this form of satire.[15] Lastly, as minstrel shows developed, a walkaround finale was often added, and this usually consisted of solo and choral song, and dancing to instrumental 'symphonies'. Emmett wrote his famous 'Dixie' for exactly such a finale section.[16] In general terms the walkaround was very much the antecedent of the finale associated with later vaudeville and revue productions.[17]

The minstrel show was thus intrinsically vibrant and compelling in structure and style of presentation, and progenitive of other popular theatrical acts and routines. That is one measure of its magnetism as an entertainment form. But minstrel shows in England would never have remained so popular, as time went on, without becoming anglicized to the extent that they did, and without the introduction of new and ever more spectacular elements. Evolution and innovation were vital to the maintenance of success. As its basic structure was becoming established, certain significant modifications were being made to the English minstrel set-up. Harmonisation and operatic music were introduced into minstrelsy by the emigré Buckley family, and thereafter harmony and fine musical arrangement became one of the hallmarks of professional English minstrelsy. Reynolds considered its quality in this respect to be far superior to that of blackface yankees, while MacQueen Pope singled out 'Pony' Moore's troupe for the way their voices blended together 'like the tunes of an organ'.[18] A further development was the addition of an orchestra, whose conductor usually acted as musical director for the troupe. There was also a new sentimentalism, developing out of the Ethiopian Serenaders' act somewhat at the expense of the earlier comic elements upon which their predecessors had relied.[19] Much of the original appeal of negro delineators and minstrels had been founded on their singularity and quaintness, the catchiness of their tunes, and the way their odd comicality gave novel features to foolery and clowning. These attractions gradually waned, making minstrelsy's links with Afro-American culture itself even more tenuous. The comic parts became monopolised by the caricature of the 'negro' dandy with his constantly unrealised pretension to grandiloquence (fig. 4.2) whereas the tatterdemalion plantation black, particularly as a result of Stephen Foster's songs, became the object, in a much more concentrated fashion, of a sentimental pathos. Essentially 'the trend' was 'away from simplicity and primitive realism'[20] towards a narrower seductive courting of the senses and affects. One aspect of this is the shift towards spectacle in attire, particularly among the court-dress minstrel troupes who 'dressed in elaborate costumes of the English court, plush coats and kneebreeches, stockings and buckled shoes, and powdered white wigs'.[21] Stage minstrelsy's era of grand extravagance had dawned.

From the mid to late nineteenth century, British minstrelsy exhibited a broad range of forms. At one end of the scale the largest minstrel companies established themselves at fixed metropolitan venues and prided themselves on not needing to tour the provinces, as the smaller companies and troupes did. The Mohawk Minstrels are a representative case in point, as are the Moore and

Burgess Minstrels with whom they eventually merged in 1900. Founded by James and William Francis in 1867, the Mohawks began as a semi-professional troupe of 12 touring suburban halls in the Home Counties. The keen (show) business sense of the two brothers underlaid the Mohawks' establishment as an important metropolitan attraction; led them to snatch up Harry Hunter, a prolific songwriter and adroit interlocutor, as well as many other men of talent; and spurred them to spread out laterally into music publishing and the marketing of theatrical props. The characteristic expansionist policy of minstrel companies such as the Mohawks was carried even further by 'Colonel Jack' Haverly, an American who set the pace for creating a new level of audience appeal in Britain after a point of saturation had been reached around 1880. Acting solely as manager and publicist, Haverly cleverly exploited the commercial opportunities offered by the changing leisure patterns and retail revolution of the late nineteenth century. His troupes provided grand scale spectacle and extravaganza entertainment, backed up by efficient organisation and Barnumesque promotion. Haverly was an empire builder, a man with an eye for the main chance, the Lew Grade of the blackface arts. He expanded his enterprises economically in both vertical and horizontal directions and, in an instance of that paradox of capitalist development, the spirit of market competitiveness he fostered contributed to a reduction of competition, with other companies forced to follow suit or go under.

Big-time minstrelsy became characterised by a division of labour between a proprietorial management and professional bourgeois (or petit bourgeois) artistes contracted to a limited liability company; by the pressures of economies of scale and maximisation of productivity; and by economic and organisational concentration and integration. But the potlatch-style staging of ever-more mammoth shows represented the decline of stage minstrelsy, and not only for economic reasons: the unique dynamic of its structure became progressively diluted, and minstrel shows became increasingly less differentiated from any other kind of variety entertainment. The elastic format of the minstrel show was made to accommodate a whole host of extraneous material, and a whole pack of different song styles and genres, working together in a now cluttered farrago with coon songs and plantation melodies, stump speeches and breakdown dances. By the 1900s, minstrelsy had effectively merged into variety, vaudeville and musical comedy.

During the second half of the century, professional stage minstrelsy could be found in various acts performed within the broad range of popular entertainment available in the various types of music hall and singing saloon, as well as in the fully fledged shows performed at variety theatres like St James's Hall in Piccadilly. Outside of these contexts the extension of blackface acts was extremely widespread and pervasive. For present purposes these can be divided into two broad, interrelated categories: street entertainment and local amateur performances. The former included minstrel acts at country fairs and wakes, chapel gatherings, race meetings, seaside resorts, markets, annual beanos and festivals, Punch and Judy shows, village and small-town concerts, pantomimes, circuses and travelling shows.[22] The vogue for burnt-cork forms of outdoor entertainment developed from the late 1840s and lasted until the turn of the century; at the seaside, after that time, pierrot entertainment became the commonest form of alfresco act. As their contexts of performance indicate, such forms of blackface acts involved street busking and setting up a pitch at any likely place of custom. As with professional stage minstrelsy, they were almost exclusively performed by men, in what has been described as 'masculine musical comedy'.[23] Often resorted to as a result of poverty and unemployment, street 'nigger' serenading at times attained an excellence of quality to equal that of professional artistes.[24]

At the other end of the scale from big-time minstrelsy, the flexibility of the form was further demonstrated by the amateur performance of blackface songs, acts and routines in community and domestic milieux. Here the minstrel mode either became assimilated into existing customary forms of vernacular drama, dance and the general structures of local song culture, or came to influence the form and content of emergent types of cultural expression and entertainment. Blacking-up was already an integral element in such popular festive activities as plough-witching, pace-egging, mumming, morris and May customs; amateur singers in town and village happily integrated plantation songs into their repertoires; local minstrel troupes were widespread; and various regional forms of popular entertainment, such as 'niggering', coconut dancing, and waffen fuffen or Tommy Talker comic bands, manifested the imprint of blackface artistry.

Having given a necessarily rudimentary outline of the development and content of minstrelsy in England, as well as an indication of its manifold adaptations and allied forms, I shall now concentrate on the most important as well as the most difficult aspects of blackface artistry in this period: the complex dissonances within the genre, and the issue of culturally stratified processes of reception. The questions raised by these aspects of minstrelsy are crucial to the major concern of this essay, which is to contribute to an analysis of the durable appeal of blackface acts and activities in England. The major problem confronting any explanation of British minstrelsy is how we read the mask; how we attempt to understand what it may have signified at the time. What is of central importance in any effort to unpack its connotative meanings is the distinction between 'negro' delineation, drawing upon plantation themes, and acts which used the device of masking to advance certain specialised stage roles and effects. The distinction should not be conceived as clear cut, as if these two basic facets of the 'nigger' minstrel mask did not cross-refer; meanings and pleasures, I would suggest, were generated by a complex and changing interaction between them, for symbolically the new form of mask in minstrelsy involved a reassembling and redefining of the blackface code, with older aspects and associations from stage and vernacular traditions promiscuously entangled with a new set of aspects and associations relating to the Afro-American 'negro'. What the mask meant in minstrelsy was not then necessarily determined by recognition of *either* 'negro character' *or* clown's regalia, for although the two could be and undoubtedly were at times seen as quite unrelated, so much of the point of a specifically 'nigger' form of harlequinade is that it offered a quite deliberate symbolic conflation. Its very success was dependent on the exuberant ambiguity engendered by this as well as on its adaptability to an English context.

What I am suggesting came to have more importance was the *degree* to which recognition was made of mask and costume as conventions or as realist motifs in a dialectical movement between the two. How can Chirgwin's famous diamond-shaped, white eye-patch be understood except as a theatrical device and trademark, particularly in view of the fact that his face was sometimes painted white and the patch black? This example probably provides us with a limit case, that could be matched at the opposite pole by an ingenuous belief in the verisimilitude of Jim Crow or Mister Bones. Sam Redfern – the 'Black Boss of the Benighted Bohemians' – could, in Reynolds's view, have 'worked his act equally well without the aid of burnt cork', but it did nevertheless contribute to his knockabout style of humour, as did his white ulster coat and Russian boots.[25] The same could be said for countless other music-hall performers. The black mask served to distinguish and signal a certain kind of act and certain kinds of comic effects. Its anonymity no doubt also served to mitigate stage-fright and first-night nerves; the mask could be dropped when self-confidence was assured or an act had been developed. Another advantage of the black mask for tyros was that their identity could be concealed from the public if the initial act they had assembled was given the bird; they could live to fight another night. Finally, the force of convention and fashion should be acknowledged. The fact that it was 'all the rage' is why so many famous music hall and variety performers – the Great Vance, Dan Leno, Little Tich among others – began their careers in burnt cork. Yet at the same time minstrelsy's distinctive feature in terms of the conventions of blacking-up was that it had introduced a whole set of relatively new associations that stereotyped the 'negro' in different ways, and that these became amalgamated with the older senses and functions of masquerade in English cultural traditions. What minstrelsy assimilated most of all from popular custom and traditional vernacular drama was the licence which blacking-up afforded, creating a cultural space bracketed off from the moral rules and regulated behaviour of mundane reality, but it did this at once via an association with black people in a new dynamic theatrical format and within a developing professionalism and commercial provision of popular entertainment. It was the coalescence of all these factors which made the minstrel mask so volatile in meaning.

What was involved in minstrelsy was that 'creative mésalliance' of modes of dress, songs and language 'that gave much of late-Victorian music hall humour its point'.[26] The humour of minstrelsy burlesque or stump orations hinged crucially on the incongruity of blackface impersonations, as did the whole effect of 'coon' love songs, which in varying degrees comically subverted the tone and content of the Victorian parlour ballad, not only by treating the theme of romance with a flippant lightheartedness, but also by using the coon buffoon caricature to ironically send up a mawkish sentimentalism: some of the songs of G. H. Elliott – the 'Chocolate Coloured Coon' – provide an example of this.[27] The minstrel mode facilitated parody. The incongruous use of existing aesthetic forms could work to expose and make comic the habitual effect of certain technical devices. To give just one example from a relatively late British minstrel song, the opening lines

An ebony tinted maid of affectation
Was loved by a gent of tawny hue

set the ironic tone for the rest of what proves to be a cleverly written comic piece precisely because of their adoption of the pompous, overblown discourse of polite parlour verse.[28] Of course talent, like murder, will out. Acts like that staged in the late nineteenth century by the Bohee brothers – two real blacks – commanded a wide appreciation of their excellent skills. But while post-bellum black minstrels were successful in England, there seems on the whole to have been a greater preference among English audiences for imitation black performers rather than the genuine article, even when that was framed within the minstrel mode. This can only be explained with reference to minstrelsy's dissonant fusions and the excitement and delight aroused by them. So long as we continue to think of minstrelsy in terms of the either/or dichotomy between realist representation and theatrical artifice which bourgeois literary ideology has insisted on for so long, then we will continue to miss or misinterpret what it was that made the minstrel mode so dynamic and successful.

Before discussing this in terms of performer-audience relations, it would be useful to amplify a little further the ways in which minstrelsy proved adaptable to an existing but at the same time evolving popular culture. This needs much more extended study, but certain key links should be noted. Firstly, caricatures were very much to the taste of popular audiences at the time, and those presented were quickly integrated into a general range of dramatic stereotypes and stock characters. Minstrelsy also proved readily adaptable to existing comic and farce routines, and contemporary dramatic genres. The weird and exaggerated distortions of early minstrelsy chimed in, for instance, with the grotesqueries of clowning in the Grimaldi harlequinade and pantomime, and was well suited to the existing popular taste for melodrama, with its abrupt changes of pace and mood, its athletic and stylised acting, and the display of emotion which was at its heart.[29] Not only was minstrelsy moulded to a John Bull anti-slavery sentiment; more broadly, as Bratton has shown, it was adapted for use in making satirical social comment on the English scene, in localising allusion and reference.[30]

Last but by no means least, the minstrel mode proved highly compatible in the Victorian period with a developing repertory of popular song types, themes and conventions, and with the new emphasis upon verbal play and techniques. The various kinds of minstrel song had their own themes and conventions, both in the comic and sentimental realms, but they shared others with music hall and parlour song generally, and in yet further ways worked parodically or became amalgamated with subjects or generic types found elsewhere in the popular tradition, sometimes with fantastic or bizarre effects. Hunter's *The Coster Coon*, whose hero is a 'nig-no-ra-mus', plays on a celebrated staple of the metropolitian music hall; *Haulie Boys*, written and sung by Joseph Garland of Haverley's Mastodon Minstrels, mongrelises the sea shanty; and the Jim Dandy 'negro' stereotype of minstrel songs entangled even further the symbolic associations and complexity of audience response involved in the tradition of music-hall representations of mashers, knuts and swells.[31] Topical reference to national events and developments continued to be made both in songs whose verses could be constantly kept up to date, as for instance in the Great Mackney's *The Whole Hog or None*, or in songs such as Hunter's *Woman's Rights* written for the purpose of contemporary social comment.[32] The pervasive Victorian taste for verbal humour was readily catered for by English minstrelsy, particularly in the shape of the pun. To take just two examples, again from the prolific pen of Harry Hunter; *Uncle Jupe Lubs Chicken Soup* ends as follows:

Old Uncle Jupe, he lubs a joke,
   Sez he's one ob de stars,
And his Ma called him Jupiter
   Cause he's a son of Ma's;
She reared him in the milky way
   And he's heard her confess
When he was christened Jupiter
   She wore a Saturn dress,
It's Sattun sure what she sat on
Was then a sat on dress

while his *I know a gal dat lubs a Coon* has the verse:

My heart is in a pulpy state
   It's in a palpitation;
My gals like dat, because she's fat,
   She's my in-fat-uation.[33]

Countless other examples could be given to illustrate this accommodation of 'nigger' and 'coon' songs to the immense pleasure of English music-hall audiences in all kinds of linguistic dalliance, but the point is I think sufficiently established.

As all these examples show, the formulas of minstrel songs could be shaped around the needs, pleasures and attitudes that were components of their English audiences' particularised kinds of interest and response. This potential of minstrelsy for extremely varied adaptation is particularly important in understanding its appeal in England: an appeal which was in significant ways quite different to its attraction in what was then still often thought of as the New World. Essentially, two major reasons have been advanced for 'nigger' minstrelsy's success in ante-bellum America: its satirical power and its function in race relations. Saxton, Zanger and Hitchcock have (among others) demonstrated the appeal to popular audiences of minstrelsy's capacity to puncture the pretensions of Eastern America's elitist culture and to burlesque resented 'high' cultural imports such as Jullien's epic concerts.[34]

Huggins' observation of the adaptation of early minstrel caricatures to pre-existent white American comic types is best developed by Toll in his discussion of minstrelsy in the context of an emergent 'common man's culture' in early nineteenth-century America.[35] Toll is also notable for focusing on minstrelsy's function in serving as an overt vehicle in the North for covert and ambivalent feelings with regard to the Afro-American population. The minstrel show's success in the 1840s was coincident with the emergence of slavery as a major national controversy. It is argued that the grossly caricatured version of 'negro' peculiarities and culture which the minstrels portrayed satisfied a deep-rooted need to conceive of blacks as radically different from free, white Americans. This was especially the case in the 1850s when slavery became the centre of a struggle to destroy the Union and to allow blacks to challenge whites for land, jobs and status. As Toll succinctly puts it: 'Most white Americans act out their need for racial subordination only when they feel that their own interests and values are challenged'. Not surprisingly, in this developing context, the anti-slavery aspect of blackface acts rapidly diminished, and the black became increasingly represented in narrow, derogatory caricatures. Coupled with this was the shift, after the Civil War, towards nostalgic retrospect centred around the type of the Old Darky, a reassuring and comforting image of the (now legally free) black 'that whites desperately needed and clung to'.[36]

The absence of any significant black population in early Victorian England clearly indicates a quite different source for minstrelsy's appeal. As we have seen, minstrelsy's main elements as a cultural form and mode of stage entertainment properly crystallised in America during the years following the cessation of hostilities with England in 1815, and as far as minstrelsy's initial phenomenal success in this country is concerned, this connected with a profound fascination for life in the New World which quite swept away the anti-American sentiments of the revolutionary period. To some extent, though it is uncertain whether he may have influenced the development of 'nigger' minstrelsy itself, the way for Jim Crow Rice in England had been paved by the actor and mimic Charles Mathews (1776–1835) with his black caricatures and rendering of the song *Possum up a Gum Tree*. This proto-minstrel song was a big hit, and his use of it 'the first certain example of a white man borrowing Negro material for a blackface act'.[37] Its success in England showed a receptive cultural context for the subsequent themes and characterisations of minstrelsy. Concern with life on the slave plantations of the South was primarily an expression of abolitionist sentiment. But as Enkvist has shown, it also related to curiosity about Negro character and culture, and should be seen as well in the context of a wider interest in things American and of the popularity, in humour and popular drama, of Yankee character and picaresque, Jonathanisms and frontier culture.[38]

The early boom period of minstrelsy was also coincident with the formation of a new, integrated, commercial popular culture of the industrialised town whose representative features included the prototypal music halls, gin palaces, the circus and travelling menagerie, a new popular Sunday press, criminal gazettes and the combination of politics and entertainment in the content of such newspapers as those run by Reynolds and Lloyd. Blackface minstrelsy during this period became very much a part of this process of cultural change, involving a reaction between and creative reassemblage of old and new. In various spheres of commercial entertainment there was clearly a demand for new material and forms. Minstrelsy in certain ways met with an appetite already whetted and amenable to it: audiences thrived on its novelty. The minstrel show has typically been celebrated by Americans as a unique and original form of American drama. There is obvious truth in this claim insofar as it was bred out of American vernacular resources and initially spoke to specifically American social structural relations. But in explaining its success in Britain, we need to note that even before its assimilation here, the idioms of Afro-American music and dance were in fact fused in minstrelsy with a mélange of British influences (Irish jigs, Scotch reels, English melodies and dance tunes). No cultural or artistic form is ever wholly original and unique. New forms always involve combinations of older genres and styles. What constitutes novelty and change in cultural practice is the means and manner in which these are mixed together with untried elements in a spirit of innovation, however opportunistic or entrepreneurial in motivation such a spirit might be.

The novelty of 'nigger' acts has thus to be qualified in terms of content and form, and in relation to the nature and extent of the receptivity with which they were met in England during the 1830s and 40s. This receptivity should be understood in terms of cultural continuity as well as change, in relation to processes of adaptation as well as adoption, and in the context of specific historical social relations.

Bratton has pointed to the fact that the minstrel show afforded such groups as the clergy, the dissenting lower middle class, petit bourgeois tradesmen and respectable ladies, their only access 'to certain liberating elements of popular entertainment'. This was due to the fact that the unsavoury reputation attached to the early music hall and to the later 'vulgar' kinds of hall was never acquired in the same way by the minstrel show, partly because of a bourgeois philanthropic concern up until the Civil War with the plight of the Southern slave, culminating in the ideological moment of Uncle Tom's Cabin, and partly because of the early emphasis British minstrelsy put upon family entertainment; anything remotely blue or risqué was likely to receive the order from the proprietor to 'wash up'. As John Abbot put it, minstrelsy 'was a form of family entertainment where a husband and wife could take their children without fear of being asked embarrassing questions afterwards'.[39] A particular kind of family is of course implied here, and it is not that of an East End docker. Minstrelsy in nineteenth-century England is particularly notable for its wide cross-class appeal, but this raises a particularly knotty problem in any consideration of its reception, for while we need to explain the nature of that broad appeal in the ways I have been suggesting, we cannot assume a uniformity of response and pleasure throughout the class society of the period.

As we have seen, the English had no strong need, either materially or psychologically, to develop and support strategies for coming to terms with 'uppity nigras', and the specifically English attitude within which minstrelsy resonated before the Civil War was one of opposition to the 'peculiar institution' of slavery. But the self-righteous anti-slavery emphasis on Britain as the land of the free would have had a double-edge in the significations of minstrelsy for many members of the English working class. The comparison between slave-labour and wage-slavery was commonly made in the Victorian age, both in defence of slavery and in the radical critique of a shallow philanthropic conscience. The middle-class hypocrisy which for some was epitomised by the Stafford House address was attacked precisely because abolitionist sentiment was seen as existing at the expense of attention to the suffering of the English poor. This was not, however, simply a matter of convenience. It was the denial of liberty by law which excited abolitionist fervour, rather than the imposition of the commodity form on to labour. Yet at the same time the particular interest of a blackface association with the 'negro' was its comparative value in relation to an assumption of Anglo-Saxon superiority. Minstrelsy was just as much about English social relations as it was about a scantily known Afro-American population. What was being symbolically worked out in minstrelsy, at a metalevel of commentary, were questions about the status of white Victorian society in the whole human social and biological order. These questions were posed within a framework of class differentiation. Race relations abroad were perceived in the light of class relations at home. It is this which links, in official and popular discourses, the derogatory images of 'negroes', Jews, Irish, hooligans, working-class 'roughs', criminals and whores: essentially they all belonged to a perpetually lower order that was defined by its antithetical contrast with English gentility.

Yet those whom Clarendon called 'dirty people of no name' enjoyed 'nigger' minstrelsy with the best of them. What we must then suppose is a negotiation of meaning influenced by existential conditions and position in the social class structure, and by educational attainment and political view. One can only speculate here. During the period when minstrelsy was booming, there was 'universal and ceaseless comparison of the American slave with the British labourer' in contemporary discussion and debate, and 'an overwhelming mass of evidence' points to the way in which some English working men, 'becoming conscious of the value of American propaganda and counter-propaganda, were resolved to bring them to bear upon their own desperate political and economic struggles'.[40] A predominantly fatalistic perspective would however have influenced a contrasting working-class response to the pathetic figure of the suffering slave or Uncle Ned stereotype, producing a rather different kind of identification with such sentimentalised victims of circumstance. Blacks, in other words, were regarded with pity from 'above' because they were oppressed people, but were perhaps regarded, by whites who were themselves oppressed, as much with a self-regarding sympathy as with a self-appeasing pity. Again, within a perspective from 'below', different (and indeed contradictory) responses may have been made to contrasting black stereotypes, such as that of the comic 'nigger': the hostility of that stereotype may have vibrated within a need to discover or invent others who were perceived as more inferior in order to compensate for the stigma of low status, and thus retain (or regain) at least a modicum of self-esteem.

In the absence of a social history of laughter, such possibilities (and one obviously think of others) must inevitably remain conjectural. At least more definite is the set of prejudicial conceptions of blacks which was communicated to English audiences generally by 'nigger' minstrelsy. Because of a lack of first-hand experience of black people, these conceptions are unlikely to have been challenged; most whites were simply not equipped with any alternative knowledge. The contradictions between popular stereotypes of blacks were manifest in the different personae and stock images of minstrelsy, which both produced and reproduced contradictions in white racial consciousness. From one side the 'negro' was the faithful, deferential servant; from another the indolent, undisciplined labourer. Turn him again, 'jis so', and one confronts the natural Christian, opposed from an opposite angle by the image of an unregenerate sinner; yet another pair of antithetical popular conceptions show him as a patient, suffering forbearing slave on the one hand, and on the other a brutal, lustful, vengeful savage.[41] Among the most prevalent derogatory elements in the popular mythology of blacks were malodorous body smell, large size of penis vs small size of brain, remarkable sexual appetite and promiscuity, tendency to savage violence, an inherent inclination to theft, work-shyness, stupidity and sloth, and of course a tremendous musicality and propensity to dance. With the exception of any explicit sexual reference, all these images were purveyed in minstrel songs.

The mythical 'noble savage' of eighteenth-century drama was obviously not adaptable to the farce and knockabout humour of minstrelsy. Consequently during the nineteenth century, there was a shift towards a more comic presentation, with blacks being depicted as lazy yet excitable, loving gaudy clothes, speaking a peculiar dialect, misusing long latinate words and commonly uttering malapropisms. Capping the image, the negro was pictured as tackling life's vicissitudes with a broad slice-of-watermelon grin. An idealised dignity and nobility was somewhat regained through the numerous dramatisations of *Uncle Tom's Cabin*, and the nostalgic sentimentalism of later plantation songs typified by the work of Stephen Foster, but the minstrel's comic aspects were not thereby supplanted and the noble savage figure only enjoyed a short, attenuated revival as a result of these developments.

Stereotypical representation of blacks in such material needs, however, to be seen in terms of three sub-categories: 'universal' physical features, typical psychological traits, and the imagery of plantation slave culture. Eugene Stratton's *The Whistling Coon*, from which his popular sobriquet was derived, concerned 'a knock-kneed, double-jointed, humpy-plumpy moke' whose basic pleasure consisted of whistling his happy-go-lucky way through life. What more could be expected from a 'chuckle-headed, hickleberry nig' with 'a cranium like a big baboon,' and a Jim Crow-type 'limpy' gait. Portrayal of the whistling coon's features was typical of minstrel songs:

He's got a pair of lips like a pound of liver split
And a nose like an in-jum-rubber shoe.[42]

Such racist images occur again and again. Aunt Deb's 'darter' has a 'mouf'
two acres wide and feet two yards long,[43] while Aunt Dinah's mouth was so
large a pumpkin could be dropped in whole.[44] India-rubber faces apparently
made the negro's mouth 'all expandibility'[45] while the black woman's
gargantuan feet left little room for anyone else to walk alongside her on the
pavement.[46] The skulls of negros were held to be exceptually thick, thus
ensuring that any blows to their heads could be made with impunity. Here, as
in other respects, we find the prejudicial imagery of popular song supported by
polite learned journals, for 'scientific' proof of this claim was being offered in the
pseudo-anthropological literature of the time. Minstrel songs similarly conveyed a consistent pattern of black psychology and behaviour including
insatiable love of racoon and possum – later chicken – meat, watermelons and
pumpkins, a 'natural' urge to steal, and an irrepressible need to sing, make
music and dance. This last feature of the negro character was integral also to
the characteristic portrayal of the carefree life of the old Southern plantation
where de banjos twanged in de ole corn-brake and a happy band of 'niggers'
danced the night away in de light of de silbery moon. Such 'magnolia' themes
contrast with another nostalgic strand in plantation pastoral where the intended
effect was one of sentimental pathos. The old darky figure characteristically
looked back over a lifetime of happy toil with fond regret, contemplating that
other shore with sanguine composure, as for instance in Will S. Hays' 'The
Little Old Log Cabin in the Lane', (fig. 4.3) which has the chorus:

Oh yes, I'm old and feeble now, my head is bending low,
And I never more shall hoe the corn again,
Yet the angels they will lead me, when my time has come to go,
From my little old log cabin in the lane.[47]

Plantation themes could work as pastoral idealisation, offering 'affirmative
utopian expression'[48] and acting as a vehicle for nostalgic and aspirational
emotional projection: the grass always seeming greener in an imagined faraway
community. More simply, they could fill the heart with what Thackeray
felicitously called 'happy pity'. As I have suggested elsewhere, in discussing the
sentimentalism of Victorian parlour ballads and the sociology of their reception,
the response to these themes is likely to have been rather different among the
habitués of Belgravia than among those for whom old age entailed the dreaded
prospect, if not the actuality, of a bleak workhouse environment and regimen.[49]

    This kind of consideration requires a more extended treatment than I am able
to give here, and I point to it now simply to indicate that the social history of
popular cultural audiences, an area that is much more underdeveloped than the
analysis of forms, institutions and even performers, needs to take into account
the concrete and situated determinants of reception rather than rely on
across-the-board assumptions of general function or effect. The contradictions

between different stereotypical images of blacks in popular culture can be seen retrospectively to have derived in large part from the pro and anti-slave lobbies of the late eighteenth and early nineteenth centuries, represented at one extreme by the plantocratic racism of Edward Long and at the other by the philanthropic humanitarianism of Wilberforce. These conflicting sets of images and conceptions entered into general currency during the nineteenth century via those processes of cultural seepage which are among the distinguishing marks of leisure in Western society. Though it would take a chapter to demonstrate it, these images and conceptions were translated into the general stock of minstrel representations in Britain. I do not wish to deny that the malign as opposed to the benign racial stereotypes of minstrelsy are those which have persisted much more vehemently, throughout the twentieth century, providing a negative counter-reference to a reformed national image and culture. This change of view reached down to all levels of society. Writing of working-class attitudes to 'foreigners' in Salford in the early twentieth century, Roberts recalled: 'Taking our cue from adult canon, we lived by the belief that all 'niggers' were congenitally stupid and funny'.[50] Few working-class people read writings by the proponents of 'scientific racism', but they did attend minstrel shows. Changes in race relations, in conceptions of racial difference and in attitudes to black people, were coincident with the development of minstrelsy. Minstrelsy was not immune from their field of force but in fact central to it, both propagating and shaping racial ideas. To see minstrelsy as only to do with negro impersonation, and to interpret it only in relation to the general discourse of race and racial ideology, is to be blind to its function as a set of generic conventions within the performing arts. But along with other influences, minstrelsy in Britain was nevertheless responsible for crystallising and establishing certain stereotypes of blacks and black 'racial' characteristics. In helping to give firm shape to these, as a symbolic lexicon which people carried away in their minds after leaving the theatres and halls, it contributed to the developement of racial prejudice, and when shifts in social structure and circumstance provided a need for scapegoats among the victims of such shifts, hostility towards blacks has had that symbolic lexicon of derogatory ideas and images readily to hand. As we have seen over the last 25 years, this ideological legacy in Britain has still to be exhausted and defeated.

But the use of black stereotypes varied according to context, conditions and circumstances, as is illustrated in the contrast between Old Joe imagery and upper-class views of the insurrectionists of Morant Bay. Lorimer's argument that during the Victorian period in England there occurred a general transformation of attitude to the 'negro' from ethnocentrism to racialism is too neat a picture. The change was not so straightforwardly 'from an object of pity to a figure of fun', for that figure of fun was emphatically there right at the outset, in the Jim Crow character as portrayed by Rice, and the 'noble savage' conception proved resurgent in the character of Uncle Tom.[51] The 'coon' songs of the late nineteenth century were also not confined to portrayals of farcical stupidity or razor-toting viciousness; on both sides of the Atlantic, as Paul Oliver has put it, the covers of such songs 'showed sympathetic lithographs of black mothers nursing beribboned "Topsy" piccaninnies, and idealized scenes of rustic cabins in a sunny, timeless Southland'.[52] As I suggested at the beginning of this essay, an exclusive focus on racism in the study of English minstrelsy can easily induce an analytical myopia.

The blackface minstrel has been compared with, and situated within, the tradition of the *commedia dell'arte* and other forms of clowning, particularly by Moody and Rehin.[53] There are undoubtedly parallels, but the minstrel blackface was a particular sociocultural form of the clown's mask. The danger of claiming archetypal features for minstrelsy is that attention may be deflected from the specific historical context in which it was embedded. The reception of any cultural text has to be understood in relation to the social conditions and situations in which it occurs, and to the consciousness which characterises particular social groups. Central to the dominant moral and institutional order of Victorian England was, of course, in one form or another, the Protestant work ethic. What was presented in minstrel stereotypes of blacks was much that was antithetical to that ethic and order. The Victorian 'nigger' minstrel offered an inverted image of all that was held comely, respectable and proper in a civilised society, and all that meant success in a commercial world and an enterprise culture. This antithesis applied to every aspect of the presentation: dress, facial and physical features referred to in song, language in corner-men repartee and in burlesque lectures, posture, dance, devil-may-care attitude, irreverant disposition and madcap conduct. For the middle class, and those upwardly mobile or with pretensions to gentility, self-restraint and deferral of gratification were crucial moral values which they attempted to live out in both private and public spheres. In contrast, as Huggins points out, the 'nigger' minstrel persona was 'completely self-indulgent and irresponsible'. He goes on:

> White men put on black masks and became another self, one which was loose of limb, innocent of obligation to anything outside itself, indifferent to success... and thus a creature totally devoid of tension and deep anxiety. The verisimilitude of this persona to actual Negroes... was at best incidental. For the white man who put on the black mask 'modelled himself after a subjective black man —' a black man of lust and passion and natural freedom (licence) which white men carried within themselves and harboured with both fascination and dread.[54]

The disguise, however, had a dual purpose, objectifying a repressed self antithetical to the kind of personality structure enjoined by the dominant sociocultural formation, and yet having a satirical and burlesquing dimension to it that was possible precisely because it was 'antithetical to respectable taste and manners'.[55] The 'nigger' caricature was meant to be ridiculous and stupid, to be laughed at and mocked, yet it could act back at the same time, in the circumscribed interval of performance, to laugh at social pretension, posturing and pomposity, and to mock the holders of authority and power. When the 'nigger' became a toff, for instance, the humour lay in the disparity, the absurd pretence, the travesty, even more so than in the ordinary swell song, but it was directed as much at the excesses and pretensions of gentlemanly fashion as at black dandies; and it may have served as well to police the rigidly defined cultural boundaries of Victorian society between male and female gender roles and identities, in the sense that the figure at times inclined towards an effeminacy and unmanly ostentation which, as Wilde discovered, could meet with dire retribution if pushed beyond the limits of institutionalised licence.

All societies need to express those 'elements of a culture's own negation which in an ordinary, un-Hegelian fashion are included within it'.[56] Symbolically, British blackface minstrelsy was a *mundus inversus* of the white world. With a social constituency wider than that for virtually all other forms of Victorian popular entertainment, the minstrel show was a non-rational form of recreation occurring in the 'betwixt-and-between, neither-this-nor-that domain' of leisure.[57] Operating within an intermediary period between shifts of labour, or other compulsions of duty and discipline, minstrelsy expressed a spirit of play and pleasure relatively absent from — indeed, in contradistinction to — commercial and industrial occupations, and formalized domestic milieux. The mockery, masquerade and clowning were the expressive vehicles of those elements of the dominant culture's own negation. The ritualistic 'Gentlemen, be seated...' marked the beginning of a ludic interval in the course of everyday time and a sense of symbolic inversion of what was normatively expected and understood, for after all, 'even "a self-improved Negro" could not rise to the elevated status of a gentleman'.[58]

The recognition and acceptance of inversion within a bracketed interval of ordinary life would have required an understanding of realist elements within a modifying context where both the construction and deconstruction of illusion jostled for prominence. This occurred not only within the structure of distribution of varying forms in a sequential programme, but also in relation to that deliberate commingling of different modes and effects which gave much of music hall and minstrel culture its singular dynamic. We have then to speak of popular audiences in the Victorian period attuned to delight at the contrivances of popular theatricality rather than to a continuous suspension of disbelief in realist drama overheard in a fourth-wall-removed theatre.

The 1843 Theatre Act paradoxically intensified the division of drama into 'legitimate' and 'illegitimate' categories, with realist drama being developed from the mid nineteenth century in the 'legitimate' theatre and the tradition of popular theatricality continuing in the halls. While the techniques and conventions of this theatricality did not demand, as in realist drama, a temporary abnegation of awareness in the fact of acting, comic sketches, stump speeches, character impersonations, situation humour, singer personae and such did not thereby of necessity lose in 'truth' value or integrity; what was depicted could be valued as a representation of some aspect of social reality and simultaneously recognised and valued as theatrical artifice. This involved a dialectical movement between involvement with the 'reality' of the performance and awareness of its simulation of 'reality' outside of its own ambit of representation. Neither mode of attention and response was then primary, or rather both were alternately primary and then secondary, in the sense of what Bethell has termed the principle of multiconscious response and apprehension in the popular tradition.[59] Minstrelsy was a form of theatre which involved acting but did not insist on a sustained acceptance of the verisimilitude of what was portrayed. The games played with words and verbal construction, in song, sketch and monologue, would have created an alternate or even simultaneous awareness of language as a medium and as an artefact, a sense of the distinction between communicational content and form. There were of course many instances of unalloyed pathos involving a suspension of disbelief in the act of presentation of some aged Sambo by a white minstrel, but the point is that this frame would not become fixed within the minstrel show as a whole, but made and then broken, again and again, in a complex sequence.

The fact of frame and frame-break, which I have attempted to show was an integral aesthetic feature of the spectacle of British minstrelsy, concerns the relation between the transmission and reception of images and meanings. If, as I am suggesting, the 'nigger' mask symbolised all that was the opposite of the bourgeois conception of the white English person, then we must consider the possibilities of differential understandings of that structured opposition, precisely because its conceptualization was produced against the template of class distinction and difference. How, for instance, was minstrelsy's inversion of the work ethic and all its satellite values received by the class enemies of aristocratic swells and gentlefolk? The blackface clown mask may, for some, have been not so much a temporary escape from internalised repressive disciplines as something that symbolised, however covertly, an abnegation of dominant values and a challenge to the agents of repression in a 'two nation' social order. It may as well have been in this respect that the blackface code connected with aspects of its function in vernacular cultures and customs, and in traditional modes of social satire and protest. This may provide us with a clue to the reason why the clowning elements in minstrelsy survived most vigorously in the music hall, with the accent on sentimentality and lavishness being made much more strongly in the separate minstrel shows. While these points are at this stage only intended as provisional, they are made here to underline the danger of assuming that the blackface code, in Victorian English minstrelsy, had been completely the victim of bourgeois incorporation.

Its subversive potential in fact continued, though perhaps less so in the respectable minstrel show than in the music hall and in 'nigger' blackface borrowings and adaptations. When the minstrel mode did begin to lose force it was because of the ascendancy of a rampant commercialism. Its symbolic inversions tended in time to lose force by becoming all too familiar, fetishized and frozen in the amber of conspicuous consumption. The minstrel mode became vitiated by its absorption in the increasingly extravagant productions of later minstrelsy where the performers were anonymous elements in a whole baroque assemblage, where what counted was grand scale, variety, extravagence and excess, where the effect was obliterative of 'the insistencies of everyday life' and where all that remained was delight.[60] It is this aesthetic which people like Ziegfeld and Berkeley adopted and developed in the twentieth century, and which was celebrated in the 'candy-floss' world of *The Black and White Minstrel Show*, a series which its producer George Inns described as 'pure entertainment'. It was, he said, 'a show you could watch without having to make any effort'.[61] The potential in English minstrelsy of symbolically inverting a socially constructed reality had become subsumed by a world which was 'totally other than the real world, a completely fabricated, artificial, separate reality'.[62]

5   *Jenny Hill: Sex and Sexism in the Victorian Music Hall*

J. S. BRATTON

Jenny Hill was 'the one woman of real genius who ever enlivened the music-hall stage', according to John Hollingshead; and to Harry Hibbert, she was without any qualification 'the supreme genius' of her generation.[1] She has not come down to modern consciousness as a leading figure in the mythology of the halls, perhaps because 'her generation' was that of the 1860s to the 1880s, and like her contemporaries George Leybourne and Alfred Vance she did not survive into the era of recordings and respectability. But like the lions comiques, was nevertheless surrounded in her own time by a more than life-size public self: an image carefully fostered and kept up on and off stage, an image compounded of glamour ('amazing chic', in contemporary parlance) and humour, and a reputation for bounce and energy – she was 'fast' in every sense, a performer who exhausted herself on stage, and off stage exhausted everyone around her, getting through agents, escorts, horses and addresses with unflagging 'go'. When she visited New York in 1891, reporters commented that she was 'a little bunch of nerves', and described 'a very little woman, trimly built, agile, nervous, energetic, with a face that is pleasing and expressive, and often grotesque beyond description when her mobile features are working'.[2] Hence her sobriquet, characteristically alluding to the latest glittering invention of the day – she was 'the Vital Spark', a flashing particle of electric wit and vitality.

Jenny Hill was a serio-comic, indeed sometimes called a 'low comedian', a phrase normally reserved for male performers.[3] Her material included the occasional sentimental number, but it was predominantly in character songs which described and celebrated working-class figures and the Londoner's life that she made her impact. Harold Scott saw in her loving portrayal of the waitress, the serving girl and the street saleswoman 'an intense instinct of class consciousness', and felt her success was due to 'a democratic appeal based on an intimacy with the poorest members of her audience.'[4] Her act included a great deal of spoken material: improvised comic patter characteristically delivered at high speed and in defiance of any attempt at censorship. She was also a sought-after principal boy in pantomime, and she could extend to burlesque

Figure 5.1   Entr'acte *cartoon of Jenny Hill dancing a hornpipe. Author's Collection.*

acting: John Hollinshead tried to persuade her to transfer from the halls to his productions at the Gaiety, and her act often included burlesque sketches. On benefit nights she delighted in involving the beneficiare, a normally non-performing manager or proprietor, in acting out cod versions of melodramas. The range of her skills and appearances should alert us both to the complexity of music-hall performance at its best, and to the subtlety of the negotiations between the halls and the theatres.

To explore the mythology which was built upon music-hall performance, and the contemporary appeal of the performances themselves, it is fruitful to take such a figure as Jenny Hill, whose reputation grew with the institution rather than being created to an existing formula, and whose image is not too thickly overlaid with twentieth-century nostalgia. The distortions created when the myth of a past hero of the halls is kept alive are discussed in Dave Harker's revaluation of Joe Wilson in Chapter 6. Since Jenny Hill is forgotten, she may more easily be placed in a culturalist/feminist perspective of theatrical history, which should illuminate the nineteenth-century music hall and the place of women within it.

It is a commonplace of the more recent music-hall history that the halls provided working-class women with a rare opportunity to make their way to independence and even to fortune. Martha Vicinus observes that women on the halls 'personified not only the outward glories of music-hall life in their chic clothing, but also the potential for freedom and joy amidst a narrow life'. Edward Lee, in a modern school textbook, promotes the halls as offering 'the beginning of a change in the position of women in society'.[5] Both give as their example Bessie Bellwood, who is supposed to have begun her career as a child labourer skinning rabbits in Bermondsey and who became a leading serio-comic and mistress of the Viscount Mandeville before dying, deep in debt and drink, at the age of thirty-nine. This new perception of the ancient doubled role of actress and courtesan should be treated with some scepticism. The elevation of certain women of obscure origins but fashionable good looks to the status of idols of the public and playthings of the great, to be admired, envied, reprobated and scandalised, is by no means a phenomenon of the music halls alone. The nineteenth-century manifestation of it has certain peculiarities, however, which shed light on the class and gender conflicts and negotiations manifest in the institution of music hall; Jenny Hill, her myth, her working life and her performances afford a promising case study.

The Myths: a) retrospective

Music-hall mythology is an aspect of the entertainment itself, an exploitation by journalists and sometimes by performers of the public interest in back-stage gossip and the conspicuous lives of the 'great'. Such writing does much to construct the culture within which it finds, exploits and fosters its materials. Victorian and Edwardian journalists identified on the whole with a middle-class professional group, and entered the music-hall world as 'bohemians', conscious simultaneously of rejecting the values of some of their social equals, and of retaining their personal superiority to those whith whom they were mixing. Unsurprisingly, there were very few women amongst these middle-class participants in the music halls; the mythology created by such self-styled 'historians' was overwhelmingly designed by and for men. Their presentation of those working-class women who achieved the prosperity and freedom offered by success as performers is semiotically complex, seeking to incorporate a phenomenon potentially challenging in both class and gender terms.

The fact that Jenny Hill made a great deal of money and spent it herself is registered by such comments as that of her obituarist in the *Era:* 'the terms she was able to secure caused many a hard-working actress on the orthodox stage to regard with envy the music hall performer's horses, carriages, and diamonds.'[6] Here the supposed envy of other women and the tacit condemnation of conspicuous consumption both signal the writer's disapprobation of lower-class, female possession of such wealth and independence. More often the threat Jenny Hill presents is disarmed more subtly, by casting all comments on her life into a form which implies that her achievements were as nothing beside the sufferings they cost her. A tone of patronising pity swamps most accounts of her life.

This is not, of course, a tone reserved exclusively for her. The usual picture presented of most of the early music-hall performers stresses their humble origins and their consequent inability to cope with the incongruous earnings their stage successes brought. This class-based perception is reinforced in the case of female performers like Jenny Hill and Bessie Bellwood by considerable unease at the breach their earning power and independence might cause in the structure of patriarchal power. It is interesting that Jerome K. Jerome's tale[7] of a female performer who verbally wiped down the hall with an interrupter whom the chairman had failed to quell, displaying an awesome power over strong men, has been attached to both these singers. Bessie Bellwood's career was rather too scandalous for much elaboration by the mythmakers; but Jenny Hill's short reign of success made ideal material.

The locus classicus for the story of Jenny Hill's life, moulded to suit its cultural function, is Chapter 8 of Harry Hibbert's *Fifty Years of a Londoner's Life* – a book praised as an accurate and valuable record by modern bibliographers.[8] He relates how Jenny Hill, 'a wan and stricken woman, in dull apartments in Brixton, told me the story of her life, soon to end, in its early forties', while 'with trembling fingers she turned over photographs, and treasured newspaper cuttings, to adorn her tale'. The story is said to begin when she was a child worker in an artificial flower factory in Marylebone, owned by Bob Botting, the proprietor of the Marylebone Music Hall: 'he would throw a few coppers to little Jenny, to make her sing: it so encouraged the other workers.' To this is added the pathetic information that in her last illness 'she found pleasure in twisting the paper flowers again'. The picture is a compelling one: the working-class child is seen in her role in the industrial society, a role to be both pitied and commended for its brave self-reliance, while her talent, later to be the cause of her removal from her place, is stolen by the wicked employer to increase production. The actual occupation, while it is productive of pity in that it is unsuitable for one whose merit is to distinguish her from the mass, is not dirty, arduous or otherwise distressingly unfeminine: the pathos of her final reversion to a childhood occupation would hardly be so effective if she had been a mate of Bessie Bellwood's at the rabbit-skinning, or even of Dickens's in the blacking factory.

Hibbert notes that Jenny Hill's father was said to be 'a cab-minder, hanging about a rank in Marylebone'. Subsequent copiests located the rank outside the various halls and theatres of the district, symbolically assigning him to the position traditionally at the very bottom of the theatrical ladder, holding horses' heads at the door. If he was really so lowly, his elevation to 'cab proprietor' on Jenny Hill's marriage lines in 1866 may have been self-promotion, or meant that he had risen to become a petty capitalist on the strength of his daughter's earnings before she was 16. But most likely the juvenile occupation of horse and cab-minding has been foisted upon him simply to maximise his daughter's rise to fame and fortune.

In describing that rise, the myth-makers do not present it as a success story. The pathos of the waif-like infant performer is followed by that of the exploited teenager. Both Hibbert and her *Era* obituarist lay much stress upon her seven-year apprenticeship to a Bradford publican. Hibbert claimed to have seen the indentures, 'the most wicked bond I have ever encountered'. He elaborates on her subjection:

> Soon, Jenny was apprenticed, for seven years ... to learn the trade of a serio-comic singer, and otherwise make herself generally useful as the household drudge. It is

all set out in the bond. The licensing laws were very lax in those days, and on market days the farmers would sit over their cups till one or two o'clock in the morning. While ever they lingered, the poor little serio-comic singer and dancer must be ready to take the stage of the "free and easy." And at five o'clock in the morning she must be alert, to scrub floors, polish pewter or bottle beer, at which she became quite an adept. At noon, the performance began again.

Here the pathos and bravery of the exploited child is reinforced by perception of her as adept in homely chores, which places her, however ironically, in a useful female role, and also by overtones of the sexual exploitation of the growing girl, the nymphet – 'poor little serio-comic singer and dancer'. The Shakespearean reference to 'the bond' has already triggered the idea of trading in flesh.

Attention turns to her sexuality immediately after this in Hibbert's narrative, when he notes that she 'married an acrobat, and he taught her his trade, none too kindly'. This was John Woodley, otherwise Jean Pasta. The early point at which this marriage broke down is nowhere recorded in the mythology. Hibbert's next frame shows her along again, but with the inevitable baby in her arms, about to be launched into the 'a star is born' sequence of the archetypal showbusiness biography, with a story of her triumph over a melodramatically villainous agent and her victorious arrival in her true home, the hearts of the audience of the London Pavilion, and also in the strong arms of the heroic George Leybourne. Hibbert concludes, 'Jenny's fortune was made'.

After this Hibbert's account begins deliberately to take account of the image that Jenny Hill's publicity created for her in her own lifetime, and to reinforce or contradict it for his own purposes. It is part of his elegiac, pathetic presentation of the oppressed and helpless little woman in the bad old days of the early music hall to assert that hers was a 'modest fortune' only, that her normal salary was only a half or one third of what she would have commanded at the time he was writing in 1916. He adds that she was pretty, but 'terribly scarred by illness, on inspection', and that as an actress, as opposed to a solo performer, 'she was a failure'. He similarly underplays the value of the greatest possession which her wealth had brought her, the 'farm' at Streatham, calling it 'a straggling, secluded bungalow ... where a royal person had once hidden a romance'. This gratuitous piece of gossip associates Jenny Hill's earnings with the idea of a kept woman. Thus by a combination of fanciful romaticising and patronising pity the potential threat to patriarchal order posed by wealth, property and land in the hands of an independent woman is thoroughly defused by his representation.

The Myths: b) contemporary – her presentation of herself

Jenny Hill saw her own career rather differently. We may gain some sense of this from what she says about herself in interviews, and in speeches. She was a determined speechmaker, something which journalists often comment upon coyly, facetiously or with covert derision, as being an inappropriately masculine talent. A report of her 1879 London season benefit at the South London Palace, for example, remarks of her 'oratorical display by way of returning thanks' that 'Miss Hall is one of the few ladies who can make a speech... to her oratory comes very naturally... Mr Charles Collette... must have been slightly astonished... that there is a lady in the Profession who is equal to him at this own game'.[9] She was also a self-publicist in print, through the medium of her 'card' advertisements which normally appeared at the head of the first column on the back page of the *Era* from 1876 until her last illness.

The speeches and the advertisements are in themselves as assertion of her independence – managers tried to silence her, writing clauses about not addressing the audience into her contracts[10] – and of her participation as an equal in music-hall society. It seems that she strove to be a full rather than an honorary member of the bonhomous coterie of the leaders of the profession. She was an active participant in the round of lavish entertainments by which the leaders of the music-hall fraternity defined their position, and she spoke up for herself in the marathons of mutually congratulatory speechmaking. She was, for example, the only female guest at a farewell party for W. G. Eaton, musical director at the Paragon, when he left for six months in Australia in 1889; she made an after-dinner speech, in 'a burst of natural an persuasive eloquence' when she took the chair on the 'Canterbury' coach trip in July 1886, on which occasion she was 'very witty'. She often financed such prestigious parties, on the Thames or at her own South London houses, and she also exercised hospitality as patronage, providing treats for music-hall children and staff, at which no expense was spared, and entertainments might include balloon ascents and parachute drops as well as music and feasting. The press reports of the social events are suitably impressed by the guest-list, the speechmaking and the expenditure, when, for example, at her 1887 'water party up the Thames', the 'commodious steam-launch Princess Beatrice' had to be accompanied by another vessel to carry the overflowing people and provisions. In her card, the hostess preferred to stress good fellowship and enjoyment, turning the business of hospitality to managers, writers and other influencial persons into a spree:

> We sailed up the river, each heart was light,
> Cheered by the strains of music bright;
> And I'm happy to say not a soul got – well,
> They were all right. – Billy.
> NB the author of this fell overboard.[11]

What she said about herself and her career in her public speeches hardly tallies with the lachrymose picture painted after her death. Her version of her childhood, for example, focuses upon her perception of herself as ambitious and eager to pursue a career which she has passionately enjoyed. She stresses her success, her advancement in the profession and its rapid changes in her time; she looks back with amusement, optimistic rather than nostalgic. At a testimonial benefit in 1890, for example, she 'displayed her well-known eloquence' and avowed that 'her work in the profession form the age of nine, when she ran away from home to join it, and sought an engagement at the Victoria Gardens, Yarmouth, had been a labour of love... Miss Hill gave a humorous sketch of the various transitions in public taste' before launching into a peroration about her pride in her reception that night.[12]

She described the 'old style' halls to a *Sketch* reporter in 1893, explaining that she made her London debut at the Dr Johnson Concert Rooms when she 'was a little thing in socks and shoes', and received three shillings a night and refreshments. She hastened to add that this was not some sort of exploitation of her personally – 'no one got any more than'.[13]

Her self-presentation in her cards is determinedly positive, often combative, never admitting anything but a triumphant self-confidence. They project, for publicity purposes, a life bubbling over with exciting activity. It is with hindsight that they appear frenetic, anxious and self-justifying. Jenny Hill's cards announce her engagements, as all the professional advertisements do, but rarely leave it at that. She returns thanks, for example, not only to artists for their presence at her benefits, as is usual, but to everyone involved – her 'always gentlemanly' agent Thomas Holmes, even the 'poor, ill-treated luggage-carrier' (5.10.79)[14]; to a Glasgow manager and his wife for 'the many pleasant drives and hours spent in their company' (25.3.82); even to 'Dr Miskim, York Rd. Lambeth and Percy Boulton Physician 6 Seymour St. W.' for their attendance (21.10.82). She takes the opportunity to blame as well as to praise, and heaps mysterious execrations on, for example, 'N.W.' (3.11.78); 'Milburn and daughter' (9.9.82); and 'the shaking Ink Slinger' (3.11.88). Her private messages also include jokes, misappropriated poetical quotations, scraps of doggerel such as the one about the water party quoted above, and the apparent overflow of high spirits and self-congratulation: 'Monday next, starring in the Trossachs, with a strong contingent from Streatham. "We're all gay" (12.9.85) or 'Permanent address, the Hermitage Lodge, South Streatham, Surrey. "Oh, we do like farming."' (30.6.88) The intention seems to be to fabricate a tantalisingly attractive picture of her life, and present it to the public as satisfactory.

More serious self-puffery focuses upon her high fees: 'Jenny Hill commands a greater salary by £10 than any single lady *Artiste* ever received in the Music Halls' (9.6.78); '£294 taken at the doors. Biggest benefit by £40 this season' (3.3.82); 'Mercer H Simpson Esq., with his characteristic pluck, having distanced all offers for her services with the biggest salary ever paid to a single artiste in Burlesque, "N'importe qui"' (22.9.88). She feels she must advertise her capacity to keep up with her punishing schedule of work: '336 turns in 108 nights. No rest. No disappointments' (13.8.87) and constantly seeks and publishes confirmation of her popularity with audiences, filling columns every year with her accumulated press cuttings after the pantomime season, and repeating snippets of praise: 'Mr Garcia says Jenny Hill has made the greatest success ever made by any *Artiste*. On the stage Twelve Times and then the audience not satisfied' (3.11.78). Running out of the words of managers, she resorts to belligerent assertions of her own: 'Folly Theatre March. Brilliant success as usual. Standing room at a premium, as usual. Magnificent finish to a highly successful Tour, as usual. Statements should be founded on facts. Principal Pantomime Boys should remember this, ere announcing themselves as being in receipt of the largest salary ever paid' (15.12.88). Eventually she simply shouts from the column '"Success, success, success. There's no such word as fail" – Shakespeare (16.6.82).

In these announcements, Jenny Hill advertises three aspects of her career. The first, given out in a welter of explicit detail which suggests that it is being presented as her professional credentials, is the amount of work she is offered and the salaries she can command. More obliquely, she boasts of the financial ventures both professional and personal in which she invests her earnings as a performer, which seem to be offered both as proof of her earning power and as the evidence of her engagement in the profession as something more than a mere worker. And thirdly, almost incidentally, as part of the image of success she is projecting, she mentions her performance and its evolution. Information from other sources can be related to each of these elements of her public persona.

The Career: a) the working life of an early music-hall star

Jenny Hill's child appearance and the years of 'apprenticeship' presumably came to an end when she married at the age of 16, in 1866. There followed a short period of independent provincial work: she shared a bill with her husband Pasta, for example, at the Victoria Concert Hall West Hartlepool in December 1869, a date billed as the 'reappearance of the West Hartlepool favourite, Miss Jenny Hill, Character vocalist and dancer'. In the next year she was billed there as 'The Dashing London Serio-comic', and had obviously established a metropolitan style, if not yet a base in town. Tracing her engagements from 1870 onwards shows the fairly rapid establishment of a pattern of work which she intensified but did not radically change while she had the strength to maintain it. She never chose to rest on her laurels. One of the most frequent comments in reviews of her performances is that 'this lady revels in her work', 'as though her business were her greatest pleasure… and this disposition to oblige always obtains a recognition, which helps to build up the structure of popularity'.[15]

The building-up of that structure began with twice-nightly engagements in London over the period from Easter every year until the end of August. She told the *Sketch* reporter that she began on 30 shillings a week from each hall, and Mr Deacon, at whose hall and at the Raglan she did her first two turns, gave her the first pair of tights she had ever seen. The London seasons were generally preceded by short North of England spring tours, and followed by longer tours in the autumn. She then did a Christmas show, at first Christmas concerts like the 'New Star Christmas Pie' at the Star in Liverpool, 1874–5, and then went into pantomimes, sometimes in London – she was at the Aquarium in *A Frog He Would a Wooing Go* in 1877–8, for example – but more often thereafter at a provincial Theatre Royal.

From about 1878 she was commanding the highest salaries. She tried burlesque acting, appearing in Buckstone's *Good For Nothing Nan* at the Grecian. In March 1878 she began to play three, and then from 1888 four, turns nightly during her London seasons; she would set off in September on extensive tours, playing up to 20 places before the pantomime rehearsal week, when she would often secure variety dates in the town where she was called to rehearse. The spring tours remained much briefer, and normally northern; some years they were squeezed to only a week or two by the extension of the pantomime, or, increasingly, by the imperative need to recuperate from her winter illnesses.

The schedule was indeed a physically punishing one. The pantomime often seems, from the reviews, to have rested upon her personal effort: *Goody Two Shoes* at the Birmingham Theatre Royal in 1886–7, for example, was said by the *Birmingham Daily Mail* of December 27 to be liable to 'collapse altogether in the later scenes' were it not for her exertions. She was regularly praised in the provincial press both for bringing a music-hall-like spirit of vivacity and 'go' to the pantomime, and also, conversely, for playing with and to the rest of the cast, avoiding the common failings of the solo performer.[16] When she stepped up her London turns to four halls nightly, she appeared, for example, in the spring of 1889 at the Canterbury at 8.25, then fitted in the Cambridge and the London Pavilion before finishing up at the Queens, Poplar, at 10.50. The distance travelled, in her personal brougham stuffed with her costumes, was considerable, extending from South London via the two West End Halls to the East End. When she fell ill, the *Era* gossip columnist observed, 'working four halls a night means much harrass of mind and weariness of body. Let us hope that Miss Hill is not overtaxing her energies'.[17] She put even more strain upon herself during some of her northern tours, when she did much longer turns, often singing over 70 songs in the week.

Jenny Hill's commitment to work inthe northern halls was partly a personal loyalty to Edward Garcia, entrepreneur of Manchester. This seems to have been a working relationship founded on mutual admiration for each other's dashing approach to the business. Some of the first compliments she repeated in her advertisements are quotations from Garcia, and the ever-increasing terms on which he re-engaged her for one or several of his halls were triumphantly turned into copy. There was on one occasion a dramatic storm between them, and a falling-out, also conducted in the columns of the *Era*, and then olive-branches and increases in fees were offered, and all set right in an equally public manner. The subject of the altercation is not stated, but seems to have been an insult not unconnected with money.[18]

The Career: b) management and investment

Jenny Hill's relationships with agents were very much stormier than her professional camaraderie with the managers. She changed her agents repeatedly, employing the magnates of the business, and patronising previously unknown men; one at least of these had a role in her life which went beyond business. The exploitation of her success is an area in which her vulnerability is obvious. The dislocations in relations with her agents seem to follow a recurring pattern. Several times, at the end of a London season, she parted company with her current agent and launched an independent venture, which required considerable investment. Thus in June 1879 she became the proprietor of the Star Music Hall in Hull; in July 1882 she took the lease of a London pub, the Albert Arms, London Road SE; and in September 1884 she bought the Rainbow Music Hall in Southampton. Each of these ventures was shortlived. She intended to install Pasta, who was presumbaly still her husband, as manager at Hull, but mysteriously the arrangements broke down at the last moment, and he returned to London inside the week to his previous occupation as catcher to the female gymnast Madame Senyah. The *Entr'acte* columnist, unable to refrain from a wiseacre 'I told you so', still professed himself glad that she had got her deposit back.[19] She remained her own agent only until the end of July.

The South London pub lasted a little longer, but cost her more. When she acquired it she paid substitutes for her first turn, in order to spend time welcoming her expected guests, and she ran a 'Sunday lounge' for friends and the profession. She raised money by selling her four-wheeled trap and a pair of ponies, and by organising a concert party at the Victoria Hall in Sunderland. This backfired: some of her employees demanded a share of the takings. By September she was forced to take on another agent. By the end of the month she was ill, presumably from overwork, and under doctor's orders to rest. She recovered sufficiently to begin her autumn tour and spend each Saturday night travelling back from Leeds or Birmingham to her Sunday At Home; but her health faltered again, and after October her cards say no more about the Albert Arms.

The Rainbow (renamed the Gaiety) was a complete disaster. She launched the place with personal appearances, superintending bookings and rehearsals for the supporting turns, then arranged her own bookings so as to stay on the South coast for a month after the opening. She returned to the Northern towns at the end of October; and in the last week of November, when she was appearing in Manchester, the hall in Southampton went up in flames.

After this she confined her essays in management to the arranging of massive social events. Her relationships with her agents remained stormy, and often interrupted, though she was never able to manage her own bookings for very long. The desire to take charge of her own career, to manage the investment of her own earnings and to make the transition, common enough for men of her generation, from performer to proprietor, was obviously something she felt strongly, but tried in vain. One can only speculate about the meaning of the repeated pattern. Perhaps the timing of these events is significant: each time she launched into a speculation it was on the full tide of her London season; her professional friends no doubt rallying round to egg her on, some of them, perhaps, with an eye to their own profit.

Artists attempted to make the difficult transition to manangement at every level of the business. In the North East concert halls, both Ned Corvan and Joe Wilson tried it, and found it hard going. In London some of the new breed of entertainment entrepreneurs made performance a stepping stone to their real goal. Joe Cave was a blackface singer and danced a hornpipe in fetters before he built and ran the Cosmotheka, and Edward Villiers who managed at various times the South London, the Canterbury and the Pavilion broke into the business by attempting to act. There were successful performers at the top of the profession who invested their earnings in ownership and management. Sam Collins took the Upper Welsh Harp and the Rose of Normandy taverns before settling at the Lansdowne is Islington and renaming it after himself. The effort to achieve this pinnacle of success would seem to have been too great, however, and he died two years later, aged thirty-nine. His widow Anne conducted the hall for three years after his death. Hers was the only route by which women normally came to management: the widow's succession was allowed by the licensing authorities, and some wives who had been performers presumably possessed the necessary expertise. But, as Peter Bailey points out,[20] gentrification soon filtered out the contribution of women managers to the family trades, in the entertainment world as elsewhere. Adelaide Stoll, left in charge of the Parthenon in Liverpool when her husband died in 1880, had to rely on 14-year-old Oswald pretending to bring messages from a fictitious manager to give credibility to her dealings with visitors and agents.[21] In this as in other businesses, the 'community of friends' at least pretended that they left their wives at home. For Jenny Hill as a woman artist, therefore, to persist not only in speechmaking and self-advertisement, but in attempting to take on proprietorships in her own name, was flying in the face of the patriarchal organisation.

It may be that her efforts at independence would have been more successful had she been able to pursue her ventures entirely in terms of her own career choices. In fact it appears that she was trying to capitalise on her own success for the benefit of family and friends. The Hull venture included not only Jean Pasta, but their daughter Lettie (later Peggy Pryde) making her professional debut at the age of 13. The Southampton music hall was managed by Edward Turnbull, whom the *Era* and Stuart and Park[22] speak of as Jenny Hill's husband. Her next summer's venture, in August 1885, may have been to finance Turnbull's entry into agency: the newly-formed firm of Victor and Turnbull became her agents at that time.

This arrangement ended in September 1887, and she chopped and changed agents until her enforced retirement. by 1889 her engagements were being repeatedly disrupted by illness, but she struggled to retain a grasp of her own career and earning power to the end. It is in some ways the familiar story of rapid earning and unwise spending. But the endemic dangers of the profession for the performer unequipped to handle sudden wealth are greatly exacerbated in Jenny Hill's case by the difficulty for a woman of seizing and maintaining financial power over her own life. Her earning power did not automatically give her the status within the profession which a successful male performer could expect; and her attempts to seize that position always seem to have been on behalf of others, and to have foundered upon their inadequacy in backing up her investment.

One element of her management of her earnings that illustrates the patriarchal reappropriation of her success directly is her use and possession of personal adornments. The publicity-directed display of dress and accoutrements as part of the swell image is explored by Peter Bailey in Chapter 3. Jenny Hill had her tiny brougham with her name engraved on its lamps,[23]; the *Pink 'un* reported such extravagancies as her promised return for the London season 'accompanied by her suite, an American waggon and a trotting mare, that can do more miles per hour than even Charliarris's famous cream-colored quad', after a farewell banquet in Liverpool where 'thousands of bottles of the Boy... were consumed'.[24] But this display was not quite the same as that in which her male counterparts indulged. A large and semiotically significant element of it consisted in the fact that her most conspicuous possessions were not purchases nor payments, but gifts. From Mr Deacon's pair of tights onwards, managers publically lavished presents upon her; and increasingly, the gifts were diamonds. Jenny Hill not only possessed, but carried about with her and constantly wore, a spectacular collection of jewellery, to which each benefit night and farewell added its portion. (Consequently she was repeatedly assaulted and robbed.) When her carriage overturned on an ordinary working night in 1884, it held not only Jenny Hill, her maid, Edward Turnbull and her current wardrobe, but also a leather handbag containing 'eleven diamond rings, a number of diamond and gold bracelets, an a splendid diamond pendant'.[25] The theft of this from the wreckage caused Didcott – not her agent at the time – to get up a testimonial benefit in compensation, with further presentations.

The possession and display of diamonds known to be gifts was a traditional part of the image of the successful actress, ever since Mrs Pepys saw Mary Davies sitting amongst the players from Lincoln's Inn Fields at a Court performance showing off a ring, worth £700, given to her by Charles II.[26] She was about to leave the stage and occupy the mansion he had furnished for her; meanwhile, the display indicated, quite simply, her possession of – and effectively, her possession by – a rich admirer. It was normal in later generations for such marks of favour to be worn on stage, regardless of the role being played; and they were so necessary a sign of success that at Charles Matthews's bankcruptcy proceedings in 1844 it was explained to the court that hire of diamonds for stage wear cost Vestris (his wife) £3 per week.[27] Such a token of conspicuous wealth signifies the actress's status as possession rather than possessor: she wears the badge of her dishonourable honours, which impresses women less well found, while warning off men whose wealth does not match that of her present protectors. In the case of a music-hall star like Jenny hill, the tradition persists, but the transaction it signifies is now between the woman and a new set of protectors, the managers and audiences with whom she finds favour. Nevertheless the sign remains powerful, enabling the patriarchy to perceive her wealth as the gift of men rather than the earning-power of the woman.

The Career: c) the act

And yet Jenny Hill's discerning audience was female. On her last tour in 1894 she found the Johannesburg audience 'so peculiar – nothing but men'; she was used, she said, to a situation in which 'women always go to the music hall and seem to appreciate you more than the men do'.[28] Her act centred upon a body of material related to the lives of women, and especially the women likely to be in her audiences: working-class wives and mothers, working girls in London trades, in shops, in service, or in the lower reaches of the entertainment business. The best known of her contemporaries did not share this focus. Bessie Bonehill's speciality was in drag performance, Annie Adams had a 'jolly' persona, to match her bulk, and though Bessie Bellwood sometimes sang about coster girls she used Irish sentiment at least as often. In the next generation there was Kate Carney, 'the coster queen', and Marie Lloyd; but of Jenny Hill's contemporaries, only Ada Lundberg seems to have specialised as she did. On February 8, 1890 the *Evening News* reported that 'this lady's sketches of types of character amongst women of the poorer class are the most genuinely clever things of their line to be seen in or out of the music hall'. She was never in Jenny Hill's bracket, however, and tended to play the minor venues: two months after this report she returned to London to play the Royal Albert Canning Town and the Britannia, Hoxton, a theatre which used variety turns between its dramatic pieces. She remains a very shadowy figure: I have never found a song of hers published. The absence is significant, and is not directly related to her low status in the profession. The abundant reviews of Jenny Hill's work describe dozens of such songs sung by her, but few of these seem to have been published either. The surviving songsheets must represent that part of her repertoire which the music dealers felt had a potential sale to female amateur singers with access to pianos; and they were unlikely to wish to perform comic character songs impersonating lower-class women. Those who appreciated these characterisations were the audience with whom she was most successful, in the northern towns and cities where she earned her largest salaries, and in East and South London where she normally began her London seasons and took an annual benefit, usually at the Forester's or the South London Palace. She appeared in West End halls, but commentators felt it worthy of comment when her 'Whitechapel' character songs were successfully transferred there.[29]

Reviewers often report Jenny Hill's female character songs in contradictory ways, suggesting that the middle-class male found the ironies of her performance incomprehensible or unacceptable. For example, when she sang a highly successful song early in her career called 'Bother the Men' or 'A Fig for the Men', she was perceived variously as presenting 'a strong-minded female speaking her mind freely about the men', or on the other hand as presenting 'in quite a fierce style the antipathy towards the lords of creation, which is manifested by an old maid who sings, and sometimes screams, "Bother the men". Her appearance as the vehement vixen was exceedingly quaint'.[30] Some commentators capacity for receiving protest as 'quaint' is manifest even more strikingly in accounts of her performances in the character of the oppressed working-class wife and mother. In June 1878 her act included two songs in this vein, *I'm determined no longer to stand it*, which was 'sharp' and 'strong-minded', and *I've been a good woman to you*, in which an 'outspoken wife' complains

I've been a good woman to you,
And the neighbours all know that it's true;
You go to the pub,
And you blue the kids' grub,
But I've been a good woman to you.[31]

In June 1879, however, a reviewer saw this as 'a fine piece of comic acting' in the character of 'a drunken wife, the inconsequential and self-satisfied burden of whose ditty is 'I've been a good woman to you.'[32] In 1882–3 she was singing a character piece by G.W. Hunt, 'excellently made up as a poor but clean woman who gives expression to her feelings in the words "Woe is the woman who owns eleven," "A woman's work is never done," and "Who'd be a mother"'. This

Figure 5.2   A studio portrait of Jenny Hill in costume – print dress, long black apron and cross-over paisley shawl suggest an honest working woman. The submissive stance, with clasped hands and slightly bent head, hints at precisely observed character acting; the presentation of the figure is markedly different from both the glamorous and the caricature 'dame' representations of women on the halls (Author's collection)

reviewer thought it an 'excellent' piece of acting; but his colleague who saw her at the same hall (the Cambridge) a year later found 'her face as she exclaimed "Woe is the mother who owns eleven" was a study of a very amusing nature'.[33]

With reporting so obtuse, and no surviving texts, the overtones of such a characterisation can only be guessed at. The music-hall songs about older women which did find their way into print are those sung by men, and in them the common music-hall trait of violent hostility to women is manifest. the grotesque harridans presented by comedians like Harry Randall, working in burlesque drag costume of which the surviving pantomime dame is a shadow, give us little clue to Jenny Hill's performances. Photographs show that she dressed these songs strictly realistically – hence the reviewers' surprise over 'convincing' make-up, as opposed to the usual red nose and outsize curlers. She did not match this with a purely pathetic rendering of the character, however; the scraps of songs and patter that have been recorded seem to suggest also the grim, the robust and the comic presentation of the experience of the women portrayed. The group of middle-aged figures is varied; besides the downtrodden mothers and disillusioned wives there are such women as the elderly widow who pathetically describes her precarious living in the 'dull and badly-built' area where she lets lodgings; but it was surely some sort of comic touch when she exclaimed 'Bathrooms! Whoever heard of bathrooms in Camden Town?'[34] We shall never know whether this was tart, knowing, disingenuous, or debunking, but no doubt it was funny. A more self-assertive character was Mrs Markham, the proprietress of a fairground shooting gallery, in a song which had the stridently suggestive cry of 'Forty in the bulls-eye!' as its chorus; one can imagine some traditionally earthy versus to match it, and at the same time the kind of realism *Era* writers loved to call 'Zola-like'.

These figures multiplied in Jenny Hill's repertoire as she matured, and were presented alongside a continuing line in servants and 'coster girls', who sang chiefly about the archetypal music-hall subject of the drunken spree, under such titles as *Every pub we saw, we went inside of it*, and *Four Ale Sal*. These songs were performed, especially inthe 1870s, in a way many reviewers called 'certainly' or 'absolutely' fast, when the singer 'daringly brushes away the artificial cobwebs of society, and tells her mind to the other sex with catching Bohemian frankness'.[35] Her rapid patter was admired, at this date, for its freedom, and occasionally one has a glimpse in the reporting of the kind of bawdy witticisms she produced, as when we learn in the *Era* that 'she gave a first-rate performance as an aspiring servant girl, who comes out fine in the clothes of her mistress, and has such a desire to marry a person of rank that she declares the ranker he is the better she will like him'.[36] The reviewer makes the patronising assumption that the girl is saying something unintentionally rude, into which men may read a double meaning; but the servant girls in the audience at the Marylebone (near the very fashionable residential streets south of Regent's Park) might well have read it quite differently. It is based overtly upon the common fantasy of role reversal between mistress and servant, the triumphant escape from social and financial servitude, and also, in such an aside, touches upon the concomitant sexual fantasy of enjoying one of the rich, well-dressed and well-fed men of the upper classes.

In other ways, Jenny Hill's young servants showed no admiration at all for their employers, and openly flouted the Victorian convention of the invisible barrier which supposedly protected the employer from the observation and hearing of his inferiors. One of her most famous impersonations was of *The Coffee-Shop Gal*, a young worker who did not bother with the expected appeal for sympathy, but instead gave a scathing commentary on the eating habits of her customers. When Jenny Hill's daughter, Peggy Pryde, was charged with indencency in her act, the number she was singing concerned the amusement of a servant at the sexual antics of her newly-married employers: the prosecution suggests that the song breached one too many respectable taboos.

When she reviewed her own career in the 1890s, Jenny Hill showed an awareness that the open bawdy and perhaps the direct social criticism of her early songs had belonged to a phase of the halls which had now passed. The early act had been 'strong' in several ways. Besides the 'fast' comic songs and the aggressively-presented lower-class female characters, it had included mocking presentations in drag of male figures like the *Boy about Town* and the chinless wonder she impersonated in *Bai Jove!* who 'gloried in putting on side' and laughed at 'those mugs of the working-man sort'. The tune of *Boy About Town*, analysed by Tony Bennett in Chapter 1, had 'jerky dotted rhythms' which he interprets as aggressively subverting the pretensions of would-be elegance. When Jenny Hill presented the loudly-dressed and bad-mannered cockney figure called '*Arry*, the surviving text shows her attitude was celebratory, enjoying the cheap finery and the noisy fun and finishing by pointedly praising her subject, because he 'works and pays his way/ While doing the la-di-dah'. The journalist inventors of the figure used it to mock working-class pretensions, and some reporters of Jenny Hill's song persisted, in spite of its unmistakable message, in taking it for a satire upon its subject; it would seem that '*Arry* is a case of the expropriation of a widely-disseminated image to a different, indeed contradictory, cultural resonance. The song is further discussed, in the context of the 'swell', in Peter Bailey's essay (Chapter 3).

As well as 'fast' and socially aggressive songs mocking and subverting bourgeois values, Jenny Hill's early performances included physical elements which, sanctioned by theatrical custom, presented as admirable behaviour diametrically opposed to the Victorian model of femininity. She practised acrobatic dancing, and exhibitionist use of the body that was built into her act in ways that may be variously understood. The hornpipe with which she frequently finished was a matter of ancient custom, an exhibition of a skill which theatrical audiences had been relishing since the Restoration period, when it was inserted into plays like Congreve's *Love for Love*. At that time, too, began their privilege of ogling fine pairs of female legs dancing in boy's clothes. The same Mary Davies who became the king's mistress and the mother of the Jacobite 2nd Earl of Derwentwater persuaded the audience at the Duke's playhouse to allow the repetition of a bad tragedy by John Caryl only for the pleasure of seeing her repeat such a performance.[37] Jigs and hornpipes were common currency in music hall. Very many minor female acts relied on dancing, a leg-show being an obvious form of subsexual display in a crinolined society. The dimension of admiration for skilled execution must have retained some reality as part of the appeal, since men danced too, but the stress upon the 'cleverness' of girl dancers found in the reporting suggests an excuse for dwelling upon the subject. It also betrays surprise at any evidence of physical abilities in women – a class-biased perception. Jenny Hill's act contained a more distinctive use of movement in her 'characteristic' dances, which were part of the evocation of figures like the Coffee-shop Gal. The 'cellar flap' dance, part of that performance, was grotesque and derisory, using a broom as a prop: one can only speculate on whether the shock of a deliberately ugly physical presentation of a poor girl was felt by the audience as an attack on the girl herself, correcting by laughter extreme deviation from female propriety, as a criticism of those whose exploitation reduced her to such an ignominious state, or as a burlesque of the cherished picture of passive and pretty female behaviour.

When Jenny Hill presented sketches early in her career, they were farcical, or burlesques of the sentimental melodrama: she did an energetic and absurd parody of the drowning of Eily in *The Colleen Bawn*, leaping from a kitchen table into a half-filled bathtub. The legacy of burlesque performance in saloon, fairground and fit-up, the anti-romantic clowning and inversion which is a recognisable element of working-class theatre, can be seen in these travesties; but they were not likely to survive into the changed music hall of the 1880s and 90s. For Jenny Hill herself, the physical demands of such an act became difficult to meet. Her obsessive response to her audience, her thirst for applause, meant that often she performed for very long periods at a stretch: when outside the constraints of the London turns system and its tight timing, she would stay on stage for more than an hour, and answer calls until she was exhausted. When the new managements began to impose tighter controls on the content of comic acts, from the end of the 1870s, Jenny Hill seems to have been ready to modify her performance to spare her own battered frame as well as the sensibilities of managers seeking a more respectable image. Her notices began to include assurances that her humour was clean and inoffensive; by 1884 reviewers were commenting that she had 'considerably toned down her too pronounced style'.[38]

This was not directly a matter of modifying her physical commitment to her stage work – in 1891 a reporter who had never seen her before was struck by her electric vivacity, and described her 'quivering with nervous excitement, passionately intent upon rendering every little detail with truth: upon making you feel it as she feels it'.[39] Rather, she changed the emotional emphasis, shifting the climax of the performance from the comic character song and the eccentric dance to sentimental and 'dramatic' set pieces.

Some of these pieces have survived in print, such as the Harrington and Le Brunn composition *The City Waif*. It is from an examination of this song that Scott illustrates his claim for Jenny Hill's 'democratic appeal', her rapport with 'the poorest members of her audience'.[40] He could only report what he believed he observed of that audience, from his own middle-class position, but it is worth considering whether it is a modern distortion to see this song's gross sentiment as in some way less authentic than her previous humour and irony. It begins by establishing the winsome cheekiness of the street arab stereotype, but then leaves humour behind, and gives a whole domestic melodrama in each verse. It was received by the press at least with the utmost seriousness, echoing Scott's judgement of its authenticity:

> As Miss Hill slowly walks on the stage at Collins's in front of the cloth which Mr Herbert Sprake has had specially painted for her, it is seen at once that her portrait of the waif is taken from the streets. Hers is no fancy sketch, but is the waif, tossing on the seething ocean of London life, deserted, alone, in perpetual unrest.[41]

It is hard to believe that the climax of the piece is quite without irony:

> A friendly policeman hears him tell a story of his own heroism… The member of the force *recognising the circumstances are coincident with the saving of a near relation of his own*, acts the part of a good samaritan, and as the curtain slowly falls he is seen supporting the boy's head and giving him nourishment [my italics]

The ironic impression is confirmed when one turns to the refrain of the printed version, and finds the line 'Out of my bed in a doorway, bobbies all hunt me down' which might be thought to correspond more closely to the perceptions of the young working-class members of the audience. There are further possibilities for a critical reading when one returns to the first four lines of the song:

> Alone, in the streets of London, my papers I sell each day,
> And notice each sight around me, though only a "waif and stray"
> I aint 'ad much eddication – it's wasted on sich as *me* –
> Except what the Ragged School gave me, or else – the Reformat'ry![42]

Here the clichés of the middle-class perception of the 'problem' of uncontrolled young people in the streets are neatly marshalled to be their own condemnation, made especially telling by the inclusion of the faux-naif 'And notice each sight around me', the possibility that these deprived youngsters would begin to 'notice' what was going on being a strong motive in the philanthropic effort to bring them in from the cold. But the sentimentality of the song's melodramatic happy ending, with the penitent policeman, must remain the dominant impression, however it might have been qualified in performance. Again, I think, we have a glimpse of a way in which music-hall style, a deliberate combination of clear-sighted recognition of the way things are with a willed enjoyment of emotional fantasies, translates middle-class values into an entertainment for the less deceived.

Jenny Hill developed this vein, which was obviously to the taste at least of management and the press, and which took so much less out of her physically, during the latter years of her career. *The Little Stowaway*, very highly praised in reviews, was a melodramatic scena so elaborated that it became embroiled in the music-hall sketch controversy and banned in 1889; by 1890 it was back in performance, along with another 'waif' piece, the *Shades of St Pauls*, and one called *Little Gyp*. This last, praised by reviewers as a real melodrama, seems to have been as lurid and sensational as it was sentimental. It told the story of a fairground child who escaped from a drunken and brutal master to marry a miner; a change of scene to the pithead village provided an idyllic moment before the arrival of the brute to reclaim her. A confrontation between Jack the miner and the brute fulfilled the melodramatic requirement of a fight between good and evil, and the sensational dénouement was provided by a fire in the mine, during which, with an interesting reversal of the normal pattern, the heroine rescued her beloved from the flames. The 'waif' pieces and *The Little Stowaway* used one or two supporting actors, but they were mere props; *Little Gyp*, although it was 'chiefly designed for the display of the versatility of Miss Jenny Hill, who seems equal to all the demands that are made on her' in fact provided her with much more support. There was the story itself, elaborate scenery including a 'splendidly built-up picture of the workings of the coal-mine', the Olympian Quintet chiming in with choral singing, and four other performers, including well-known coster singer Hyram Travers, playing the showman and singing a song of his own that was sufficiently important to be printed and sold in its own right.[43]

The changes in Jenny Hill's act in the 1880s and early 1890s were no doubt provoked by a combination of factors: her own failing health, the managerial clamp-down on risqué material, and perhaps the changing tastes and composition of the audiences. We have her own assertion that her own sex appreciated her best, and Harold Scott's testimony that she did not lose touch with her first audience, and that she was conscious of and loyal to her class origins. This is I think borne out, however tenuously, by clues in the manner and substance of the account given of her in music-hall myth. Such a clue, for example, as the jocular uneasiness with which H. Chance Newton registers her rejection of all 'side', when he hears her voice jeering at him from the grave when he writes '*Miss* Jenny Hill'. But history is in his hands, and he can soon put her in her place, as a 'cockney damsel', 'saucy little Jenny', who was a 'real little artiste', 'my little friend and fellow-worker' (the diminutives pile up quite oppressively) who had been 'ill for a long while... And no wonder, for like so many women in her profession (and out of it), she had been very unlucky and unhappy in her two or three marriages'.[44] Such reductive familiarity and easy and patronising pity is the last, but not the least effective, of the manoeuvres by which the most talented woman could be defeated in her attempt to take an independent place in the patriarchal institution of the music-hall.

6   *Joe Wilson: 'Comic Dialectical Singer' or Class Traitor?*

DAVE HARKER

If Joe Wilson is known at all, outside North-East England, it is as the author of *Keep yor feet still! (Geordey hinny)* or *Aw wish yor Muther wad cum*, two songs which get sung occasionally by NE people in pubs, clubs, on radio or TV, and in 'Olde Tyme' revivals tapping the markets for regional patriotism, nostalgia or tourism. Yet populists of the right and the left have felt Wilson to be important, and have even struggled to claim him for their own selective traditions of working-class culture. And while this contest might appear to be, at first blush, somewhat eccentric, it is in fact the case that the left and right myths of Joe Wilson do relate to real and significant historical issues. As usual, the struggle tells us more about the mediators of Wilson than about the man himself, let alone about his significance in NE culture of the period 1864–74; but we need to know how both myths were constructed, and what historical and ideological functions they perform.

For this reason, my chapter is retrospective: the myths are traced back from the present day to the specific political, economic and cultural conjuncture in which Wilson and his work were produced. I am aware that the traditional academic procedure would be to arrive at these 'conclusions' with apparent ease, after starting from an analysis of Wilson's early life; but to do so would be dishonest and in many ways more confusing than this backwards chronology. My own mediation of Wilson, then, is intended to be a polemic with contemporary socialist cultural practitioners, and with historians who have come to recognise that cultural products and practices are potentially useful sources, but who don't know what to do with them, since their training in orthodox sources did not fit them for such work.

In 1971, the Tyneside Theatre Trust presented *Joe Lives!*, 'being the life and times of Joe Wilson, bard of Tyneside'. It opened in the Gulbenkian Studio of Newcastle's University Theatre, and was a one-man show, starring the well-known stage and TV actor, John Woodvine, who was brought up in South Shields. The script constituted a series of Wilson's songs, linked by patter written by Alex Glasgow, the socialist singer-songwriter and journalist from

Gateshead who had got into the theatre after the success of *Close the Coalhouse Door* in 1968. The Musical Director was Bill Southgate, who later left for New Zealand to conduct an orchestra. The 'period' handbill credits the apprentice carpenter, the proprietors of Scottish and Newcastle Breweries, who loaned a beer keg, and the local music shop, J. G. Windows, for the loan of a tambourine.

The key material support, however, came from the Labour-controlled local councils, and from the national and regional Arts Councils, since there was little anticipation that the production would attract more than the customary theatre-goers, members of the liberal petit bourgeoisie, and perhaps a sprinkling of socialists and trade union bureaucrats. Working-class people were not expected to arrive in strength; yet Glasgow 'decided that his predecessor and hero Joe Wilson should be revived afer a century of neglect', implying that Wilson was something of a socialist, or at least fit to be placed in the labour movement Valhalla. (Martha Vicinus was later to confirm this perspective when she characterised Wilson as one of the NE's 'traditional working class song-writers', and, along with Ned Corvan, one of the 'two most successful Northumbrian dialect writers'.[1]) Is this true? Was Wilson a working-class person who wrote songs for working-class audiences? Is there a 'tradition' which links Wilson to an overtly socialist song-writer like Glasgow? Was he the best of his time? Did he write 'Northumbrian dialect'? Why did a 1970s socialist songwriter need such a man as 'hero'? What was heroic about Joe Wilson? Does the Joe Wilson of *Joe Lives!* tally with what we know about Joe Wilson the historical figure?

Part of the impetus for Glasgow's play was the appearance in 1970 of a reprint of Joe Wilson's *Tyneside Songs and Drolleries, Readings and Temperance Songs*. Yet this book did not represent the major source of continuity in the publishing of Wilson's work, since, for over half a century before, the Newcastle music shop of J. G. Windows had reissued a four-volume piano edition of *Tyneside Songs*[2] which contained 10 of Wilson's pieces – over 20 per cent of the total, and far and away the largest single contribution. The first three volumes had 'pianoforte accompaniment' by C. E. Catchside-Warrington, and were published in 1911–13, allegedly because while the words of Tyneside 'Folk Songs' had been preserved, 'the tunes are in danger of becoming forgotten and extinct.'[3] Evidently, Wilson's material (and all the other items by known authors) needed reviving *as songs*, if not as 'poetry',[4] in the piano-owning section of the community, following John Bruce and John Stokoe's 1890s project to revive 'Northumberland' tunes amongst bourgeois and petit-bourgeois people, in which Catchside-Warrington had played a part.[5] Yet Catchside-Warrington had a weather-eye open for the expatriate market, too, and 'our friends and relatives' helping run the Empire were explicitly thanked in Volume II, as '"Geordies" abroad, from Vancouver to Aden, from South Africa and Australia to Shanghai,' for their 'faithful allegiance to the "Aad Tyneside Songs."'[6]

A later edition of Volume II also noted the 'great appreciation' the songs had met 'both in print and as Gramophone records'.[7] Catchside-Warrington had been making records for Edison in London at least since 1893, in the form of master soft wax cylinders. He sang 'popular songs of the day', sometimes 'imitating the original singers', and he used the assumed name of 'Eric Foster', apparently to avoid paying income tax.[8] But he also recorded 'about 33 items of dialect humour and song;' and he made appearances on the music-hall stage, and at events organised by his fellow Freemasons.[9] In such ways – but especially through the songbooks – Catchside-Warrington's selection of older Tyneside songs penetrated several cultural strata, and acted as raw materials for repertoires and as models for 'community singing, as dance music and as concert items,' right through the 1910s and 1920s. The songbooks were frequently reprinted, and were used not only by the indigenous and expatriate bourgeoisie and petit-bourgeoisie, but also by solo singers on concert platforms, in some workers' clubs, and in the parlours or front rooms of better-off workers' houses, such as Alex Glasgow's parents' home.[10] These songs also became part of the stock-in-trade of brass bands, school choirs and the established adult choirs of the region – notably, the Felling Male Voice Choir – right through until our own day. Yet the cultural trajectory of these pieces was definitely not towards greater use amongst the mass of working-class people, as Catchside-Warrington acknowledged in his publication of a large 'Vocabulary of Local Dialect' in each songbook,[11] and this is not surprising, given the ideological tendency of much of the material he reissued.

Volume IV of *Tyneside Songs* was published (probably in 1927) with pianoforte accompaniments done by Samuel Reay, Mus. Bac., who helped sustain the original connection with what the bourgeoisie had come to term 'Folk-lore' and 'Folk Song'.[12] Wilson was placed squarely in this context, just as he had been when Reay had cooperated with John Stokoe to produce *Songs and Ballads of Northern England* in 1893, where *Cum, Geordy, Haud the Bairn* is proclaimed one of the 'Characteristic Songs and Ballads of Northern England', and as the 'best local song of the best of the latest local songwriters', a man of 'blameless life, not possessing a robust frame' who died 'leaving a vacancy not yet filled'. Stokoe and Reay were quite confident that 'Some of his songs will be sung as long as Tyne runs to the sea;'[13] and when Catchside-Warrington paid homage to these editors this was precisely the aim he had in mind, even if most NE people were willing to allow Wilson's songs to fade away!

If anything, Stokoe's revivalist fervour went deeper, when he cooperated with Bruce in the Newcastle Society of Antiquaries' project – begun at the behest of the Duke of Northumberland in the 1850s – to publish 'Northumbrian' tunes.[14] The *Northumbrian Minstrelsy* of 1882 was one result; but the raw material contained in that work was aimed at only a small section of the NE bourgeoisie, and was *then* used in cultural missionary work amongst working-class people, as part of an attempt to popularise a safely selective and mediated version of NE musical culture. The antiquarian and populist bourgeois tradition in which this project stood included not only Richard Oliver Heslop, latest in a lengthy line of bourgeois antiquarians in the region, but also elements of the radical bourgeois 'popular' press, including the influential *Weekly Chronicle*, and elements of the commercial song-publishing trade, notably Thomas and George Allan.

T. & G. Allan published their 578-page final edition of *Tyneside Songs and Readings* in 1891, complete with 'Lives, Portraits, and Autographs of the

Writers, and notes on the songs'.[15] They published no music; but this was already the sixth edition of a work originally issued in a much cheaper format in 1862, and gradually increased in size and quality until the fifth edition of 1873. Joe Wilson's work formed only a tiny part of the 1891 edition, with four songs – two from the 'Author's Manuscript' of 1869, and two more from the 'Author's Copy' dating from 1863 and 1864 – yet Allan claimed for Wilson that status of being 'Beyond all comparison...the most successful of Tyneside song-writers'.[16] In fact, Wilson's 'works' had been accorded the status of a separate full-size book, only a year before, in 1890; and though Wilson is recorded there as having seen himself as a song-writer, and not as a poet,[17] it is as *poetry* that his songs are published in the 472 pages of *Tyneside Songs and Drolleries, Readings and Temperance Songs by Joe Wilson*. Again, not a note of music appears in this 'collected edition'; and while the volume is said to have been 'noticed most favourably by the highest literary papers of the day',[18] the Allans' intention was evidently to consolidate Wilson's status as a 'dialect' poet, alongside the Lancashire rhymers of the later nineteenth century. (This was also the intention of William Andrews, who included three Wilson pieces in his 1888 edition of *North Country Poets*.[19])

Such pretensions had not been evident in the Allans' previous involvement with Wilson's work, as, for example, when they published an edition of his *Temperance Song*[20] which appeared in twopenny numbers, carefully copyrighted, in 1874, or even in the 292-page revised edition of his *Tyneside Songs, Ballads and Drolleries*, which appeared the same year, at half-a-crown apiece (or 2/2d for ready cash), or in sixpenny 'Parts' and penny 'Numbers'. This edition was an expanded version of that issued in 1873, which had only 212 pages;[21] and there may also have been an 1872 edition, the 'companion volume' to the Allans' *Tyneside Songs* of that year, advertised in the second number of the penny *Joe Wilson's Budjit ov Tyneside Drolleries, Sangs and Funny Stories*.[22] So, the parallel republication of Wilson's 'works' and the Allans' more general Tyneside songbook represents not only an unmistakable sign of Wilson's pre-eminence in bourgeois eyes, but a clear, conscious and inexorable drift up-market in the period after 1870 – once the Allans had secured copyright – from the cheap and ephemeral to the relatively costly and monumental. Joe Wilson, and the tradition of song-writing he was deemed to epitomise, were being systematically *enshrined*.

Part of this process was the association of Wilson's work with one form of radical populism. The 1890 'collected edition' of the songwriter's work was dedicated to Joseph Cowen, Esq., one who, according to the brothers Allan, 'always partial to what is "racy of the soil," has, from his earliest days, toiled for the elevation of the masses'.[23] In fact, Cowen was the son of a 'self-made' man, a Blaydon brick-maker, who moved from being a Radical in the period 1815–19 to become a Liberal MP for Newcastle and, eventually, a knight.[24] Joseph Cowen was, therefore, a scion of the emergent bourgeoisie, and had some early links with radicalism. He had some connection with Chartists in the 1830s and 1840s, received Garibaldi and Kossuth on their visits to Tyneside, set up the radical *Northern Tribune* in the mid 1850s, was associated with the post-Chartist *Republican Record* in 1855, worked in the Northern Reform Union after 1857, and became Secretary of the Northern Union of Mechanics' Institutes in 1859.[25] Perhaps his most important intervention in public affairs, however, was his purchase of the *Newcastle Chronicle* (also in 1859), which he staffed with old republicans and radicals. By 1871, he employed

> one man who had taken part in the liberation of Italy. One gathered that Tyrannicide was capable of justification and it would have been possible to meet a quiet, white-haired, dignified gentleman who had carried over from London to Paris the pistols which played their part in one of the attempted assassinations of Napoleon III. Another member of the staff had edited a Republican journal; a fourth had played an active part in securing the escape of more than one patriot from the prisons of European despotism.[26]

By 1873, the year before Cowen first became MP for Newcastle, the *Chronicle* had a circulation of 35,000, a total not exceeded by any other provincial daily, let alone by any other provincial organ of 'advanced Liberal' opinion.[27] Its editorials called for vote by ballot, equal electoral districts, representative government in the counties, women's suffrage, national compulsory education, disestablishment of the Church throughout Britain, the improvement of the position of agricultural labourers, reform of the game laws, and the abolition of corporal and capital punishment.[28] In other words, Cowen and his paper represented the most advanced sections of the *progressive bourgeoisie*; and *this* was the tradition to which Wilson's work was being assimilated.

No longer, by the 1870s, was Cowen the fiery republican of his youth, when he and G. J. Harney acted as joint secretries of the Republican Brotherhood of Newcastle, and called for 'a government of the people, for the people, by the people, by substituting for that which is nominally a Monarchy, but really an Oligarchy of aristocracy and mammon, A COMMONWEALTH OF FREE MEN.'[29] By 1874, Cowen disowned these sentiments and adopted an overtly reformist standpoint, in order to consolidate his power-base within the post-1867 Reform Act electorate. On Tyneside, and in Newcastle above all, that meant appealing to skilled male workers in shipbuilding and engineering – whose numbers were to double, nationally, between 1851 and 1881[30] – and to the radical and progressive petit bourgeoisie. The women he didn't care to cultivate; and though he spoke in favour of women's suffrage, privately he dreaded being successful, since he believed that 'the ordinary run of women are all Tories and greatly under the influence of the Priests'.[31] Enfranchised men, though they remained a tiny fraction of the working class, were evidently a political power in the land, and had to be taken very seriously indeed.[32] Hence Cowen's championing of the miners' leader, Thomas Burt, as parliamentary candidate for the Liberals. With Robert Spence Watson's help, Cowen saw to it that Burt went unopposed, and this no doubt paid dividends when Cowen was himself returned for Newcastle quite against the national trend.

At this period the tradition of revolutionary socialism was, of course, hardly known to British workers, and when Frederick Engels analysed the results of the 1874 elections, he did so for a German periodical, *Der Volkstaat*:

The second Parliament elected under the Reform Bill of 1867 and the first by secret ballot has yielded a *strong conservative majority*. And it is particularly the big industrial cities and factory districts, where the workers are now absolutely in the majority, that send Conservatives to Parliament. How is this?[33]

His answer to this question involved a socialist analysis which could not guarantee a readership in the country where at least skilled workers felt they had benefitted materially from capitalist development and the beginnings of systematic imperialist expansion, and where engineering and armaments workers – who were so important on Tyneside – had done better than most in the period before what was to be termed the 'Great Depression'.[34] Undeterred, Engels argued that whereas Gladstone had attempted a sort of 'coup d'etat' by means of the elections, he had not fully taken into account the new electoral situation, and especially the recent provisions for the secret ballot, which now allowed workers to vote with impunity against their employers, many of whom were not only 'big barons of industry', but also prominent members of the Liberal Party. In a country where John Bull was 'dim-witted enough to consider his government to be not his lord and master, but his servant', and where socialism had yet to take a lasting hold on any sizeable section of the working class, the only way in which the political representatives of the big bourgeoisie would be able to hold on to power by electoral means was to make alliances with 'respectable' men who acted as 'labour leaders' – they were, of course, all men – and thus head off the formation of a separate workers' party. And at a period when the economic motor of Chartism had been stalled through a sustained boom, and its political sting drawn by a careful implementation of three of the famous Six Points, what had to be done was to encourage men like Thomas Burt to stand for membership of the 'most fashionable debating club of Europe', thereby ensuring that the bourgeoisie maintained class control through its ideas as well as through its economic power.[35] The struggle for the hearts and minds of Tyneside workers has to be seen in this context; and so when Cowen bought up the *Chronicle* he did not stop there. In 1867 he built the Tyne Theatre and Opera House, bang in the middle of Westgate, and extremely convenient for the engineers of West Newcastle – many of them employees at Armstrong's engineering works – who formed his political power base, first as an alderman, then as MP. And one of the biggest favourites of those same engineers was the concert hall singer-songwriter, Joe Wilson.

In terms of his origins, Joe Wilson was *not* typical of Newcastle working-class people as a whole.[36] Apart from the fact that there are quite unusual and lengthy records of his life, it is also important to understand that his birth, upbringing, education and apprenticeship to trade were by no means the normal experience for a Newcastle boy born in 1841.[37] His father – whose own family hailed from Alnwick – was not only a skilled joiner and cabinet-maker, but also a freeman of the town, with all the rights and privileges that entailed, such as voting as part of the minority at Corporation and Parliamentary elections. Joe's mother had worked as a straw-bonnet-maker, but she probably left off working outside her home after bearing twins and, subsequently, two more children. Joe and Tom were born in recently-built Stowell Street, but not long afterwards the family moved around the corner into Gallowgate. Then, in 1844, the father died, apparently of tuberculosis, and the mother had to take on the role of bread-winner in order to keep herself and her children out of the Workhouse. The twins went to St. Andrew's Church School in Percy Street, and Joe became a free scholar,though at the cost of wearing the ridiculous uniform which marked him out as a recipient of charity.

When Joe was 10, a thoughtful uncle treated him to a seat at the Olympic concert hall, on the Forth, which had not long been open; and there they saw Ned Corvan, already established as a local singer-songwriter for an audience (and a market for printed songs) composed largely of working-class people.[38] When he was 14, in 1855, Joe was apprenticed to one of Newcastle's deepest-rooted trades, printing, in which several men had developed into songwriters; and in 1858 he printed his first 'beuk' of sentimental songs and poems. (Only one of those pieces survives, since his later success as a song-writer drove him to seek out every copy he could find and to destroy them.) In 1859, his master, Frank Robson of Market Lane off Pilgrim Street, gave up the trade, and Joe then worked at various printing offices, including that of the *Newcastle Guardian* newspaper, until he had finished his time. He also worked at Howe's of Gateshead, and published a couple of his own songs in a comic almanack they were printing in 1860; but his fondness for singing – he sang in the Church of England All Saints' Church Choir until early manhood[39] – and his talent for making colleagues laugh, pushed him more and more into songwriting.

In 1862, newly out of his time, Joe was able to set himself up as a printer – indicating at least a certain level of capital accumulation – though he took advantage of a room in a Marlborough Crescent pub kept by his sister and her husband. At first, trade was slack, but the enforced leisure enabled him to set up his own compositions and, with Tom inking the roller, to run off a few copies for private distribution, and, eventually for sale to the local shopkeepers, barbers included. In between jobs, Joe did waged work for other printers, such as Mr Beall, who in 1862 got the contract to print the first book of local songs which had appeared for 13 years. This was to be the first edition of the Allans' *Tyneside Songs*, which was inspired as much by the success of the local concert hall songwriters – whose work had made J. P. Robson's *Bards of the Tyne* very dated – as by that of the local bookbinder, poet and prose-writer, W. H. Dawson, one of whose effusions on the Stephenson Monument had recently sold well as a rather anachronistic broadside.[40]

Not long after this, Wilson had enough confidence in the marketability of his own work to produce penny 'Numbers' of song and verse; and at least six eight-page Numbers of *Joe Wilson's Tyneside Songs and Ballads* appeared in 1864. Wilson acted as his own agent, and sold six Numbers stitched together for sixpence; but he also used the wholesaling network of T. France in the Side, Newcastle, who published Robson's old songbook, and acted as an outlet for trade union and political literature in the town.[41] Eventually there were 15

Numbers, which, according to Thomas Allan's careful eyes, were 'editions for the million' and sold 'amongst the working men of Tyneside by the thousands; while the volume, also made up from penny numbers... had a large sale'. Wilson allowed some of his work to appear in *Charter's Comic Tyneside Almanack*, as for example in 1865, but the first three editions of the Allans' songbook contained no Wilson songs at all, the writer being canny enough to hang on to the copyright. Unlike Corvan, who was near death and hard up, Wilson had the security of his trade to fall back on; and, as yet, there was no incentive to have his work exploited by a middleman for cash down. But as the 1860s wore on, Wilson's and Allan's paths came closer together, as their interests coincided.

Wilson's crossover to professional singing was hardly a major risk, since the institutional base was firmly in place. Out of public-house 'free and easies' there had developed the commercial concert halls, notably in Newcastle but also in other Tyneside towns; and Wilson was able to try out his performance at the Mechanics' Institutes and Reading Rooms, whose managers he canvassed in a footnote in his booklet of songs. He used his print-shop as a base[42], and sang at People's Concerts in Newcastle's Lecture Rooms on Saturday evenings, using the London-disseminated 'ordinary sentimental songs of the day' – things like *Nelly Gray* and *I'm leaving thee in sorrow, Annie* – as well as testing out one or two of his own pieces. When the Working Men's Club was founded (specifically to counter the attractions of the pubs)[43], Wilson was one of the first members, and wrote a rhyming appeal on its behalf. He was no doctrinaire teetotaller, however, and was for years the 'Bard' of the Highland Society, an up-market benefit society then chaired by Sir John Fife, a one-time Radical who had moved up the social scale and to the right in politics, taking a leading role in opposing the Chartists on the streets of Newcastle.[44] Another member of the society was Mr Bagnall, who took over the chair from Fife; and when Bagnall bought the old Wheatsheaf pub and concert room from John Balmbra, in 1864, and along with Mr Blakey rechristened it the Oxford, it was Wilson who was asked to sing there on the opening night.

Blakey doubted that Wilson's voice could be heard in the hall, however 'tuneful and sweet' it might have sounded in a workshop, a parlour, or in smaller, non-commercial rooms;[45] but his misgivings were proved wrong. Wilson opened in December 1864, and by January 1865 he was being 'repeatedly encored':[46] the management extended his booking for three months, and his benefit in March was oversubscribed. After that, he moved straight into the Tyne Concert Hall, an establishment run by the former Theatre Royal manager, Mr Stanley, who had encountered serious licensing problems with the local Tory JPs (who had shares in the legitimate theatre). Then it was back again to the Oxford, probably until early June. It was at the Oxford that Ned Corvan saw his new rival – George Ridley having died the previous September, aged 30 – singing *Aw wish yor Muther wad cum*:

> A friend who was sitting beside him said, "A good song that, Ned." "Yes," said Ned in a voice which towards the end had become almost a hoarse whisper. "Yes," said he huskily, "a gud song, but aw'm writin' one that'll knock its end in."[47]

On May 30, 1865, Wilson took part in a benefit performance for Corvan, who was 'ill, and in a condition of great distress'.[48] The show was staged at the Lecture Room, and Joe sang his own songs to an audience of people connected with the concert hall and song-publishing trades:

> the manner in which he rendered them won for him many admirers. His voice was sweet though somewhat thin, but he had a very happy way of imparting varying shades of pathos and humour to suit the words of his melodies, which was very pleasing and telling with the audience.[49]

Whatever good this did for Wilson's career, it was of little use to Corvan, who died on August 31, 1865, in his 35th year, leaving the field wide open to Joe Wilson as what a reporter termed a 'comic dialectical singer'.[50]

Corvan and then Ridley had established the role of local songwriter-singer in the NE concert halls, during the 1850s and 1860s, and Corvan had developed the old broadside and chapbook trade into slip-songs and songbooks.[51] Both men provided Wilson with models for songs – Corvan on domestic situations and social comment, and Ridley on sporting events and heroes[52] – and he gratefully adapted both. Nor did he remain a NE entertainer, for he followed their footsteps down into Durham and the North Riding, then further afield. In fact, concert-hall managers needed someone to fill Corvan's and Ridley's shoes, so Wilson slotted in nicely at Stanley's new Tynemouth hall, and was passed on from there along the developing circuit of NE halls. With his mother as companion, and selling his songbooks as he went, Wilson toured northern England at a period when the regions most distant from the capital were enjoying something of a boom in so-called 'dialect' writing. Writers in Lancashire as well as in the NE were being patronised by regional patriots drawn from among the petit bourgeoisie and elements of the bourgeoisie, and it may be that this prompted the fostering of 'cockney' writers and singers in the London halls, which had hitherto been almost wholly parasitic on talent sucked in from the provinces.[53] Whatever was the case, when Wilson returned to Tyneside in 1867 he was firmly established as a minor celebrity amongst other 'clivvor cheps' like the poet and part-time journalist, J. P. Robson – who had sniped at Wilson through his weekly newspaper column[54] – and the editor of comic almanacks, J. W. Chater (who also published Wilson's re-named *Tyneside Songs and Drolleries*).

Nor was Wilson popular only in the concert halls. In June 1867, he advertised himself as being available 'for a short season, to engage for concerts, soirees' and suchlike one-night-stands in the workers' clubs and institutes of Tynside,[55] before settling down to lengthy engagements at both the Tyne and the Oxford. In July, he was the only performer based outside London to be engaged at the reopening of the Wear Music Hall in Sunderland; and he could rely on a series of bookings at South Shields, West Hartlepool and Middlesbrough, right through until the end of November. All the while, and unprecedentedly, his career was reported in Cowen's *Chronicle*; and Chater advertised Wilson's songbooks as 'Sung by him with unparalleled success at all the Principal

Concert Halls in the North of England'. Chater had also become Wilson's agent, based in the Clayton Street shop, and Howe Brothers (his former employers) continued to print and to reprint his songbooks, as did Mr Fordyce, himself a veteran of the defunct broadside trade.[56]

Income from these sources made Wilson moderately secure, financially; and in 1869 he married a Miss English of Jarrow. Soon they had a child, and though the family spent nine months at Spennymoor, in the burgeoning central Durham coalfield, when Joe was managing a new concert hall, the end of that engagement forced him back on to the road once more. Though he went 'singing his songs as successfully as ever at the various concert halls of the North', he took the separation badly, and the travelling got him down.[57] (Even his song-writing suffered: in 1870, an unknown pitman's song won the annual prize in the *Weekly Chronicle* competition, while Wilson's effort received only an 'honourable mention'[58].) In the end, he decided to try to take over the Adelaide Hotel in New Bridge Street, Newcastle, and run it as a free and easy, using his own reputation and singing as the draw. This was in 1871; and yet he continued to advertise himself as 'At liberty for concerts, Soirees, etc, singly or with company'[59] in order to help pay back the capital he had borrowed from his petit-bourgeois acquaintance. Almost certainly, one of the two teetotallers involved was Thomas Allan, who later averred that 'instead of a guarantee for so much the amount was advanced as a loan (afterwards honourably repaid)'. So the name of JOsEph WILSON (looking at first sight like JOE WILSON) appeared above the pub door; but there is some suspicion that the security for the loan may have involved the copyright of Wilson's songs. Allan had already published Wilson's pantomime, *Pilferini*,[60] in 1869, where the copyright is 'Deddycated tiv Ivrybody' – no doubt in jest only – but once Wilson had abandoned the pub in 1872, Thomas Allan's fourth edition of *Tyneside Songs* of that year became the first to contain any of Wilson's songs.

Wilson's unsavoury experience at the Adelaide seems to have speeded his transition form the skilled, 'respectable' working class to the even more 'respectable' petit-bourgeoisie, not only in economic but also in ideological terms. Though he could still write a song in favour of the engineers' strike in 1871, the gap between his ideas, attitudes and beliefs and some of those of his more proletarian customers was no doubt widened by his having to cope with drunks at closing-time. He had never been strong – he had 'defective limbs'[61] as well as tuberculosis – and on one occasion he let fly at a man who insulted his wife. Like Corvan, he was often treated to drink beyond his capacity to enjoy it, but was called a 'surly beast' if he refused any more. According to Thomas Allan, whose petit-bourgeois ideology Wilson more and more felt drawn towards, Wilson was 'Worsened in every way, disappointed and sickened with the whole business'. He gave up the pub after about a twelvemonth, joining the Good Templars at the same time, writing, singing and then publishing material in support of their cause. In turn, the well-placed petit-bourgeois stalwarts of that organisation, Thomas Allan among them, rallied round to see to it that their influential recruit got work. Happily for Wilson, they were well represented in the print trade, so he was offered an opening in journalism, and given work by Mr Fordyce in setting up nearly all the type for the Allans' 1872 *Tyneside Songs*, throwing in acrostics, notes and other material as he did so. Then, with the help of contacts from his concert hall days, Wilson put together an 'entertainment' with which he toured schoolrooms, Liberal Clubs, workers' clubs and institutes, in between his professional engagements at the halls. The move to further 'respectability' and to 'poetry' naturally followed.

By 1873, if not a little earlier, the Allans were publishing a separate book of Wilson's *Tyneside Songs, Ballads and Drolleries*, in a collected format of 212 pages, but evidently using the eight-page Numbers as a basis – the ones Wilson had himself set up 'upwards of Six Years' before. The Allans may well have recouped at least part of their loan by securing copyright of Wilson's early songs, and certainly by May 1874 Thomas was buying the copyright of another batch of Wilson songs, then inscribing '26 or '27' on his copy, as if to indicate which new Number the particular songs should appear in.[62] In February of that year a 'New Edition' of the Wilson songbook, bigger by 80 pages, was published at 2/2d (nominally 2/6d), but still available in sixpenny Parts and penny Numbers for the less affluent.

Simultaneously, the Allans published twopenny parts of *Joe Wilson's Temperance Songs, Readings and Recitations* in a 36–page format, the third of which appeared during 1874, carefully marked 'Copyright'. Evidently, Wilson needed the ready cash to supplement his income from the halls, even though he was puffed as having become a 'Household name throughout the North, where his songs are universally adimired and sung.[63] Twice he was booked so far away as Glasgow, and it was in that city, probably at the Britannia, that the disease which killed his father first struck Joe Wilson down on stage. His last professional engagement was at the Royal Star Theatre, Stockton-on-Tees, where he had a benefit early in September 1874. After that, only the charity of friends, colleagues and fellow entertainers kept him going. Rowland Harrison, another local singer-songwriter,[64] put him up at his Commercial Hotel at Winlaton. In mid October, a benefit concert was arranged by Thomas Allan, W. H. Dawson and Robert Stephenson, the musical landlord of the Lord Nelson Inn. Allan tried to keep Wilson's name before the public by using the newspapers, and may have suggested that Wilson play an important part in getting going a Tyneside equivalent of the 'Lancashire dialect' *Hartley's Clock Almanack*; but it was all useless. Wilson died on February 12th – some accounts say the 14th[65] – 1875, at the age of 33. Two months later, his infant son was buried in the same unmarked grave.

On the very day that Wilson's death was announced in the *Chronicle*, the paper carried an advertisement for 'Mr Fordyce's collection of Joe Wilson's songs', which was later amended to 'Mr Allan', Fordyce being only the printer[66] – thus getting two advertisements for the price of one. On the 18th, the *Chronicle* gave notice of an appeal for the benefit of Mrs Wilson and her three children;[67] yet in spite of the fact that subscriptions were to be acknowledged in the *Daily Chronicle*, the response from concert-hall managers was feeble indeed. Stanley gave two guineas, Bell (of the Wear) gave three, Bagnall chipped in a pound, as did the managers of the Oxford at Middlesbrough. Thomas and George Allan managed three guineas between them; yet even a whip-round at the Adelaide produced two and a half guineas. A Templars' Lodge collected eighteen shillings.[68] Thomas Allan made sure that he was one of the pall-bearers, however, and he continued to hold the earning power of his almost complete set of Wilson copyrights in high respect, decades after the fund topped £1000.[69]

Profit margins on Wilson's *Temperance Songs* remained very high, even in 1886. Allan ran off a thousand at a time, and enjoyed a 200 per cent mark-up, yet the October 1890 edition of Wilson's 'works' had a print run of only 2,000, with a projected profit of 29 per cent. Three months before this book came out (in time for the Christmas trade),[70] Allan had seen to it that a stone was erected over Wilson's grave, after a decade and a half of neglect. This 'private munificence' – costing some £38 according to the bill kept by Allan – was allowed to 'leak' to the *Chronicle*. (The stone was photographed for the song-book, and the newspaper hinted that a 'complete edition of the works of the earlier songwriters' of Tyneside might be a good follow-up. Allan's 1891 edition of *Tyneside Songs* coincidentally appeared a few months later.[71]) The Wilson songbook was dedicated to the *Chronicle's* proprietor, who had dropped out of the Democratic Foundation when it became Socialist.[72] A presentation copy also went to Thomas Burt, who resolutely opposed the building of a workers' party to the end; and another was sent to the Chief Constable of Gateshead, who was said to have been instrumental in persuading Wilson to go on the stage in the 1860s.[73] Joe Wilson, and what he stood for, had by this date become the cultural property of the liberal bourgeoisie, as they moved economically upwards and politically to the right, at differing speeds. There were no Parts and no Numbers for these books of the 1890s. The market which had sustained Wilson (and the Allans) in the 1860s and 1870s had, apart from the teetotallers, turned away from the man and his works. When we examine the trajectory of Wilson's songs, as they exhibit his changing attitudes towards workers and working-class culture, we can see why this bourgeois 'capture' was not contested.

Of the sentimental verse which Joe Wilson wrote in the 1850s, only *The Twin-Twin-Brothers' Birthday* survives.[74] It is truly dull stuff, worse even than J. P. Robson's verse – 'Dear brother Tom,/ Our birthday's come,/ And now we're seventeen'. But there were few other models available. Ridley and Corvan may have established the vogue for idiomatic songs written for the working-class concert-hall audiences, but Wilson could not well compete directly with, say, Corvan's broad humour, burlesque tone and acid wit. However, Wilson seems to have attempted to imitate Corvan's bubbly prose and over-the-top patter for *Wor Geordey's Accoont o' the Greet Boat Races* in 1863. This piece and the accompanying song, *The Cockney's Lament*, continued the regionally-patriotic vogue established by Corvan and Ridley; but whereas the older writers' work feels authentically idiomatic, Wilson's song gives the impression of having been conceived in standard English, and then as it were *translated*. In fact, he admits as much by having his factitious 'local figure', Jacky Broon, claim that the song was overheard being sung by a cockney, and, thinkin that ye mebbies cuddent read thor ootlandish twang,...got his Uncle Bob, a weel eddycated man, te translate it inte the Newcassel dialect, so as onybody can understand it.[75]

The truth is that Wilson's song can equally as well be translated *back* into standard orthography with absolutely no difficulty apart from the occasional idiomatic word, since grammar remains unaffected; and this fact reminds us that many of Wilson's songs were written specifically for the audience for printed (and not simply sung) material, and that all of them were written with print in mind. Since Wilson actually set up much of the type for his songs, he well knew that 'Newcassel tawk's a queerish thing te reed';[76] but the question arises, why was it printed that way at all, when any Newcastle worker reading standard English would speak it idiomatically, to a greater or lesser extent? What *was* Wilson's audience? Or were there different and overlapping audiences for his singing and his published verse, some of whom simply enjoyed the 'phonetic' spelling, and others who needed it to get into the swing?

If Corvan and Ridley had succeeded in differentiating themselves from the older, petit-bourgeois song-writing of the period 1800–40, J. P. Robson remained at the fag-end of that tradition. His were the models which Wilson used for his non-idiomatic pieces, and Robson's status as a 'poet' was shored up by the young aspirant in a fulsome acrostic.[77] But Wilson's audience seems to have been markedly different, judging by what we can glean from hints scattered through his songs and verse: it was predominantly male, skilled workers, usually employed in a Tyneside factory, and in engineering works above all. Such men probably shared with Wilson an interest in getting out of wage slavery and 'getting on', and harboured ambitions of becoming self-employed or even of employing other workers. Thus, while 'Tyneside lads' are often invoked or celebrated, and *The Lads upon the Wear* get a whole song, women tend to figure as *personae* for Wilson, and only occasionally as workers outside the home – as in *She's Gyen te Place at Jarrow, That Factory Lass* or *The Pork Shop Lass*.[78] Usually, women appear in their capacity as potential wives rather than as people capable of selling their labour-power. Similarly while many songs assume a detailed knowledge of Newcastle streets and people, 'country' pitmen very rarely figure in Wilson's songs – apart from the compulsory exercise *In Memory of the Hartley Catastrophe*. Keelmen, who were in any case a dying trade after the 1820s, but who lingered on Tyne and Wear past mid century, appear hardly more often.[79]

If people in his songs are not defined in terms of their economic independence – as in the long list of self-employed relations of *Maw Bonny Gyetside Lass* – then it's the 'workman that's first class' who is used as Wilson's standard. Most often, these men are from Stevenson's, Hawthorn's, Hawks's or Armstrong's engineering factories, and they are used to skilled, heavy work, such as forge work, and to the shift system.[80] *Maw Bonny Injineer* is perhaps typical, in that the lad just out of his time at Hawthorn's is looking forward to 20 or 30 shillings a week, with the chance of overtime and the prospect of one day setting up for himself.[81] Such 'stiddy cheps' – at a time when 16 shillings a week did not satisfy the housemaid in another Wilson song – could always get a job; and it was their working and leisure-time standards against which other men were measured, by Wilson and (according to him) by would-be wives. No more did such men go 'on the tramp' to look for work: that was deprecated;[82] though strikes and slackness of trade did interrupt the steadiest of jobs. Even for an engineer, it was always possible to get the sack, through clocking-on late, being 'sawsy' to the foreman, or through 'bad times' in the market; and Wilson recognised that only by continuing to sell their skilled labour-power could these men hope to remain 'freed frae sad poverty's pang'. (Wilson went so far as to claim affinity with those who had been 'oot o' wark, like me-sel', though he had always had his own skilled trade to fall back on.)[83] Losing a quarter of an hour's pay through sleeping-in could still be a problem, for engineering workers were by no means immune from poverty. They, like Wilson, doubtless had close experience of tenement living, of *The Meun-Leet Flit*, of lodging houses, of having only two unbroken china cups in the house and of needing to scratch around when wages were low or non-existent.[84] In his early songs, Wilson never assumes that his audience is immune from such pressures, or ignorant of shop-floor culture. Indeed, it was the shared fear of falling back into the abyss of the the urban poor which motivated them and him, since going up the social scale was one of the best safeguards against going down. Meanwhile, these were the people who also had the spare pence to buy Wilson's song-books, and the leisure-time to go to hear him sing.[85]

Given this was the kernel of Wilson's audience – a view echoed by Thomas Allan, and by George Stanley, who paid tribute to the 'intelligent and independent artisans'[86] who bought seats in his halls – it is interesting to examine the attitudes, values and assumptions which are built into the songs. When Corvan was alive, Wilson did not venture too far into the burlesque, but struck out in a curious direction, as his fellow-poet and print-trade worker W. H. Dawson noted in 1869. Compared to the 'frothy, unmeaning, and ephemeral trash termed comic songs' – by which Dawson may well have meant Corvan's as well as London-made material – Wilson's pieces were characterised by the 'depth of moral tone that pervades them':

> Indeed, his *hardiesse* in that respect has often been to us a matter of surprise. Let it suffice that he has scarcely written a piece without endeavouring to make his listener the better for it... The slight tincture of dialecticism that pervades his songs only adds charm to their homeliness.[87]

It is not simply that Wilson could make certain assumptions about his audience's culture, as in his references to *Sporting life*, Cowen's *Chronicle* and even the dispute between the 'consart' owners and the manager of the Newcastle Theatre Royal, Davies.[88] Nor is it only a question of material ambitions, such as the way a skilled worker might choose to swap his 'fustin claes' for both a light and a dark suit and a 10–shilling hat when funds allowed, or his wife might aspire to a muff.[89] What *is* revealing is the way Wilson appears to articulate the ideas which went along with a skilled hand 'hard and brawny' – how he helps us understand the answer to Engels' question.[90]

Work was at the centre of this set of ideas. Men who cadged for beer were exhorted to 'Try wark, aw's sure ye shud'. Other work-shy individuals are lampooned – 'He diddent fancy wark/ So he's gyen te be a Bobby'[91] – and far from Wilson perceiving class-based antagonisms between 'maister an' Man', he proclaims that their interests coincide. *The Draper's Appeal* is overtly on behalf of both employer and employee, and 'Economy' was deemed to be the 'study' of both.[92] Being without work is a social stigma, as well as an economic problem: 'Ne wark yit! to tell them aw really think shem', since 'dependence is painful', even on parents.[93] In courtship as at work, Wilson's audience was warned that 'Ye'll find uthers i' yor place/ If ye dinnet shuv aheed – an' fettle reetly;' yet there were other pitfalls familiar to the mass readership of Samuel Smiles' *Self-Help*: 'Be careful, – if ye want te raise,/Be canny wi' the beer'.[94] With work went a particular status, a 'stayshun' whose demands should be met while men or women remained there, right down to matters of appearance – 'A fact'ry lass wad nivvor seem/ Curl-paypers iv her heed' – and of accent – *Affected Bella* is denounced not for speaking idiomatically, but because she 'mixes the dialec se' with would-be Queen's English.[95] And while work sometimes caused problems at home, as when a father is absent on night-shift, and cannot be used as an immediate threat to wayward children,[96] the absence of work during a dispute such as the Nine Hours engineers' strikes in the NE during 1871 brought out Wilson's fundamental attitudes towards capital and labour.

Wilson was distantly related to John Burnett, the engineers' leader, and he must have known that his own hero, J. P. Robson, had risked writing some mealy-mouthed verses in support of the great NE pitmen's strike of 1844.[97] Robson, his 'great rival', had died in 1870, and while Wilson did not go so far as Corvan did in 1851 – when the songwriter published strike songs at his own expense[98] – September 1871 found Wilson singing in Newcastle's Town Hall. Four months into the strike, he came out in public support of the men on strike, and he

> contributed a local song, especially written for the occasion, and the sentiments therein contained in favour of the strike hands were greeted with immense enthusiasm.[99]

Joe Lives! represented Wilson as having the lights turned out on him by outraged agents of capital;[100] but the truth was more mundane, and in any case, *The Strike!* was in no way subversive of capitalist orthodoxy. If anything, it could be accused of slightly patronising the 'mony poor fellows on strike' rather than advocating a rush to the barricades after the Parisian fashion. In fact, capitalist social relations are assumed to be permanent, unshakeable, and probably satisfactory all round in Wilson's song, which contented itself with reminding some 'greet Maisters' that a 'Mechanic' was 'ne slave'. Wilson accepted that the demand for a nine-hour day was acceptable because it was not 'unreasonable', whether or no 'lang oors Industry increases' – possibly, a reference to the ludicrous notion that employers' profits were made only at the end of a working day.[101] 'Let them that condemn'd hev a try on't,' Wilson tells the advocates of a longer day; and he points out the economic irrationality of masters turning a blind eye to the 'Forriners' who had been shipped in to scab, but who acted as though they were – horror of horrors – 'thor awn maisters' and worked 'just when they'd a mind'.

All through this song, Wilson assumes that labour-power is a commodity to be bought and sold on the basis of 'reasonable' self-interest. There is no hint that there is either the possibility or the necessity of transcending these social relations: 'if Maisters is meant to be Maisters,/ Let them find tho's Men meant to be Men!' And that's it. If this sort of stuff really was 'greeted with immense enthusiasm' by the strikers in the Town Hall, then, presumably, they shared Wilson's ideas, and looked to a future where the increasing price of their sole commodity could be cashed in terms of increased leisure-time, rather than money. It is hardly surprising, then, that the limited trade union reforms of the 1870s appeased many of them.[102] And this fits in with what Wilson presents as the engineers' ambition to become self-employed and small employers, and with his own transition from the 'respectable' working class to the even more 'respectable' petit bourgeoisie. In this sense, Wilson succeeds in articulating the culture of the aspiring, skilled working class.

On the face of it, Wilson's early 'hit', *Aw Wish Yor Muther Wad Cum*, 'or, wor Geordy's notions aboot men nursin bairns', is mildly progressive in its attitudes towards women. He wrote the song 'throo seein me brother-in-law nursin the bairn the time me sister wes oot, nivor dreaming at the time it wad turn oot the "hit" it did'; and he dresses up sententiousness in archly idiomatic language:

> What a selfish world this is,
>   Thor's nowt mair se than man;
> He laffs at wummin's toil,
>   And winnet nurse his awn;...

Now, it is true that Wilson knew he could make women in his audience laugh at Geordy's having 'ne skill', and at his constant wish that the mother would come back; but the truth was that Geordy well recognised the work the woman felt forced to do to service his and his child's needs. Yet still he craves praise for nursing his child when she wanted him to do it, rather than when he chose to play the proud father. Even so, the song was sufficiently open about male attitudes to get some support from women in his audience. After a three-month season at the Oxford, 'on the occasion of his benefit',

> a lady friend gave him a large dressed doll with which he came on to the stage and sung his "Aw wish yor Muther wad cum."[103]

Everything in Wilson's performance was made subservient to his moralising verse. Until he was given that doll as a prop for *Aw Wish*, he had always sung the song with two handkerchiefs made up into the figure of a doll; and this was one of the ways in which Wilson sought to differentiate himself from Corvan, who frequently dressed in character (as did Ridley), wore over-the-top clothes, and used props. Instead, Wilson adopted a rigorously minimalist position; and there is no evidence that he wore a ludicrously 'loud' suit as used in *Joe Lives!* In fact, such pictures as we have of Wilson on stage show him in a sober, dark suit, with a waistcoat, a necktie, and a handkerchief in his jacket breast pocket. On what might be a late photograph, he is shown with a neatly-dressed pianist, while Wilson – without a beard, but retaining a moustache – wears highly polished shoes and an even smarter three-piece suit, complete with a watch and hunter. (A photograph of Wilson posed in a photographer's studio shows him as a young man, book in hand, with a matching waistcoat and trousers and a darker, more casual jacket, for all the world like a person aspiring to be a poet; and this seems to be the original of the line drawing used on the cover of his sixth Number of his own songs, published in 1864.) this was *not* the 'ordinary dress of a working man' at this period, as Vicinus claims,[104] but that of the 'respectable' stratum of that class which formed the backbone of his audience.

Wilson's singing may sometimes have been barely audible, but his manner was evidently 'sweet'. In this, also, he relates more to Robson's tradition than to Corvan's or Ridley's. The *Chronicle* usually called him 'Mr Joe Wilson' – an honour rarely if ever accorded to Ned Corvan or George Ridley – and noted with evident satisfaction that some new local songs were 'cordially received' by the audience at the Tyne Concert Hall. Corvan was never described as one who 'warbles his pleasant ditties', let alone as a writer of songs 'characterised by mingled pathos and humour,... to which he lends an additional interest by his unaffected and simple style of vocalisation'.[105] Nor did anyone ever record Corvan having experienced problems like those faced by Wilson in the New Town Hall, where he was

> all but inaudible and could not have been heard by those in the gallery. Yet after singing "Aw wish yer Muther wad Cum" he was called back again, and substituted another local song in its place.[106]

Quite clearly, Wilson wished to make the words of his songs the centre of interest in his performance, and everything else – dress, pose, props and delivery – was tailored to this end. His motives were up front: 'Me constant aim's te please, instruct, amuse;' but he also wanted badly to make a distinctive niche for himself in the concert hall and as a sententious *poet*, disclaimers notwithstanding.[107] Time and again he crops up in his songs about local heroes and celebrities. He uses Corvan and Ridley tunes, especially in his earlier songs, and sometimes imitates Corvan's 'daft' patter. The titles of his own pieces appear repeatedly in his later songs, sometimes dragged in by the scruff of their neck, and Wilson wasn't above giving Thomas Allan's shop a free plug.[108] Everything about Wilson and his performance had to be 'respectable' in ways which suited both the labour aristocracy and the petit bourgeoisie, his patrons. Compared to Corvan, Wilson was not only politically and ideologically safe, but he was really useful in helping to popularise the values, attitudes and ideas espoused by the bourgeoisie, and by those who aspired to that status. No lampoons on civic corruption were ever likely to flow from his pen; no satires of the emigrant trying to escape from capitalist social relations in Australia, and no class-conscious or republican sentiments would stain the ideological purity of his stage performances or his songbooks. Instead, in *Prepare for what's te cum*, even a first-class workman is lectured about taking a glass of rum after twelve hours' graft, and hectored about deferred gratification which extends beyond this life to 'anuther an' a better world te cum!' In *What Gud can Sweerin de?*, all and sundry reminded that they 'run thor sowls i' deadly sin' should they chance to vent an oath; and only those models of bourgeois individualism such as Cowen, Chambers, Stephenson, Armstrong, Renforth and Burt – heroes of sport or industry[109] – get singled out for praise, after an earlier bow to Garibaldi. So while, as Vicinus says, 'almost all of his songs were based on actual events',[110] it remains the case that those events are used as pegs on which to hang obtrusive advice on social behaviour and on mores in general. So scrupulous was Wilson that he wrote whole songs about acceptable and unacceptable forms of *Pride*; and he executed another piece, *Varry Canny*, which is devoted to explaining (for the benefit of a 'cockney' performer, according to Wilson's brother, Tom)[111] why a phrase that apotheosises the unexceptionable and unexceptional represents Wilson's idea of perfect social behaviour. He evidently saw himself as some sort of custodian of 'respectable' working-class moral welfare; and only very occasionally does any sense of fun get communicated in his songs. His repertoire – even before the Adelaide fiasco – is packed with very, very sensible and very, very tedious ideas. Yet Wilson not only believed his own propaganda, he aimed to translate it into practice in his own life:

> An' if wi' me sang aw shud please a' the foaks,
> 　Aw'll whisper, cum Joey, maw manny,
> Ye maynit de owt like sum greet bleezin star,
> 　But yor reet if ye de "varry canny."

The social abyss which Wilson and his audience knew to exist seems to have yawned open to him after his experience of the lumpen customers at the Adelaide; and while he could treat the story of bed-sharers in a riverside lodging-house with something like humour in *Keep yor feet still!*, later on in his career he denounced the excesses of the poorest people in the town. In this, he was articulating that gut-churning *fear* felt by all 'respectables' in the community for the underclass in general; just as, in *Glorious Vote be Ballot*, he gives voice to the utter contempt felt by the well-to-do for poor voters. Instead of advocating a change in the social arrangements which led to the creation of the sometimes lurid culture of the urban poor, Wilson, like the good petit bourgeois he had become, preached fervently in attacking the symptoms rather than the disease.[112] Above all, drink was defined as the central problem, rather than the palliative; and so the results of alcohol abuse were seen as fit for violent retribution. Whereas before 1871 he might appeal to 'Wimmin o' charity' and 'men o' sense' to help relieve an old woman expected to survive on half a crown a week (half of which went in rent), and the moderate use of beer by working men was recommended in preference to 'dorty pledges', after that date Wilson homed in hard on the victims of bourgeois economic and human relations.[113] When a woman died of drink, not only are her 'crimes' against respectability set out at length without a thought about what drove her to them, but Wilson feels it necessary and right that he should pronounce the community's verdict on her:

> Cum, print us a funeral caird, Mister Printer,
>   An' put a bit verse on te let the folks see
> That aud Drunken Dolly i' jail's kickt the bucket,
>   An' not before time's the opinion o' me!
> They tell ye the falts o' the deed te forget, man,
>   But sum heh se mony ye cannet de that;
> For when leevin she nivvor did gud te nebody,
>   An' noo she's gyen deed like a venimus rat.[114]

Occasionally, as in *Tom Broon*, Wilson's subjects come back from the brink, in this case, typically, because of the leniency of a magistrate; but for most of his extremely intemperate 'Temperance' songs, Wilson's own fear of the masses vents itself as almost uncontrolled viciousness. 'Fightin Dan,' the subject of *Flog'd in Jail!*, spells out Wilson's (and his class's) fear of those who can 'use thor fists' against anybody with property, but only when Dan is safely in jail awaiting the execution of his sentence! It's impossible to miss Wilson's pleasurable *frisson* as he builds up to the climax:

> For days he waited i' the jail,
>   Till one day, tiv his ward,
> The turnkey com te tell him he
>   Wes wanted in the yard.
> He seun wes stript an' fastened up –
>   'Gan at it! – hit him hard!"

And so it goes on, until bourgeois law and order had extracted its vengeance from one who dared to challenge its rule; and then Wilson could pronounce a verdict with some confidence that he was speaking for the 'respectable' community as a whole:

> Ne pity for the hardened wretch;
>   Ne sympathy or fear:
> Thor's ower mony like him, an'
>   We divvent want them here:
> Thor's sum wad commit ony crime,
>   Ay, murder, for thor beer!

And that's that. No remorse. No understanding of the basis of the need to get drunk. No sympathy. The answer is a form of moral rearmament, not a change in a system which produces Fightin Dans and Drunken Dollys as a matter of course. What was needed, according to this view, was more legal repression and, preferably, the return of public hangings.[115] (Wilson also used 'jew' as a *verb*, and blacks are always 'Niggers'.)[116] By thus showing the reverse of the coin of 'respectability' Wilson helps us understand how populism can be pulled both ways, politically, including in the direction of what we now know as fascism. And while we do not know if he used all of this material when he went back on the concert-hall stage, it is now clear why his material found a welcome in 'respectable' culture long after Wilson's death.

Which brings us back to the myths. Alex Glasgow now recognises that he invented the scene where Wilson gets the stage lights switched off for a 'good dramatic effect to finish the first act', and that he tended to make him 'more radical than he actually was, so that I could identify with him more closely':

> The other Big Lie is in the second act when Joe's temperance songs scale staggering heights of bigotry. I suppose I could have let him die a despicable, consumption-ridden misanthrope. Why didn't I? Fifteen years later it's hard to know. Perhaps, having created a hero I wanted to get him off the hook. Not to make a "happy ending" because it was far from that – But to allow for dignity in death. He spent most of his short life writing and singing marvellous songs for and about the working class of Newcastle. He deserves a decent memorial.[117]

Yet we have seen that Wilson wasn't any kind of a socialist, or even a trade unionist. He was a self-employed professional printer turned concert-hall singer and songwriter, who made money from printing his own songs, and gradually levered himself out of the 'top' end of the skilled working class. He was far less politically progressive than Ned Corvan, but then, Corvan's repertoire and class-consciousness were not widely known until the 1970s, thanks to the mediating of Thomas Allan and Catchside-Warrington, and to the fact that we academics had not done the necessary work. Neither is it Glasgow's fault. Where, in the 1970s, was a socialist songwriter to turn for inspiration and for some sense of belonging to a tradition – even one who had known very well what it was to get into bother by singing for workers occupying factories, and who was to come back from Australia in order to sing for the miners during their great strike of 1984–85? Only Joe Wilson appeared to be available, and so Glasgow set about editing what he could discover about the real Joe into something like a plausible radical. In practice, however, this meant so much reconstruction in order to wrest Wilson from the bourgeois culture that *Joe Lives!* just doesn't stand up as a historically-credible tale. It's not only a question of dramatic licence: that's fair enough in something that is not meant to be a documentary. Rather, it's that everything we know about Joe Wilson marks him off as a reproducer of bourgeois ideology. Joe Wilson can't be rehabilitated; and in any case socialist intellectuals and artists have a more important role to play in politics than trying to make the likes of Wilson into something like a presentable precursor of some continually delayed socialist culture of the future. There is no point in desperately seeking non-existent socialist ancestors. Even Corvan had his share of nationalism, though his tradition is nearer to Glasgow's own in other ways. And there is absolutely no justification for mystifying the harsh realities of workers' culture at the high-point of capitalist expansion. Our job is to try to *understand* that culture, warts and all, for what it really was. That way, we can hope to be better able to intervene in the present, just as Alex Glasgow and thousands of others did in the Great Strike of 1984–85.[118]

7 'Harmless Nonsense': The Comic Sketch and the Development of Music-Hall Entertainment

LOIS RUTHERFORD

In 1909 a Home Office memo summarised the Lord Chamberlain's assessment of music-hall sketches:

> They injure the theatre both financially and artistically. They withdraw from the theatres many who are tempted by the freedom, the smoking, the promenades and the drinks in the auditorium of the music hall, advantages the the theatre cannot have ... And they tend to produce a degraded taste for hurried, and frivolous and brainless drama.[1]

Officially then, music-hall sketches were not given the respect and attention accorded to legitimate drama. They were not considered to be pieces of 'culture' in what Raymond Williams has termed the 'ideal' or 'documentary' senses, and therefore they were not worthy of critical reviewing and appreciation.[2] By contrast, emphasising a 'social' conceptualisation of popular culture, the free-trade-in-amusements lobby, music-hall professionals and proprietors, and otherwise unemployed actors insisted that sketches did much to raise the tone of music-hall entertainment. Sketches were often held up as symbols of progressive cultural improvement from within music-hall enteratinment itself.

From the 1860s to the 1900s a number of arguments were advanced, petitioning for the legalisation of 'stage plays' in the halls on the grounds that they raised both the standards of behaviour and performance in the halls and variety theatres. Invariably it was not the comic sketch, but the moral melodramatic type that was said to have an edifying influence upon the uneducated masses. With due care for the intellectual and moral shibboleths of the middle classes, sketch supporters claimed that they elevated sensibilities, induced concentration and reduced drinking.[3] In 1867 the playwright Boucicault praised the music-hall profession as the 'stepping stones from the sensual enjoyment of the public house to the intellectual entertainment of the theatres'. During the 1890s *Era* was recurrently arguing that sketches were ideal for audiences who were in a 'transitionary state', moving from 'mere idle amusement to the appreciation of something better, more intellectual and elevating'.[4] The professional press was not unaware of the effects of Board School education upon their youthful and adult audiences. After 1900 it was less essential for variety professionals to employ moral justifications for sketch productions. As one director, Henry Tozer, told the Select Committee on Censorship, the sketch

> has greatly improved the tone of the music halls; secondly, it has greatly added to the diversity of the entertainments; thirdly it has stimulated the regular music hall artiste to improve both the style and attractiveness of his entertainment.[5]

Thus, whereas the chorus singing, vulgar and jolly comic song was peculiarly associated with the pub-based music hall, sketches were regarded as positively contributing towards the music halls' aspirations to be accorded the status of 'variety theatre' from the 1870s onwards. Because sketches, comic or dramatic, were a relatively theatrical form, it is no coincidence the they were connected with the demise of the comic song as the epitome of music-hall entertainment.

Similarly, sketches were associated with the improvements implemented to attract wider audiences, including the wealthier and more educated middle classes to the variety theatre. This is not the place for a discussion relating to data indicating shifts in audience composition; but it is important to point out that the middle class 'taste public' for music hall was by no means homogeneous.[6] Company records at the Public Record Office suggest that members of the leisured, business and professional middle classes readily purchased shares in variety theatre enterprises, reducing the predominance of the drink trade's investment in the economic structure of the business. the 'family' middle-class public also progressively participated as consumers of sheet music, cylinders and records, and of course, as seat purchasers. Consequently, several interested contemporaries commented upon the narrowing of the hitherto wide social gulf between the illegitimate and legitimate stage.[7]

Although the focus of this essay is upon sketches as a specific genre, itis also concerned with the question of the impact of middle-class participation in the music hall and variety theatre. Over the past two decades this has become one of the central issues in recent music-hall historiography. There have been essentially two separate, inter-related approaches to the problem, and each has some bearing on the role of the comic sketch in the variety theatre. On the one hand there are historians of working-class culture and politics, who have taken up the general line of earlier popular or sentimental writers. Music hall here is seen as class conscious, but because audiences were not confined to the working classes it is deemed to have failed to meet the need for working-class self-assertion, and become strangled by 'suburban gentility'. Stedman Jones, Vicinus andothers have concluded that music-hall culture 'never gave class a political definition'. Rather, as the mid-century 'class perspective' gave way to the late Victorian 'mass perspective', the stereotyped comic working man became an object of laughter for all classes. The halls are seen as a product of 'middle class self-congratulation', and the subordinated working classes seek recourse in 'irony or disdain' as an expression of class antagonism. Mass commercial culture therefore emerges as an agent of popular cultural suppression.[8]

By contrast, literary and social historians approaching music-hall culture from leisure and popular cultural studies have sought to examine the class culture complexities within the music hall as a subcultural institution. As places of entertainment, the music hall and variety theatre are treated as opportunities for socialisation, offering reassurance, confirmation and experiential information about learning 'how to live', as well as 'space' for working-class and middle-class subcultures to flourish, especially among the young. As sources of social morality the halls and the songs are as important as the modern media. Similarly, the learning process is facilitated by the personalisation of social, political and sexual issues, rendering the characterisation and images readily accessible and familiar. From the standpoint of public order, this approach also acknowledges that the late nineteenth-century variety theatre was welcomed by the authorities; internal reforms and legislation induced relatively quiescent, manageable public behaviour. But it is also agreed that the imposition of middle-class respectability could not have been absolute, upon individuals or institutions.[9] We do not yet know enough about the forms of resisting the discipline and mores of 'respectability', either in the auditoria or stage subculture. Furthermore, we should not presume that it was only patrons from working-class backgrounds who would be eager to withstand the strictures of bourgeois propriety. As leisure and entertainment also became affordable and acceptable to the lower middle and middle classes unshackled by the constraints of Nonconformity, we should consider how popular variety entertainment developed to accommodate the recreational needs of those social groups. As McKechnie wrote in 1930, variety comedians said things that were 'definitely class conscious, yet made everyone laugh'.[10]

In the following discussion I shall examine the comic sketch as a case-genre demonstrating the complexities inherent in the shift upmarket towards the dominant class culture, towards the more literate, sophisticated entertainment presented in the variety theatre. The evidence lends itself to an interpretation based upon the concept of cultural hegemony expounded by Gramsci and developed by Raymond Williams.[11] In so far as the rise of the sketch is brought about by the relative weakening of the dominance of the chorus-singing comic song (associated with stereotyped working-class galleries and exuberant inebriation), it may be regarded as part of a 'hegemonizing process'. This wider process, to which I have alluded, was affecting both the economic structure of the business and the social composition of audiences. However, a closer analysis of music-hall sketches (as opposed to theatrical ones) suggests that their popularity on the bills depended upon what Williams terms 'the complex interactions of control, selection, incorporation': and also that their acceptability to mixed audiences resulted from sketches expressing 'the reproduction of dominant values ... or a more subtle process of negotiated redefinition'.[12]

Thus, this essay seeks to build upon Peter Davison's recent suggestion that the music hall and variety theatre kept alive certain traditions of popular drama and participatory audience response during the nineteenth century, when the legitimate theatre was shifting towards more passive observance of 'realistic' drama. In particular, he points out that the halls nurtured the 'fanciful and absurd' elements in popular theatre, and concludes

> that the theatre has not lost its capacity to arouse wonder, its power of sheer theatricality, nor its audiences their ability to respond to direct address and to 'overhear' in the same act is largely due to music hall.[13]

This discussion will be organised into three main sections. Firstly, I shall look at the theatrical antecedents of the variety sketch, to substantiate its claim to be regarded as a popular dramatic genre, and to see how closely it resembled legitimate comedy. Secondly, I shall consider the indigenous music-hall qualities of the comic sketch, its contribution to what Davison termed the 'music hall tradition', drawing attention to the stage presence and personality of the leading comic actor. Thirdly, I shall examine the social significance of sketches as pieces of dramatic writing especially suited to the tastes of mixed audiences, discussing their moral and social content with illustrations from the scripts of some of the most popular sketch performers. The examples chosen suggest that class cultural tensions provided the basic material for the dramatic zest in many sketch productions.

There are literally hundreds of sketch scripts awaiting analysis in the Lord Chamberlain's papers in the British Library, but due to anomalies and quirks in the licensing system before the 'dual licence' of 1912, the inclusion of music-hall scripts is extremely hazardous.[14] It would be impossible to make a comprehensive analysis of all this material. Instead I have selected those scripts which are identifiable as the property of well-known music hall authors and sketch actors. It should be added that this essay is not primarily about the use of music in comic sketches. They can be analysed along a continuum from basic song and dance routines, through to comic operettas or musical 'duologue' sketches, through to the more theatrical type where the musical input played a secondary part. The source material rarely describes musical directions, but where possible I have indicated the role occupied by music in the scripts. However, the focus of this essay is more upon the kinds of sketches which did not primarily employ musical devices to achieve their dramatic imput.

Theatrical antecedents of variety sketches

How valid is it, then, to consider the music-hall sketch as a popular theatrical genre? The textual model which provides the closest pattern and spirit is offered by Anthony Caputi's study of *Buffo*, in which he examines the tradition of 'the humorous, the ridiculous, the ludicrous or the funny', excluding such 'sophisticated issues as irony, satire, wit, parody and burlesque'. Caputi traces a line of development from primitive rituals, especially medieval Carnival and the Feast of Fools, through to the vulgar comedies of the sixteenth century. From the Carnival scenario, he identifies the trial and combat after the demonic Misrule, as the 'essential episode'. The conflict itself 'provides the model for most of the struggles found in other ritual revels, and for a good many of those found in elaborated form in vulgar comedy'.[15]

Caputi describes the Renaissance 'revue play', using examples from Elizabethan love-songs and plays, French sotties, and Italian *commedia dell'arte*. These short dramas consisted of one or more units of material from the Carnival scenario. He lists six units, amongst which are found thematic patterns that reappear in variety sketches. These include dramatic combat, such as struggles between husband and wife, or youth and age; the destruction of the Old Man, in the defeat of all authority figures, from husbands to judges; wooing, leading to sexual union; human intractability as it is revealed by stupidity, animality or amorality; and the generation of a frenzy by energetic and subversive pranks.[16] He detected a process he calls 'concretisation', whereby these elements of the revel scenario grow into 'character centred comedy' with stock figures, and are progressively identified less with myth than with aspects of ordinary life, especially domesticity. Caputi's thesis stems from popular, pre-industrial texts, and in a rapid romp through the centuries he suggests that 'buffo' was romanticised in the eighteenth and nineteenth centuries, as satire, sentiment and didacticism subdued the coarseness and amorality. Rather implausibly, he suggests that true 'buffo' suddenly surfaces in the zany silent film comedies of the early twentieth century.[17] However, the works of Leo Hughes, Richard Bevis and Peter Davison, covering the illegitimate stage from the seventeenth to the nineteenth centuries as well as aspects of modern variety, cast doubt upon Caputi's projection. Their studies show important continuities between styles of jesting and clowning in Renaissance and Jacobean times, theatrical farce and pantomime, and the semi-dramatic forms that flourished in the music halls and variety theatres.[18] Thus it would be sensible to look to the Victorian and Edwardian music hall for the artistes and traditions that nurtured the early silent films of Chaplin, Keaton and others, and also to look to popular forms on the nineteenth-century stage for elements of inspiration to variety sketches.[19]

It is impossible to locate the dramatic continuum here in full, but two important cultural signposts may be established. Firstly, the antics of the pantomime clown and the pattern of construction of the harlequinade fashioned by Joey Grimaldi in early nineteenth century both influenced the shape and spirit of music-hall sketches. Grimaldi's Joey was himseld a hybrid, as Findlater has shown, of traditional English and Continental influences, combining to produce an 'urban English clown', artful, sly, mischievous, gluttonous, crude but lovable. Joey was a 'Cockney incarnation of the saturnalian spirit, a beloved criminal free from guilt, shame, compunction or reverence for age, class or propriety'.[20] The harlequinade sequences associated with Joey's clowning were not limited to pantomimes. They were sometimes appended to theatrical burlesques in the mid nineteenth century, and show a more robust sensibility than is usually thought of as Victorian. As Hippisley

Coxe has aptly written, the Clown in theatre and circus is both 'iconotect' and 'iconoclast', setting up images and situations only to break them down, at someone else's expense.[21]

It is worth quoting one example to illustrate the similarity between the harlequinade Clown and the comic-sketch protagonist. The 'Comic Business' of *Boedicea the Beautiful or Harlequin Julius Caesar* (1865) consists of four unconnected scenes.[22] The first is the interior of a railway station, followed by a schoolroom episode, a drawing-room party and finally a 'Grand Volunteer Review'. In each of these scenes Clown, Pantaloon, Harlequin and Columbine conspire to wreak havoc upon their victims and each other. The settings are a mixture of contemporary realism and complete nonsense. For example, the railway station is festooned with absurd placards and advertisements, saying such things as: 'To Buenos Ayres and back for 6d': 'All the way there and no mistake, two shillings'. Similarly the schoolroom is bedecked with maps, which have to show continents misnamed, 'Asia' being called 'Europe' and vice versa. Clown is the main instigator of the chaos brought to the ordinary individuals in each scene, the rail travellers, schoolchildren, or party-goers. In each instance he takes over control, putting himself in charge as the Station Master, for example, anticipating the fun of this, and proceeding to treat persons who ought to be respected with utter disregard for age, status or infirmity. The Clown is also the only character who addresses the audience directly, and relates to the rest of the cast. He reiterates catchphrases such as 'Now then' or 'Now, look here', and 'What did you do that for?', which make the physical clowning even more explicit. The piece is fairly evenly balanced between patter and physical slapstick, and each scene ends in an eruption, in the form of a sham fight, a procession, or 'universal hilarity'. It is interesting to note that theatrical effects are supplemented by music throughout. In the rail scene, bells and the noise of blowing steam set the scene, and 'music ad libitum' accompanies the dances. In the schoolroom, the directions indicate that 'hurried music may be played throughout – some lively air like The Burlesque Galop'.

At least one theatrical clown, 'Whimsical' Walker, argued in his memoirs that 'nearly every artifice in the so-called "comedy" films is based on the "business" of the old harlequinade'. He praised Chaplin's 'facial fertility', but insisted that his productions were at bottom 'Clown's business', where the 'crowds laugh at the grotesque situations ... and this I needn't say is the object of the Clown's antics and the practical jokes he plays'. Walker makes a further point, which is born out in the memoirs and autobiographies of other clowns and music-hall comedians, namely that their stage personae and behaviour pervades their off-stage lifestyles and professional conduct:

> The influence of clowning is very difficult to shake off. It gets into the blood and pursues one outside the theatre. The essence of harlequinade humour is practical joking, and no matter where the clown may be he finds it hard to resist a chance of taking someone in after the fashion of footlights fun.[23]

It seems likely that the pattern of this humour influenced their narrative style and presentation of the stories and escapades in their careers, as well as conditioning the acts they created onstage.[24]

The second signpost from the legitimate stage is theatrical farce. In this genre the characters are exaggerated and developed through their eccentricities, and unlike romantic comedy, they have little time for sentimentality in relations between the sexes. The pieces are strung together by repetition, disguises, physical violence and discomfort, with rapid complications needing swift unravelling. Most comedy forms deal with 'manners rather than morals'. and often in nineteenth-century farces the characters have their roots in comedy of humours' labels.[25] As with the variety sketches, there are hundreds of legitimate farces and comedies amongst the Lord Chamberlain's papers. A superficial gleaning suggests that they belonged to the same cultural milieu as the late nineteenth-century comic press: the sporting, theatrical and socially introverted carefree world of *Ally Sloper, Judy* and *The Sporting Times*. These publications, and similarly, music-hall songs, were aimed at the lighthearted leisure interests of the middle and lower middle class. The dominant theme in both the comic press and theatrical farce was 'mashing' (or courtship) between lascivious old men and uppity young ladies. Sexual attraction and flirtatious pursuit among different age-groups was a popular subject, and was often refracted through the rollicking licence of the 'spree'. This is not insignificant, because the 'spree' was more normally associated with the socially unacceptable behaviour of working men, indulging in a release form the restraints of the workplace and the home.[26] As a dramatic device, the 'spree' afforded a convenient stage environment for licensed misbehaviour regardless of social class. However, whilst these theatrical farces provided the sketch writers with a fund of contemporary stereotypes to supplement those from the comic songs, and afforded a superior model to emulate in terms of dramatic pretensions, they differed from the music-hall comic farce in a few important respects.

Firstly, there is a sense in which the language and attitudes of the educated middle classes are presented as the norm. For example, William Brough's farce, *Trying It On* (1853) revolves around 'Mr Walsingham Potts' and his efforts to court 'Fanny Jobstock'.[27] 'Potts' resembles music-hall comedians to the extent that he addresses the audience directly, refuses to observe social conventions and reiterates his catchphrase, 'six and twenty years of age, five hundred a year, good expectations, good health and the best of spirits'. But he also speaks in more witty, sophisticated terms than was usual for music-hall comic heroes:

> Walsingham Potts: don't forget the Walsingham… the elegance of my christian name is the only reparation I can possibly make for the utter vulgarity of my surname. Walsingham is a sort of currant jelly in which we swallow the bitter pill, "Potts"!

In the 1880s there is a more relaxed and slangy tone in some of the farce scripts, with plenty of back-chat and precosity among middle-class characters, engaged in pursuing 'awfully jolly' activities, especially at the seaside. Tom Park's *A Domestic Mash* (1888) and Mark Melford's *Seaside Swells or the Prize Fighter's*

Daughter (1889) are both about summer-time flirtations disregarding age, class and family barriers.[28]

Secondly, most such farces end with a certain neatness of form, with a resolution of chaotic situations and relationships. *Seaside Swells* finishes with the prize fighter 'Mr Bounder' having fought off the middle-aged 'Mr Sneezer' from his daughter 'Charlotte' (who's delicate catchphrase is 'Ga- get out!') and he accepts that she is to marry 'Jim', the blackfaced minstrel, saying 'We all meet our match sometime or other'. Often there is a positively moral overtone, as in Arthur Barclay's *Shorthand* (1889).[29] 'Tom Earlytoaste' is badly treated by his greedy employer, 'Mr Peticup', and knows when he is offered a drink, 'They always feed the prisoner before his execution'. It ends with 'Tom' losing all hope of an inheritance, but instead he escapes his job by gaining a widow he loves, and reflects upon who are his real friends.

The third, and perhaps most significant difference is that the female characters invariably play more dominant, positive or socially provocative roles. In *The Curate*, a comic operetta by Charles Wilmot, the lovely actress 'Violet Vanderville' is courted by both the 'Rev'd. Septimus Surplice' and his nephew 'Sydney'.[30] By sheer force of sexual power, logical argument and a demonstration of the harmlessness of her dancing skills, she shows up clerical prejudice against actresses, teaching the moral 'actresses are not entirely bad'. Moreover, she exposes the hypocrisy of the older man, supposedly in a respectable public position, having custody over the propriety of his timid nephew. In *Good Business* by R. K. Henry (1887) 'Polly Warboys' is an 'uppity miss' with affinities to 'Tootsie' in *Ally Sloper*.[31] She loathes having to clean the house for her mother, and has scant respect for either of her parents. Her father was an actor, who has retired into respectable suburban oblivion, and her mother is pressurising her to marry the wealthy 'Mr Stallybrass', who revolts 'Polly' with his 'false teeth and died whiskers'. She wants to be a stage dancer, and lives for the hours she spends at the 'Frivolity Theatre', with her lover, 'Dick', a comic actor. Eventually the social and familial tensions are resolved by 'Dick' achieving respectability as a manager, and 'Polly's' parents consent to their union, and even move in with them.

Comic sketches and the 'music-hall tradition'

Music-hall entertainment has traditionally been recognised for the special quality of relationship it creates between the audience and performer. Peter Davison has recently distinguished between the nineteenth-century illegitimate stage and the legitimate theatre in terms of the difference between the music-hall presenting drama in which 'continuity can frequently be broken whilst the act retains its integrity', and the theatre which 'involves total suspension of disbelief'. In other words, in music hall and variety, it is the audience's 'complexity of response' that is so vital to the way the performer addresses and handles them.[32] Davison implies that only certain types of music-hall act achieved this special rapport, notably the comic singer and later variety comedians and monologuists. I want to suggest that the closeness between music-hall artistes and audiences was indeed preserved into modern variety, largely because many artistes, including sketch artistes, did not relinquish this intimacy and informality despite the progressive 'theatricalisation' of some genres within music-hall entertainment, notably comic sketches.

Although comic sketches were, on balance, more 'theatrical' than 'musical', musical interludes and accompaniments were important to the overall production. In some pieces such as 'comic operettas' or 'musical dualogues', rhyming couplets were sung throughout. In others, where music is not obviously built into the structure of the sketch, music is used to set a scene, such as minstrel songs to indicate blackfaced entertainment in a seaside beach scene. Sometimes song interludes are included during a sketch, or at the finale, 'binding' characters together, or creating a pause in the plot, but rarely involving audience participation in choruses. Music also appears in stage directions to fulfil a simple accompanying function, especially for fights and dance sequences. And finally, music was used as a 'cueing' device. Unfortuately, in most of the variety sketches, the authors do not specify what pieces or tunes they require to evoke, say, a courtroom or a prison. One can speculate that the musicians in the halls and theatres carried a repertoire of tunes for varied purposes.

Some contemporaries were aware of the sketch growing as a natural course of development from existing, less sophisticated music-hall genres. As Vesta Tilley recalled, 'we had the comedy and dramatic sketch in the earlier days of the music hall, in a very crude form'.[33] The profession experienced a significant increase in semi-dramatic acts befoe the late 1870s, when the influx of theatrical sketch artistes first became a visible trend. Proprietors booked sketch acts to fill the holes in their bills when music-hall acts crossed over into the theatres to work in pantomimes. The *Era Almanack* lists for 1868 to 1879 show that comic duos rose from 75 to 236, trios from 8 to 52, and pantomimist troupes from 25 to 41. In the view of some theatre managers, sketches were also the 'outcome of that species of entertainment … supplied by small nigger troupes', which had grown into 'more serious dialogues and light and airy sketches for three persons', finally escalating into thieved 'mutilated' stage plays from the theatre.[34] Whilst it is the case that nigger bands offered entertainments consisting of different episodes, vocal, instrumental and comic, there was also a tremendous variety of other kinds of sketch touring the halls in the 1870s and 1880s. The trade press reviews offer brief descriptions of some of these different types of semi-sketch production. For example, trios might present an 'acrobatic grotesque and miscellaneous entertainment', which was criticised for not being 'anything in particular', but praised for its burlesquing of the 'feats of the ordinary acrobat'. Another trio were said to be

> excellent 'fancy skaters', and are exceedingly mirth provoking in the knockabout portion of their 'show'. Juggling of a very meritorious kind also forms part of their entertainment

Rather differently, some sketch duos aspired towards refinement, such as Mr and Mrs Mark Johnson who offered 'Living Models of Marble Gems', pretending to be marble statues of figures with symbolic or historical interest.[35]

It is noticable that the most theatrically ambitious managers encouraged artistes to present more lavish sketches, even with a small cast, tending towards some realistic productions, whether serious or comic. For instance, the political sketches at the Pavilion were renowned for being 'got up' creditably, with dresses and sets free from the '"cheap and nasty" look'. Charles Godfrey's entertainment, 'The Wreck: of a Sailor's Life at Sea', represented a ship sinking, catching fire, and the survival of the mariner, and attracted praise for the manager of The Foresters Music Hall, for his mounting of the piece.[36] In more frivolous vein, the duo Mr Brown and Miss Kelly played in 'Archer Up', with Miss Kelly as the stable boy and celebrated jockey, and Mr Brown playing 'Nobby Nailem', the tout, and 'Mr Grayball', the bookie. The reviews commented not upon characterisation, but upon the moral temptation and the 'realistic scenery and effects'.[37] With regard to the alleged 'mutilated' stage plays, it is interesting to see that *Era* reviews inthe 1890s went to the trouble of noticing if a variety sketch was cribbed or distilled from a theatrical piece. For example, *Too Much Married* at the South London Palace in 1894 was an adaptation of 'Les deux Noces de Bois Joi', produced at the Palais Royale in 1871, and subsequently at the Strand Theatre in 1873. Significantly, the music-hall audience laughed most 'consumedly over the farcical business' of the harlequinade, rather than the Offenbach melodies.[38]

Throughout the decades when these semi-sketches were flourishing, albeit illegally, in the halls, the repertoire of comic singers themselves was becoming progressively more theatrical. From the 1870s onwards comic singers had expressed dissatisfaction with their role as 'choirmaster to the gallrey boys', as Arthur Roberts put it.[39] Some artistes nthe 1879s and 1800s still cultivated very direct relations with their public, increasingly to the chagrin of time-conscious proprietors and stage-managers. One reviewer observed, for instance, how the comic singer Walter Laburnum was 'at home' particularly with the audiences in the East End, 'judging form the conversations he has with some of them'.[40] But from the mid 1880s it was certainly more commonplace for comic singers to publicise themselves as 'character comedians', 'descriptive vocalists', or more elaborate labels that denoted their specialisation or acting capacity. Some artistes, such as Charles Godfrey, reverted to the operatic tradition of 'song scenas'. Another vogue was that of 'illustrated songs', whereby the artiste sang the story to the accompaniment of additional performers miming around him on stage.[41] The 'patter song' usually required less theatrical surroundings, for it was simply an extension of the chorus song, whereby the participatory choruses were interspersed with passages of scripted dialogue intended to relate a story and cultivate a character simultaneously. All of these sub-genres of comic song offered the artiste an opportunity to engage with the audience directly as well as more scope for dramatic imagination and artistic expression. Arguably, the late nineteenth-century comic sketch was an equally effective and flexible vehicle through which character comedians could achieve greater theatrical aspirations, while still using their stage personalities to maintain a direct and responsive relationship with their public.[42]

It is fortunate that there are surviving records which reveal the extent to which sketch artistes maintained a box office appeal equal to that of the leading comic singers in the variety theatre. The salary and takings book of the London Music Hall, Shoreditch, from 1906–12, shows that the initial and recurrent bookings of some sketch artistes frequently attracted takings above average for a particular season or year.[43] For instance, in 1906, the weekly average was £496, but Joe Elvin drew in £605 in March and £573 in June: in 1912 the average had fallen to £417, but Elvin's weeks averaged £452 over five appearances that year. Throughout the period 1906–12, the takings for the weeks when Charles Austin was playing averaged £475, Fred Karno's troupes drew £420 and Harry Tate's weeks averaged £397. These artistes were all experienced in performing or writing comic songs, and they participated in creating their own sketch productions. But, increasingly, sketch writers were becoming a more important professional group. Their contribution was to construct simple scenarios through which the artiste's known personality could vibrate, and set the social and moral tone of the stage environment.

One of the most famous relationships between a sketch writer and and artiste, albeit one that has received little attention subsequently, was that between 'pals' Wal Pink and Joe Elvin. Wal Pink died at the age of 60 in 1922, with friends in the music-hall press claiming that he 'might have been one of the most successful dramatists of the day'. Originally trained as a gas fitter, his variety career progressed from comic singing in smoking concerts in the 1880s, to comic song writing in the 1890s, sketch acting in the 1900s, finally 'retiring' in 1907, as he said, to devote 'his entire time to authorship' – sketches, one act dramas, revues and West End musical comedies.[44] He produced patter songs and illustrated osngs for many of the stars of the 1880s and 1890s. His working friendship with Joe Elvin began inthe late 1890s, when they were both members of the convivial music-hall society, the Grand Order of Water Rats. Thereafter, Pink did more than anyone to enhance and consolidate Joe Elvin's popularity as the foremost stage Cockney working man, untainted bythe sentiment of Chevalier's work. Whereas Wal Pink began his music-hall career with comic singing, Elvin was schooled in pantomime and melodrama, with his actor-father Joseph Keegan.[45] They toured melodramatic and comic sketches in the 1870s and 1880s, attaining top of the bill status in the mid 1880s with Elvin's hilarious farce *The Tinker's Holiday*.[46] In this he created for himself the part of 'Tom Tweedlam', the Cockney out on a spree, or 'beano', for the day, causing havoc amongst the domestic staff of 'Lord Crumpet's' mansion. Eventually the chaos rebounds upon 'Tom' and order is restored. Elvin established the basic ingredients of his stage personality in this sketch. Over the next three decades Wal Pink re-worked Elvin's personification of the Cockney working man, and latterly he also elaborated upon and sharpened the cultural and political elements in that persona.

Although Elvin was of theatrical stock, his charismatic personality and rapport with the public qualified him as one of the most consistently popular *variety* artistes in the early 1900s. Reviews spoke of his 'methods and mannerisms' being 'all his own'. By comparison with Gus Elen's carefully cultivating acting of the stage Cockney, Joe Elvin's persona was not dissimilar from his naturally gregarious and sportive character. One friend recalled his Cockney voice, 'somewhat ebullient, but bubbling with kindly good humour'. The *Morning Leader*, commenting on Elvin as 'Tommy Jenkins', Cockney butcher and Gordon Highlander in *One of our Boys* (1898), explained his appeal thus:

> Mr Elvin is decidedly 'one of the boys'... there is an atmosphere about him reminiscent of a jolly night in town, of a merry day at Doncaster ... He is brimful of that boisterous fun which has brought big business wherever he has gone. What Mr Elvin doesn't know of sporting slang isn't worth picking up ... His shows are one man turns.[47]

Consequently, Elvin's sketches had the illusion of instant accessibility, informality and familiarity demanded by music-hall audiences. His arrival on stage was preceded by a musical introduction, or cue; and as another comedian remembered, Joe's catchphrase 'I ain't barmy' was taken up from one sketch and 'after that the gallery boys would shout it out directly he came on the stage', whatever piece he played in. Similarly, Charles Austin, of the 'Parker PC' farcical sketches had his stage entry met by 'prolonged cheering'.[48] This boisterous, informal response from audiences was not normal for sketch artistes, but occurred with particularly popular performers. The same comedians are also those for whom there are surviving sketch scripts. Their material may be used to analyse the strengths and appeal of comic sketches as a genre which reached its ascendancy with the mixed audiences of the fin de siecle variety theatre.

The social and moral significance of comic sketches

For the remainder of this discussion I shall consider comic sketches as pieces of popular, but not class specific, stage comedy. They may be regarded as products peculiarly suited to the variety clientele, encompassing both sexes, a range of age groups and social classes, including the educated and 'family' middle-class public who were traditionally looked upon as typical patrons of the legitimate theatre in the later nineteenth century. The fact that sketches were increasingly associated with a wide public, and grew to resemble the lighter genres of the stage, had important implications for their acceptability amongst middle-class contemporaries. In moral terms, sketches were likely to receive relatively superficial consideration by the Examiners of plays because they were similar to the light comedy which was already passed as 'safe'. Discussion arising from the Select Committee on Censorship in 1909 revealed that the establishment believed the physical and emotional power of stage performances threatened public morality more than newspapers and novels, and the majority of rejected dramatic pieces were disallowed on moral grounds. At the turn of the century

the greatest moral threat was perceived to be lurking in the social and sexual
ideas vaunted in the 'new' drama of the legitimate theatre. Serious dramatists
and social commentators complained that morality had been confined to sexual
morality only. In the midst of this banal impoverishment the Censorship
prohibited plays of 'intellectual power' and 'plain speaking', preferring instead
'frivolity' and 'a great deal of innuendo'. As Herbert Tree bemoaned, sensitive
topics like adultery would pass if they 'could be made more comic'.[49] In such a
climate, music-hall sketches were unlikely to receive interference when
performed under a stage licence, unless they were indecent or blatantly
subversive.

Contemporary middle-class perceptions of variety sketches as pieces of
popular entertainment were naturally conditioned by their own cultural values.
Essentially, sketches were regarded with a more resigned toleration than comic
songs, yet were not accorded the depth of seriousness of attention paid to the
legitimate theatre. By the early 1900s there had been a shift in the terms with
which educated observers assessed music hall stage culture. In previous
decades critics had expressed apoplectic disapproval at the demoralising
inanity and sexuality of comic singers and the content of comic songs. During
the 1880s it was not uncommon for moral purists to find offensive material in
some of the less refined sketches touring the London halls. For instance, in 1889,
the London County Council vigilante, Mr McDougall, objected to Johnny
Hanson's *The Doctor*, in which he noted:

> The doctor's assistant, attired as a woman, after walking about the stage discovers
> he has no dress improver on. He looks about for something to make one, and he
> finds a newspaper, but that is not sufficient. Then he observes a birdcage, which in
> the presence of the audience, he endeavours to place underneath his dress – I grant
> that he ultimately goes behind the stage but he does the whole thing in a glaringly
> indecent manner.[50]

He also objected, predictably, to a sketch showing women boxing in a pub, and
another in which two gentlemen share a bed. The vulgarity and blatancy of this
suggestiveness was indeed a generation behind the neutralised lunacy of many
early twentieth-century productions. It is testimony to the relative depoliticis-
ation and refined sophistication of variety entertainment that the *Times* in 1910
could sanguinely assert the

> the variety stage is not a place on which any sane dramatist would attempt the
> serious discussion of moral problems or ideas: and as to mere indecency, the
> managers and the public between them may be trusted to take good care of that.[51]

However, some social commentators were worried that the modern music-
hall stage culture lacked both elevating or refined images and laudable models
of speech or behaviour – especially with regard to the exploitation of the
'affectations' of lower middle-class lifestyles.[52] Concern was mainly channelled
towards the aura of sexual and lavatorial innuendo on the variety stage. The

Lord Chamberlain's censors were superficially vigilant in detecting comments and gestures in sketch scripts, anticipating most trouble from artistes and writers who allowed for impromptu acting in 'bus' episodes. Arthur Roberts, for instance, was known as an 'improvisatore who never sticks rigorously to his text', whose sketches gave 'opportunities for suggestive business and jokes such as used to give a piquancy to "The Sporting Times". Wal Pink, the author whom we shall draw for most, was not seen as the 'pink of refinement' by the censors, and the blue pencil appears in some of his domestic comic sketches.[53] Interestingly, Oswald Stoll confirmed for the Select Committee in 1909 that there was still a public for 'spicy performances'. Consequently, managers had to be wary of sketch companies carrying two versions of their scripts, one 'decent' for licensing, and the other 'risky' for audiences where a more club-like atmosphere prevailed. It appears that although managements like Moss Empires would prosecute artistes with too 'elastic' scripts, there was less fear of innuendo corrupting than in songs. One manager pointed out that the chorus song repeated offensive phrases far more noisily and sustainedly than in sketches, where the speed of production and dialogue prevented patrons dwelling upon questionable passages.[54] In terms of sexual morality then, sketches were not a major source of consternation and offence.

The social morality underlying the comic sketches does not offer any obvious class specific viewpoints or sympathies. However, it seems more than accidental that their composition frequently dramatises different modes of challenging and disobeying the dominant social values of middle-class respectability. In many, there is a simple plot which derives its dramatic impulse from the stylised and stereotyped expression of contemporary class cultural conflicts. Most commonly, the sketches are set in the workplace, home and leisure institutions of the working, lower middle and middle classes. Sketch authors, particularly Wal Pink, carefully specify the details of social status in the creation of a character or setting, by means of clothing or furnishings. The dramatic tension stems from the interaction of representatives of different clas cultures, with the comic sketch protagonist controlling the pace and spirit of the subversive alternatives. To an even greater degree than was the case with comic songs, the chief means of characters communicating their refusal to accept the hegemonic cultural apparatus is the verbal medium. A tremendous amount of energy flows from the pre-eminence of word-play and quick-fire dialogue between antagonists. In effect, verbal slapstick replaces or supplements physical slapstick and musical accompaniments. The noise, activity and confrontation encapsulated in the dialogues reduces any complexity of plot to subordinate interest. Furthermore, attention is deflected from any potentially disquietening social comment in the stage characterisations because the star sketch artistes were credited as popular actors, and enthusiasm was voiced about their performance skills rather than the social content of their material.

With regard to the comic sketch as the expression of class cultural and subcultural tensions, and scripts fall broadly into two patterns of construction. Both patterns draw heavily from Caputi's carnival scenario, especially the units of domestic combat, the defeat of suthority figures and the creation of a frenzy.

The first pattern is found most frequently in the pantomimic farces perfected by artistes like Fred karno, Fred Kitchen and Charles Austin. In these, the energy and impetus is directed towards the entry and sustenance of a reign of public chaos. Within the fantasy world of irresponsibility so created there is a reversal of normal standards and relationships. Thus the protagonists are those who would usually be socially discounted: scroungers, burglars, impoverished employees and rascals. Their targets are those who normally wield social power – employers, teachers, lawyers, policemen, politicians. The important characteristic about this sub-genre is that, as in all farce, ultimately the chaos is terminated, and a modicum of order, if not dignity, is re-established without any significant developments having occurred or circumstances meaningfully changed.

Fred Kitchen's sketches provide illustrations of pieces in which the basic material could have been socially sensitive, even politically charged, but the images and ideas are continually defused and reduced to absurdities before any real point can ever be made. Kitchen progressed from being a member of Karno's troupes to becoming a lead comedian in his own right. He played various characters, including those called 'Perkins' and 'Potts'. The 'Perkins' series involved him taking power over an institution or being handed the reins of control in ridiculous circumstances. In *GPO*, for instance, the Postmaster interviews him, culminating with the announcement,

> I like you, I like your eyes, I like your nose, and above all, I like your cheek. Now I am going to promote you.

Left in charge of the Post Office and petty cash, 'Perkins' proceeds to reverse all usual rules – he sacks girls for refusing to kiss him, and he plans a robbery. This sketch ends in moral retribution, and anticipates the bitter sweet sentiment of Chaplin's films: 'Perkins' is discovered and sent on his way with a 'kiddy', completely friendless. In *Perkins MP* he plays a demagogue with an irrepressible flow of nonsensical political promises. Putting himself up he cries,

> It doesn't matter about being nominated. I've been vaccinated. Gentlemen, I have stood in this market place for the last fifty years and my father before me and I can assure you that my ointment ...

He even courts the suffragettes, one of whom says to him, 'If you stick with us you'll get to the top of the pool', to which he replies with a typical music-hall pun, 'Yes, and if you stick to me you'll be up the pole'. This sketch ends in victory for Perkins and votes for women, but not through his efforts: he and his young accomplice 'Jotty' are eating bread and cheese in Parliament, contemplating turning it into a skating rink or swimming baths.[55] A similar inconsistency of moral attitude is demonstrated in Charles Austin's *Parker PC* sketches. As the officer in charge of the 'Swell Street Police Station', 'Parker' colludes and conspires with local burglars and gamblers. He occasionally stands up for justice and social equality, when for instance he is shunted on for playing marbles, retorting,

That's right. The rich can go to their clubs and play poker and Baccarat for hundreds of pounds while the poor working man can't even play marbles.

Yet, after petitioning for the release of a starving woman who has stolen a loaf of bread, he arrests her himself. The scenario collapses with Parker's exposure and arrest by the real police force.[56] To judge from the comments of one theatre-going clerk in Nottingham, Austin's sketches were regarded by some lower middle-class observers as providing an authentic picture of lower-class culture. Sydney Race, a critical enthusiast, noted of the *Parker PC* performance at the Empire,

VERY VULGAR but sometimes absurdly funny, his assistants though are hooligans and loafers inthe lowest degree and his 'wife' is either made up to be or is a fearful slum tart.[57]

Another artiste who perfected a style of burlesquing the culture of respectable society was Harry Tate, for whom Wal Pink wrote several sketches created around the persona of a 'would be' gentleman. In his productions such as *Motoring, Fishing,* or *Gardening,* Tate played up the pretensions of the wealthy amateur, who was actually very stupid, easily duped, and incapable of commanding respect from his social inferiors. This failure to grasp control was mostly expressed in rapid repartee, bursting with puns and malapropisms. Harry Tate relied less upon catch-phrases and more upon the devices that Davison calls 'cross talk' and 'mistaking the word', with line after line full of deliberate errors of pronunciation and comprehension.[58] There is a sense in which the audience is being invited along with the performers to discover and triumph over these absurd inaccuracies. There was rarely any other point to his scenarios, except for the creation of confusion and a climactic collapse at the finale. Again, the verbal chaos accompanies the physical noise and slapstick, particularly at the finale. In *Fishing,* for instance, Tate has been introduced to the pastime at his club, but has bought along a gun in case there are any rabbits. Much comedy arises from his misapprehension of the Cockney slang used by the servants and lower-class figures that he has to rely upon. The 'Puntman' tells him,

Hold that in your Dook
In my Dook?
Yes, your German Band, your hand.
Oh, in my hand, what extraordinary language you fellows use.
German Band. Why not Grenadier Guards?

The 'Cabman' insults Tate by telling him he is not fishing at all – he 'calls that drowing worms', and the whole scene ends in a water fight with punts, legs and bottles crashing against each other.[59]

The second pattern of comic-sketch construction is built upon the exploitation of confrontations between antagonistic class cultures. Frequently this

overlapped with tension between the sexes, for women were often stereotyped into the role of encouraging 'posh' pretensions and responsible behaviour. Wal Pink's scripts for Joe Elvin offer examples of sketches in which the underprivileged challenge and frustrate the exercise of official and social authority, in domestic and institutional settings. Elvin played the comic Cockney who would neither be suppressed by the opinions and power of his social superiors, nor intimidated by the discipline of responsibility expected by his female partners. The remarkable characteristic about these pieces, in contradistinction with those outlined above, was that there was no reversal of the normal order, no fantasised chaos. Consequently, neither was there a convenient resolution of conflict, and no overriding acceptance of one superior and corrective class morality which was reaffirmed in its hegemony.

The comic songs that Wal Pink wrote in the years before he began his collaboration with Elvin suggest that he was used to producing music-hall formulae out of the ordinary nuisances and pretensions of lower middle and middle-class life. There are a handful of songsheets in the British Library, either of songs Pink wrote independently or with the cooperation of other song sketch writers. *That's Where The Trouble Begins* (1891) was sung by W. F. Moss, and described successive domestic situations degenerating from confident pleasantry to embarrassment or disappointment. These were standard music-hall examples, such as being 'mashed' on holiday, but falling flat on your face instead of winning a kiss, or having a mother apply to marry her son. *Sticking It Out* (1897) by Pink and Herbert Darnley, was also about the perils of trying to create a good impression in public and in courtship. Pink and Darnley wrote a more elaborate patter song for George Robey, burlesqung suburban refinement and conjugal bliss. The patter of *The Subbubs* (1898) was presented with Robey in a battered bowler, umbrella and rednose, and it painted vignettes of domestic situations around the garden, the wife and the 'residence'. Throughout the patter episodes, Robey repeatedly asks the audience to accept his pretensions, and then takes them beyond the bounds of reality by destroying the image in absurd and self-deprecatory terms. For instance,

> But there we are in this beautiful garden, just like Adam and his wife, (only of course, dressed differently) and there we stand looking at each other. Happy! Happy! I throw a kiss at her, and she throws a tomato at me – beautiful – its like new life.

Pink and Arthur West collaborated to produce *My Brother Jack* (1894) for Miss Rose Sullivan. This was a chorus song, in the familiar music-hall mould of hero-worshipping an anti-authoritarian 'jolly little rollicking, frollicking rake'. Jack swears as if to 'awaken the dead' and threatened with contempt of court, cries 'forty bob is a sum far too small to express the contempt that I feel for you all'.[60] Many of these themes resurfaced in his sketch scenarios, with the difference that instead of a narrator presenting a character, or the singer indulging in self-mockery, the points were made by the dramatised interaction of working-clas and petit-bourgeois stereotypes. In a way, the respective stereotypes existed not so much as characters in their own right, but in order to expose each other's social vanities and idiosyncrasies, and the absence of common cultural values.

The farces in which Elvin played the stage husband nearly all pulsate with Joe as a thorn in his wife's flesh. Some are more light-hearted than others. *Another Winner* and *Billy's Money Box* were opportunities for Joe to revel in domestic irresponsibility, motivated soley by the urge to win on the horses.[61] The characters he plays remain impervious to his wife's insults, and their interchanges are nothing if not rude by polite middle-class standards. In *Another Winner*, 'Bob Buster' comes to breakfast at 1 p.m. complaining it is bacon again,

> Bob: If I keep on eating bacon like this, when I die I shall turn into a pig.
> Hilda (his wife): Very likely, you frequently act like one now.

The domestic farces contrast with the domestic comedy sketches, in which a much sharper vein of social comment emerges. Whereas in the farces Elvin's husband characters are lazy, greedy, cunning and unreliable, in the comedy sketches all these qualities are employed much more pertinently to frustrate the social pretensions of his wife or mother-in-law. *What's In A Name* is especially illustrative of these comic conflicts.[62] The Censor dismissed it as 'merely a discussion between "Jimmy Riley" and his wife "Clorinda" and their respective parents ... as to what the Riley baby shall be called ... simple fun, vulgar but harmless'. 'Jimmy Riley's' disregard for social graces and good taste is signalled in his burlesque outfit, which Pink describes in detail. 'Jimmy' wears

> a frock coat too small, tiny white waistcoat, horrible shepherd's plaid trousers, a small coloured shirt front with collar attached is sticking out, brown boots. Carries old fashioned high hat which is two sizes too small for him

At times he is stupidly zany. 'Clorinda' asks for the £2 required the christening robe, fearing correctly that much of it went on booze. 'Jimmy' says:

> He can have a pair of my old trousers.
> Clorinda: He can't be christened in your old trousers.
> Jimmy: I'm not going to lend him my new 'uns anyway.

This sketch includes pieces of dialogue and prepartee that *Era* summarised as 'Elvinesque', none more so than the discussion of the social significance of babies' names. 'Clorinda' and her mother have aspirations for the child, 'Clorinda's' father having been a doctor. They are keen on 'Marmaduke Henry', and will not hear of 'Jimmy' as a name 'for a lad who is going to enter some profession or other!'.

> Jimmy: Profession – he's going to be a musical instrument maker, like his father.
> Mother-in-law: A nice profession – unskilled labour.
> Jimmy: Unskilled, I'd like to see you do it. Here have I been all day pushing the

wind into four big drums – unskilled. As fast as you push it in at the top it
comes out at the bung hole.

Clorinda: He shall go into Parliament.

Jimmy: He shan't. I'm not goind to let him be the first to disgrace the family.

The sketch ends with unusual complexity (unnoticed by the Censor) as
'Clorinda' flings the unpaid bills at 'Jimmy', who is left contemplating his
failure as a husband and father, to the strains of 'Home Sweet home'. However,
'Jimmy' still has the audience's sympathy, for his isolation is largely imposed by
the insufferable 'Clorinda' and her mother. These two women are thereby
denied their moral victory, their code of social mobility is undermined and at
the same time 'Jimmy's' faults are subtly exculpated.

When Elvin played the single Cockney working man, or young employee, the
characterisation allowed even greater scope for social licence and irreverence.
There several examples that could be cited, but in each, Elvin's working-class
persona succeeds in questioning the assumptions of his social superiors, laying
bare their social foibles as well as his own cultural deficiencies and lack of
'breeding'. Again, it is his articulation of street slang and sheer cheek that
ensure his survival. Furthermore, those sketches tend to have a social bite to the
dialogue that distinguishes them from the ordinary farces. The full weight of
middle-class culture, education and refinement is galvanised in vain to suppress
the challenge embodied in the outspoken insubordinate. For instance, in *Under
Cross Examination*, Elvin played 'William Nutt', a witness for the defence of his
friend being tried for the theft of a violin.[63] 'Nutt' appears late before 'Mr
Sollid', the magistrate, and shows his contempt for the law. He defends his own
record of convictions saying:

'Cause you find a farthing on a man he ain't bound to be a thief – you might as
well say if you find an egg on him, he's a sparrer.

At which, predictably, the prosecution takes him to task over his pronunciation
– 'Not "sparrer" – sparrow'. They attempt to make him admit complicity, or at
least to quell him into respectful submision. The prosecution attacks 'Nutt's'
writing and asks if he knows the difference between 'N, U, and I'. 'Nutt' replies
'The (he*n*) can lay an egg – and (yo*u*) and *I* can't'. At this, 'Mr Sollid' dismisses
the case in exasperation and the sketch ends with 'Nutt' and the prisoner
shaking hands, preparing to go to the pawnshop to collect the stolen violin!

The sketch in which there is the most explicit conflict between contemporary
class cultures is *Who Ses So?*[64] Licensed in 1912, it elicited a cursory summary
from the Censor:

The disillusion of a couple of theoretical philanthropists who come across a real
specimen of the "working man" and find his tastes, his requirements and also his
manner of expressing them, so wholly unlike anything they had imagined that
their charitable impulses die out, slangy but inoffensive.

It clearly did not occur to the Censor to examine the sketch from any other angle than that of the middle classes. Moveover, there was hardly any need for a plot as such, because the sketch consisted essentially of conversations, or question and retort sessions, between 'Jimmy Juggs' and his temporary bourgeois hosts. The sketch is set in the house of a self-made man, 'John Willoughby'. The directions note that the set should be 'as smart as local circumstances will permit', with 'curtains wherever possible'. 'Willoughby's' wife, 'Clara', has evidently come from a more wealty and cultured background, and she is matched by the cultivated 'Dr Hutchins'. It is they who are fascinated when 'Jimmy Juggs', a working painter, is brought into the house, suffering from a street accident. The irony is that 'Hutchins' has just delivered a lecture about the working classes and inevitably, he patronises the working man. 'Willoughby', the directions reveal, is the only one of the trio who is really familiar with manual work, and he alone 'realizes' and 'chuckles' at 'Juggs' answers to 'Clara' and 'Hutchins'.

'Jimmy's' recovery is induced by 'Clara's' brandy bottle, and he behaves like a perfect scrounger, rebuking her for 'nursing' the bottle, and hardly tempering his language in front of her: he can't say where he's been hurt, but he adds, 'I can walk all right – but it's a good job I'm not a jockey'. On the one hand the roughness of Stepney is revealed in comments about knocking down lecturers, facing bailiffs, and 'scragging' the suffragettes. Yet, 'Jimmy' strips bare the doctor's text-book knowledge and the fatuousness of 'Clara's' questioning, removing her right to assume superior social status, even under her own roof. He baits her saying that the womenfolk of Stepney's favourite pastime is drinking gin, and that they are 'rotten cooks'. When 'Clara' begins to pass judgement, saying 'that's bad', 'Jimmy' swiftly rounds on her, asking,

Is it? Who Ses So? Who Ses So? How are you going to be a good cook when you don't have enough grub to practice on?

His behaviour and attitudes are thus excused in terms of the relative deprivation of his background, but he never once admits to recognising this inferiority, preferring to tell them to stay away, for they would be as 'much out of place as a hot cross bun on a Christmas tree'.

To conclude then, the main theme of this essay has been the relationship between the rise of music-hall sketches and the shift upmarket which broadened the social base of the public for variety entertainment. I have argued that sketches were an intermediate dramatic form, an uneasy fusion of theatrical and music-hall elements. In terms of their construction and spirit, comedy sketches closely resembled the vulgar comedy of the pantomime harlequinade, echoing back to primitive carnival scenarios, with their reign of Misrule and ultimate defeat of King Carnival. As Caputi noted, these revels evolved into popular dramas, very often based on contemporary and domestic images. The late nineteenth-century sketches borrowed most immediately from the social stereotypes found in contemporary theatrical farce and comic magazines. Although the ascendency of sketches in the variety theatre represented artistes and writers deferring to middle-class sensibilities, I have also argued that sketches did not necessarily entail the wholesale 'theatricalisation' of the music-hall stage. To borrow Davison's concepts, some sketches belonged more to the illegitimate tradition than to the legitimate, measured in terms of the mutual ties between performer and audience. The sketch stars who played more in the music-hall style were adept at maintaining a vibrant and direct relationship with their audiences, using both their acted characterisations and their wider stage personalities.

With regard to the social and moral implicationsof sketches attracting a wide and mixed public, I have suggested that they escaped public censure relatively lightly compared to comic songs, partly because they were thought ot be comparatively more artistic, mentally demanding and stimulating. However, this did not mean that sketches were fashioned by the imposition of undiluted middle-class values. The content of the scripts and the class tone of the performers was never clearly identified with one social group more sympathetically than another. Characters representing the hegemonic middle-class culture were as vulnerable to ridicule as the comic working man, and there were many instances of their social superiority and moral authority being undermined by the lower-class comic protagonist. In some sketches the period of irresponsible licensed anarchy was resolved, but in others a more complex void was left between the cultural antagonists. In a society experiencing rapid social mobility and the consequent cultural insecurity, it is not surprising to find popular comedy written for, and performed by, individuals from lower-class backgrounds which reflected the intensity of the contemporary preoccupation with status consciousness. Variety sketches aspired positively to entertain, rather than to criticise the status quo, and few observers expected anything beyond vulgar humour and boisterous comic acting. Nevertheless, within these limitations, the leading music-hall sketch writers and artistes constructed plots and stage personae that were based upon the tensions arising from contemporary expressions of class cultural conflict. And although these images did not ultimately represent a political challenge to the social structure, our knowledge of unresolved cultural struggle on the popular stage would benefit further from more investigation into the 'harmless' passive subversion allowed in the variety theatres.

Notes

Place of publication is London, unless otherwise stated.

Introduction

1 C. Pawling, ed., *Popular Fiction and Social Change*, 1984, p. 5.
2 In P. Macherey, *A Theory of Literary Production*, trans. G. Wall 1978, pp. 159–248.
3 D. Suvin, 'The sociology of science fiction', *Science Fiction Studies* 4, 1977, p. 224.
4 C. Sanders, 'Structural and interactional features of popular culture production: an introduction to the production of culture perspective', *Journal of Popular Culture* vol. 16 no. 2, 1982, pp. 66–74, p. 66.
5 'Communications as cultural science', *Journal of Communication* vol. 24 no. 3, New York, Summer 1974, pp. 17–25 p. 22.
6 *The Long Revolution*, (1961) rev. ed. Harmondsworth 1965, p. 69.

Chapter one

1 For a brief guide to the chronology of music-hall development see Peter Bailey's introduction to *Music Hall: The Business of Pleasure*.
2 See Chapters 3 and 4, and D. Höher, 'The Composition of Music-Hall Audiences 1850–1900', in Bailey, *Music Hall: The Business of Pleasure*.
3 William Makepeace Thackeray, *The History of Pendennis*, 1850, vol. I, p. 335. The principal action is set during the 1830s.
4 Charles Dickens, 'Music in Poor Neighbourhoods', *Household Words*, vol. XII (1856), pp. 139–40.
5 *120 Comic Songs sung by Sam Cowell, circa* 1855, p. 46.
6 *120 Comic songs*, p. 47.
7 Cowell's version is in *120 Comic Songs*, p. 46. For the version sung by Bannister see sheet music [1807]: British Library H.1650.g.(5).
8 Not to be confused with the *Bobbing Joan* tune reprinted and discussed in Claude M. Simpson, *The British Broadside Ballad and Its Music*, New Jersey, Rutgers University Press, 1966, p. 46–7.
9 *120 Comic Songs*, p. 4. The original ballad by M. G. Lewis had been published in 1797.
10 Bertrand H. Bronson, 'Samuel Hall's Family Tree', in his *The Ballad as Song*, Berkeley and Los Angeles, 1969, pp. 18–36.
11 For an attempt to apply comparative statistical analysis to this and two socially contrasted repertories, see Vic Gammon, ' "Not appreciated in Worthing?" Class expression and Popular Song Texts in Mid-Nineteenth-Century Britain', *Popular Music 4*, Cambridge, Cambridge University Press, 1984, pp. 5–24.

12 *120 Comic Songs*, reprinted as *D'Alcorn's Musical Miracles* [No. 1], H. D'Alcorn & Co., [1876]. Price One Shilling.

13 For the growing availability of pianos during the nineteenth century see Cyril Ehrlich, *The Piano: A History*, 1976. He estimates (p. 221) annual production figures in England as follows: 1850, 23,000; 1870, 25,000; 1890, 50,000.

14 Charles Dickens, 'The Age before Music-Halls', *All the Year Round*, new series vol. XI (1874), p. 180.

15 Compare the band of nine boasted in 1855 by the Eastern Concert Hall in London's East End, newly enlarged to seat 1,200 (*The Era*, 23 December 1855).

16 Letter from Joseph R. W. Harding, *The Era*, 28 September 1879, p. 3.

17 Letter from Frank Harcourt, *The Era*, 26 October 1879, p. 4.

18 'A Chat with Felix McGlennon', *The Era*, 10 March 1894, p. 16.

19 'A Chat with Joseph Tabrar', *The Era*, 10 February 1894, p. 16.

20 'A Chat with Felix McGlennon'.

21 Sheet music, Hopwood & Crew, [1876]: British Library H.1257.(50).

22 Sheet music, Hopwood & Crew, [1868]: British Library H.1846.ww.(12).

23 'A Chat with G. W. Hunt', *The Era*, 17 March 1894, p. 16.

24 Sheet music, Charles Sheard, [1867]: British Library H.1650.e.(9).

25 Reprinted in *Francis and Day's Comic Song Annual* No. 1, London, [1882]. Unless another source is noted, songs cited subsequently and music examples are to be found in this series, which provides a useful cross-section of successful contemporary songs. Each number carried some 17 or 18 songs. For other collections see Laurence Senelick, David F. Cheshire and Ulrich Schneider, *British Music-Hall 1840–1923: a Bibliography and Guide to Sources...*, Hamden, Connecticut, 1981.

26 These observations from a large number of songs (though necessarily a tiny and indeterminate fraction of the total *corpus*) are supported by a year by year comparison of the *Francis and Day* Annuals for the 1880s.

27 For example: 'Gestic music is that which enables the actor to exhibit certain basic gests on the stage. So-called "cheap" music, particularly that of the cabaret and the operetta, has for some time been a sort of gestic music.' Bertolt Brecht, 'Über die Verwendung von Musik für ein episches Theater', trans. John Willett in John Willett (ed.), *Brecht on Theatre*, 1964, pp. 84–90. See also *ibid.*, pp. 33–42; 104–106. Compare Kurt Weill, 'Ueber den gestichen Charakter der Musik', *Die Musik* 21 (1929), pp. 419–23, trans. Kim H. Kowalke, *Kurt Weill in Europe*, Ann Arbor, Michigan, 1979, pp. 491–496.

28 Sheet music, Hopwood & Crew, [1884]: British Library H.3565.(12).

29 Composed by Edward Jonghmans. Sheet music, R. Maynard, [1894]: British Library H.3565.(24).

30 Sheet music, Reynolds & Co., [1891]: British Library H.1931.(10).

31 Sheet music, Howard & Co., [1895]: British Library H.3627.a.(35).

32 Sheet music, Francis, Day & Hunter, [1894]: British Library H.3602.(84).

33 Re-issued on *Music Hall Top of the Bill*, EMI World Records SHB 22 ST 221/222. For a select discography of music-hall songs see Senelick, *op. cit.*, and for an extended survey Brian A. L. Rust, *British Music Hall on Record*, Harrow, Middlesex, 1979.

34 Sheet music, Reynolds & Co., [1892]: British Library H.1654.yy.(6).

Chapter two

1 See among others P. Bailey, *Leisure and Class in Victorian England*, 1977, pp. 154–5.
2 B. Waites, 'The Music Hall', *The Historical Development of Popular Culture in Britain 1*, 1981, pp. 43–76, p. 56.
3 D. Höher, 'The Composition of Music-Hall Audiences, 1850–1900', in P. Bailey: *Music Hall: The Business of Pleasure*.
4 Waites, *op. cit.*, p. 57.
5 P. Summerfield, 'The Effingham Arms and the Empire: Deliberate Selection in the Evolution of Music Hall in London'. E. & S. Yeo, *Popular Culture and Class Conflict 1590–1914*, 1981, pp. 209–240, p. 221.
6 V. Gammon, ' "Not Appreciated in Worthing?" Class Expression and Popular Song Texts in Mid-Nineteenth-Century Britain', *Popular Music 4* ed. R, Middleton and D. Horn, 1984, pp. 5–24, p. 5.
7 Summerfield *op. cit.*, p. 209.
8 G. Martin and D. Francis, 'The Camera's Eye', *The Victorian City, Images and Realities*, ed. H. Dyos and M. Wolff, 2 vols., 1978, vol. 2, pp. 227–246, p. 228.
9 I am not concerned here with the middle-class mediation of the character of the working man, as seen for instance in many coster songs or in the North-Eastern figure of Bob Cranky (though this is also a significant part of the bourgeoisification of music hall) but with the existence of middle-class man as a song stereotype.
10 British Library h.1783.e.(24).
11 R. Pearsall, *Victorian Popular Music*, 1973, pp. 74–97. See also Chapter 1, note 13, in this volume.
12 Eg. Pearsall, *op. cit.*, p. 79.
13 Waites, *op. cit.*, p. 65.
14 Ibid., p. 65.
15 G. Stedman Jones, 'Working Class Culture and Working Class Politics in London, 1870–1900: Notes on the Remaking of a Working Class', *Journal of Social History 7*, 1974, pp. 460–508, p. 490.
16 See R. Mander and J. Mitchenson, *British Music Hall*, rev. ed. 1974, pp. 9–20, and Höher, *op. cit.*
17 G. & W. Grossmith, *Diary of a Nobody*. First published in book form 1892. Penguin edn. 1979, p. 64.
18 [1864] British Library H.2581.(17).
19 Written by B. Leonard, composed by F. Eplett, [1899] British Library H.3980.r.(37).
20 See for instance G. Stedman Jones's note on the struggles of the Marx family, *op. cit.*, p. 465.
21 *Daily Telegraph* 8 January 1869, p. 5. 'The Young Man of the Day' is also the title of a song by Vance; the portrait cover shows him in costume for the role.
22 Stedman Jones *op. cit.*, p. 493.
23 See W. Thackeray, *Vanity Fair*, 1848, Chapter One.
24 See *The Late Lamented Jones, or, the Widow*, sung by Alfred Vance, composed by A. Lee, words by F. Green, Harvard Theatre Collection.
25 See *Up Comes Jones*, composed and sung by Arthur Corney, [1887] British Library H.1260.c.(7).
26 Composed and sung by Alfred Vance, [1877] British Library H.1779.p.(15).
27 M. Willson Disher, *Winkles and Champagne*, (1938) Bath, 1974, pp. 78–80.

28 'Music Hall Songs, and Music Hall Singers', *The Era Almanack* 1872, pp. 38–41, pp. 39–40.

29 [1865], British Library H.1264(6).

30 Sung by Harry Liston, written and composed by G. Hunt, Harvard Theatre Collection.

31 [1867], British Library H.2510.a.(36).

32 *Daily Telegraph* 12 January 1869, p. 3

33 *Daily Telegraph* 11 January 1869, p. 3.

34 Sung by Vesta Tilley, composed by D. Fitzgibbon, words by W. Jerome and W. De Frece [1894], Harvard Theatre Collection.

35 Written and composed by T. Lonsdale [1876], British Library H.1778.z.(33).

36 [1868], Harvard Theatre Collection, 'Adapted to Fred Macabe's celebrated melody "Early in the Morning Merrily, O"'.

37 Quoted in J. S. Bratton, *The Victorian Popular Ballad*, 1978, p. 26.

38 See for instance Alfred Vance's song *The Maze at Hampton Court*, and Vesta Tilley's *The Afternoon Parade*.

39 Written and composed by G. Leach, Harvard Theatre Collection.

40 *Pretty Jemima*, sung by Alfred Vance, written and composed by F. Hall, Harvard Theatre Collection.

41 [1865], composed by G. Hunt, British Library H.1257(7) [1865].

42 The version quoted here is in the British Library, H.1264, under the title *Isabella the Barber's Daughter* [1865]. The British Library also has a version printed in Boston in 1864, titled *Isabella and her Gingham Umbrella*, H.1780.a.(40), in which her father keeps a barber's shop in South Boston, and all the names have been changed accordingly. Harvard has *Isabella the Barber's Daughter* and another American variant, *Isabella with the Gingham Umbrella*, referring to the town of Weehawken and the Hudson River.

43 Written, composed and sung by Harry Clifton [1864/5], British Library H.1264(5), and Harvard Theatre Collection. T. Ramsey's *Georgina Brown* (printed in *The Clipper song Book* (n.d.)) borrows the tune.

44 [1864], British Library H.1780.l.(8) This, and another version held in the British Library, are both American variants. The cover of the original British version is reproduced as the frontispiece to M. Willson Disher, *op. cit.*

45 Composed by F. French, written by W. Thornton, Harvard Theatre Collection.

46 Sung by George Leybourne, written and composed G. Hunt [1878], British Library H.1257.a.(9).

47 Written and composed H. Norris [1897], Harvard Theatre Collection.

48 Written, composed and sung by Harry Clifton [1865] British Library H.1264(10).

49 Subtitled *Awf'lly Jolly Girl, Don't you Think So?*, written and composed E. Rogers [1894], British Library H.3981.o.(46), (1904 Harvard Theatre Collection).

50 [1884], British Library H.1260.b.(38).

51 Sung by Harry Freeman, composed by C. Rodney, words by R. Morton and C. Rodney [1894], British Library.

52 Sung by J. H. Stead, written and composed by J. Cherry [1870], British Library H.2510.b.(18).

53 Sung by James Fawn, composed by E. Jonghmans, words by G. Wall [1881], British Library H.1787.i.(19).

54 Written, composed and sung by Albert Chevalier in the role of Abanazar in *Aladdin* [1888], British Library H.3980.i.(33).

55 Sung by Arthur Lloyd, written by G. Palmer, Harvard Theatre Collection

56   Waites, *op. cit.*, p. 52
57   Sung by Fred French, composed by E. Whitehouse, words by G. Hunt, [1895], British Library H.1773.j.(21), and Harvard Theatre Collection.
58   Sung by Vesta Tilley, written and composed by H. Norris, Harvard Theatre Collection.
59   Sung, written and composed by Harry Clifton [1870], Harvard Theatre Collection.
60   Sung by George Leybourne, written and composed by G. Hunt, Harvard Theatre Collection.
61   Written and composed by Arthur Lloyd [1882], British Library H.1269.g.1.
62   G. Stedman Jones, *op. cit.*, p. 499.

Chapter three

I should like to thank the Social Sciences and Humanities Research Council of Canada for their generous support of my work in the history of the halls. I am grateful too for discussions with David Kunzle on the swell, though he will not agree with me in some of the interpretation.

1   *London, a Pilgrimage*, New York, 1970, p. 166. The drawings were done in 1869–71.
2   *St. James Gazette*, 21 April 1892. See also correspondence on Leybourne in *Era*, 24 June 1893.
3   R. Williams, *The Long Revolution*, 1965, p. 291; G. Stedman Jones, "Working-Class Culture and Working-Class Politics in London, 1870–1900", *Journal of Social History*, 7 (Summer 1974), p. 495, now reprinted in his *Languages of Class*, Cambridge, 1983.
4   For the latest attention to Leybourne, see P. Honri, "Leybourne! Lion Comique of the Halls", *Theatrephile*, (September 1984), pp. 65–67, and the recent dramatisation of his life by Christopher Beeching and Glyn Jones to whom I am grateful for generously sharing their own research findings. See also H. G. Hibbert, *Fifty Years of a Londoner's Life*, 1916, *passim*, and H. Chance Newton, *Idols of the Halls*, 1928, pp. 57–63.
5   C. Coborn, *'The Man Who Broke the Bank': Memories of Stage and Music Hall*, 1928, pp. 56–57.
6   *Era*, 26 February 1865; 11 November 1866. Other durable Leybourne hits were *If I Ever Cease to Love* and *The Daring Young Man on the Flying Trapeze*.
7   For extracts from the contract, see *Era*, 12 July 1868; for Holland, see my "Community of Friends: Business and Good Fellowship in London Music Hall Management" in the companion volume to this, Peter Bailey (ed.), *Music Hall: The Business of Pleasure*, 1986.
8   *Entr'acte*, 2 November 1872.
9   *Era*, 17 June 1893.
10   Jay Didcott interview, *Era*, 23 July 1882; *Evening Transcript*, 17 October 1884, quoted in L. Senelick, "A Brief Life and Times of the Music Hall", *Harvard Library Bulletin* (October 1971), p. 387. A. Roberts, *Fifty Years of Spoof*, 1927, pp. 99–100, retells the 'friends' and teashop stories.
11   There are many comparative references to Vance in the literature on Leybourne, see e.g., Hibbert, and Newton, *loc. cit.* See also the obituary in *The Times* (a recognition significantly not conferred on Leybourne), 28 December 1888; *Era*, 5 January 1889.
12   *Era*, 6 April 1865.
13   H. Jennings, *Chestnuts and Small Beer*, Birmingham, 1920, p. 203.

14 For biography in general, see R. Busby, *British Music Hall: An Illustrated Who's Who*, 1976, and L. Senelick, D. F. Cheshire & U. Schneider, *British Music Hall, 1840–1923: A Bibliography and Guide to Sources*, Hamden, Conn., 1981.

15 Bailey, "A Community of Friends", *op. cit.*

16 Select Committee on Theatrical Licences, *Parliamentary Papers* (1866), vol. 16, qq. 460–464, 2792. For the graphics, see W. H. Morton & H. C. Newton, *Sixty Years Stage Service, The Life of Charles Morton*, 1905.

17 For competitive tensions in the profession, see *Musician and Music Hall Times*, 4 June 1862. L. Rutherford, "The Professionalisation of Variety Artists", in Bailey, *op. cit.*, notes a significant increase in the number of comic acts in the 1870s.

18 See, e.g., *Entr'acte*, 14 May 1870.

19 *London Society*, April 1862.

20 M. Booth, *English Plays of the Nineteenth Century*, vol. III, 1973, pp. 146–53; D. Mayer, *Harlequin in His Element: the English Pantomime, 1806–1836*, Harvard, 1969, pp. 61, 165–8; "How Dundreary was Created", *Era*, 4 January 1874.

21 M. Vicinus, *The Industrial Muse*, 1974, p. 258.

22 Morton & Newton, *op. cit.*, p. 40.

23. M. W. Judd, "Popular Culture and the London Fairs, 1800–1860", in J. K. Walton & J. Walvin (eds.), *Leisure in Britain, 1780–1939*, Manchester, 1983, p. 23.

24 E. Moers, *The Dandy: Brummell to Beerbohm*, 1960, p. 215; J. Laver, *Dandies, 1968*.

25 C. Kent, "The Whittington Club: A Bohemian Experiment in Middle-Class Social Reform", *Victorian Studies*, 8 (1957), pp. 31–55.

26 *Town*, 12 May 1838; Ritchie, *The Night Side of London*, 1857, pp. 146, 211–220.

27 "Taverns", in the John Johnson Collection, Bodleian, Oxford. J. W. Sharpe was recalled as the lion comique of the 1840s, see F. W. Robinson, "Our Comic Singers", *Home Chimes* (February 1866), p. 29.

28 *Era*, 18 May 1895 recalls the selling of the song to its original publisher Sheard. I have used the 1925 edition, reproduced in P. Davison, *Songs of the British Music Hall*, New York, 1971, p. 17, and have generally treated the text as source as unproblematic. I have too left aside the role of the (mostly petit bourgeois) song writer — death of the author? — for which see Senelick, "Politics as Entertainment: Victorian Music Hall Song," *Victorian Studies* (December 1975) pp. 149–80, and am ill-equipped to deal with the music, for which see R. Middleton, "Popular Music of the Lower Classes", in N. Temperley (ed.), *Music in Britain: the Romantic Age, 1800–1914*, 1981, pp. 63–91 and A. Bennett, Chapter 1 in this volume.

29 On method and some theoretical models, see V. Gammon, "Problems of Method in the Historical Study of Popular Music" in P. Tagg & D. Horn (eds.), *Popular Music Perspectives*, Gotenburg, 1982, pp. 16–31 and D. Laing, *One Chord Wonders: Power and Meaning in Punk Rock*, Milton Keynes, 1985. Most of the songs treated here were consulted in the British Library, though a number of references are from the trade press. There are helpful comments on the swell song as a type in C. Pulling, *They Were Singing*, 1952, ch. 2; Senelick, "Brief Life and Times", pp. 386–88; Vicinus, *op. cit.*, ch. 6; Davison, *op. cit.*, pp. 15–18; R. Pearsall, *Victorian Popular Music*, 1973, pp. 43, 77; J. S. Bratton, *The Victorian Popular Ballad*, 1975, p. 177.

30 *Birmingham Stage & Concert Hall Reporter*, 13 July 1867.

31 *Era*, 5 January 1862.

32 A. L. Simon, *History of the Champagne Trade in England*, 1905; *Champagne*, 1934.

33 *Era*, 10 January 1864, 24 December 1865; *Wine Trade Review*, 15 September 1867; *Canterbury Music Hall Advertiser*, Sheffield, 17 October 1864.

34 A. E. Dingle, "Drink and Working-Class Living Standards in Britain, 1870–1914",

Economic History Review, 4 (November 1972), p. 616; *Saturday Review*, 17 June 1882.

35   *Era*, 18 September 1864; *Beehive*, 10 June 1871; B. Spiller, *Victorian Public Houses*, Newton Abbott, 1972, pp. 24, 71. For the importance of 'brightness', see S. Yeo, *Religion and Voluntary Organisations in Crisis*, 1976, passim.

36   W. Tomlinson, *Bye-ways of Manchester Life*, Manchester, 1887, p. 71.

37   *Era*, 6 September 1868; 7 January 1866.

38   P. Fitzgerald, *Music Hall Land*, 1890, p. 4; *Era*, 23 February 1895.

39   J. Tozer & S. Levitt, *Fabric of Society: A Century of People and Their Clothes*, 1983, pp. 113–114.

40   T. E. Pemberton, *A Memoir of E. A. Sothern*, 1890.

41   *Era*, 6 June 1872. Weston's had been equipped with mirrored walls and stage early in its career, *Concert Room Reporter*, 17 March 1858.

42   "Our Music-Halls", *Tinsley's Magazine*, 4 (April 1869) p. 216; *Entr'acte*, 15 November 1873; T. Hopkins, "Music Halls", *Dublin University Magazine*, 2 (August 1878), p. 195; Newton, *Idols of the Halls, loc. cit.*

43   *Era*, 15 October 1865; *Diprose's London Guide, 1872.*

44   T. Kennick, *Comic Singing Made Easy*, 1869, p. 26.

45   *I Like to Remember*, 1925, p. 272.

46   I owe this point to Jane Traies.

47   *Daily Telegraph*, 12 January 1869.

48   R. de V. Renwick, *English Folk Poetry: Structure and Meaning*, Pittsburg, 1980, p. 11, presumably echoing Barthes who contended that all interpretation should be extravagant.

49   *Era*, 19 August 1877, on Leybourne's "magic bottle".

50   The penny pick was a Pickwick, a cheap cigar. For Page's recollections, see *Era*, 10 June 1893; for the missile incident, *Daily News*, 28 December 1885. As with several other swell songs, including Champagne Charlie, Power's hit was taken up in the theatre, though the song was more conciliatory, suggesting that the swell would still come up trumps when his country needed him.

51   Wright, *Some Habits and Customs of the Working Classes*, 1867, pp. 180–181.

52   *Era*, 5 September 1880; W. F. Fish, *The Autobiography of a Counter Jumper*, 1929, pp. 36–37, 70–72; Okey, T., *A Basketful of Memories*, 1930, p. 54. For further discussion of songs for and about the clerks in the music hall, see Jane Traies, Chapter 2 in this volume.

53   G. E., 'Music Hall Songs and Singers', *Era Almanack*, 1872, pp. 38–41.

54   P. J. Keating, *The Working Classes in Victorian Fiction*, 1971, pp. 141, 154, 280n42; Tomlinson, *op. cit.*, pp. 196–206. See also J. S. Bratton, Chapter 5 in this volume.

55   *Era*, 30 June 1883.

56   Gammon, *op. cit.*, p. 29.

57   For various aspects of the language and practice of incorporation, see H. E. Meller, *Leisure and the Changing City*, 1976; T. R. Tholfsen, *Working Class Radicalism in Mid-Victorian England*, 1976; Bailey, *Leisure and Class in Victorian England*, 1978.

58   G. E., *loc. cit.* C. Ginzburg, *The Cheese and the Worms: The Cosmos of a Sixteenth Century Miller*, 1980, p. 84, notes that the songs of primitive utopianism carried a coda mocking those who would believe such fantasies, suggesting a long tradition of folk wariness.

59   (A. J. Mackay), *Bohemian Days in Fleet Street*, 1913, pp. 225–27.

60   J. K. Cook, "The Labourer's Leisure", *Dublin University Magazine*, 40 (1871), pp. 174–92.

61   For the swell and gentility, see also Hopkins, *loc. cit.*, and "The Genesis of the Cad",

Tinsley's Magazine (March 1869), pp. 178–181. Cf. P. N. Furbank, *Unholy Pleasure: The Idea of Social Class*, 1985, pp. 94–106.

62 Williams; Stedman Jones, *loc. cit.*

63 Hall, "Deconstructing the Popular," in R. Samuel (ed.), *People's History and Socialist Theory*, 1981, pp. 227–40.

64 On the suit as hegemony, see J. Berger, *About Looking*, New York, 1980, pp. 34–35; on the cap as uniform, E. J. Hobsbawm, "Mass-Producing Traditions: Europe, 1870–1914", in Hobsbawm & T. Ranger, *The Invention of Tradition*, 1983, pp. 287–88.

65 Factory Inspector Reports, *Parliamentary Papers*, 1875, vol. 16, pp. 332–333.

66 *Entr'acte*, 23 September 1871; W. H. Fraser, *Trade Unions and Society: The Struggle for Acceptance*, 1974, p. 41.

Chapter four

Though its content is my own responsibility, I would like to thank Michael Banton, David Glover, Barry Troyna and the volume editor for giving me the benefits of their comments on this chapter.

1 There were of course successful black troupes, solo performers and song writers (most notably James Bland), and their achievements have been ignored or uncelebrated; even Master Juba's outstanding contributions to the development of popular dance are under-acknowledged. But minstrel songs and acts remained primarily by whites for whites.

2 Michael Banton, 'The Idiom of Race: A Critique of Presentism', *Research in Race and Ethnic Relations*, vol. 2, 1980, pp. 21–42, p. 21.

3 E. H. Carr, *What is History?* Harmondsworth, 1975 edn, p. 84.

4 See particularly, Hans Nathan, *Dan Emmett and the Rise of Early Negro Minstrelsy*, Norman, Oklahoma, 1962; Robert C. Toll, *Blacking Up: The Minstrel Show in Nineteenth Century America*, New York and London, 1974; David Ewen, *All the Years of American Popular Music*, New Jersey, 1977, pp. 23–25, 36–50; Carl Wittke, *Tambo and Bones*, Connecticut, 1971 edn; Marshall and Jean Stearns, *Jazz Dance, The Story of American Vernacular Dance*, New York and London, 1968, chapters five to eight; and Berndt Ostendorf, *Black Literature in White America*, Sussex and New Jersey, 1982, chapter three. Unfortunately I did not read Ostendorf's chapter on minstrelsy until after this essay was completed, and so I have not been able to take it properly into account. I should be said, however, that it is analytically the most sophisticated treatment of American minstrelsy that has appeared to date.

5 Harry Reynolds, *Minstrel Memories: The Story of Burnt Cork Minstrelsy in Great Britain from 1836 to 1927*, London, 1928, pp. 76–78. These operas pre-figured the burlesques that later became an essential ingredient of the second part of the minstrel show.

6 Nils Enkvist, *Caricatures of Americans on the English Stage Prior to 1870*, Helsinki, 1951, pp. 78–81, and *The Origin of Jim Crow*, (anon.) 1837. See also John Briggs' *The History of Jim Crow*, 1839, a book written in what now seems a cloyingly grandiloquent style; and Reynolds, pp. 78–82.

7 *New York Times*, 5 June, 1881, cited by Alan W. C. Green, ' "Jim Crow", "Zip Coon": The Northern Origins of Negro Minstrelsy', *Massachusetts Review*, vol. 11, 1970, pp. 385–97; Charles Mackay, *Through the Long Day*, 2 vols., 1887, 1, p. 132. Mackay referred superciliously to 'Jim Crow' as 'a very silly, if not utterly stupid song' (p. 133). For Rice, see Toll, pp. 27–28, Wittke, pp. 20–31; Nathan, pp. 50–56.

8 Reynolds, p. 78.

9 Ibid., pp. 85–87.

10 Hans Nathan, 'The First Negro Minstrel Band and its Origins', *Southern Folklore Quarterly*, vol. 16, 1952, pp. 132–144; and 'The Tyrolese Family Rainer, and The Vogue of Singing Mountain Troupes in Europe and America', *The Musical Quarterly*, January 1946, pp. 63–79.

11 Reynolds, p. 93.

12 E. P. Christy was perhaps the most formative influence on the initial crystalisation of the minstrel show format.

13 Richard Moody, 'Negro Minstrelsy', *The Quarterly Journal of Speech*, vol. 30, 1944, pp. 321–28.

14 Albert F. McLean, *American Vaudeville as Ritual*, Kentucky, 1965, pp. 25–26.

15 Charles Townley, *The Mohawk Minstrels' Book of Dramas, Dialogues and Drolleries*, 1878, pp. 31–34.

16 Ewen, pp. 38–39. For two English examples of walkaround songs, see 'Jack on the Green', *Mohawk Minstrels Magazine*, vol. III, no. 7, and 'The Nigger's Jubilee', *Mohawk Minstrels Magazine*, vol. II, no. 33.

17 Moody, p. 324.

18 W. MacQueen-Pope, *Ghosts and Greasepaint* 1951, p. 116.

19 Reynolds, pp. 85, 88.

20 Nathan (1952), p. 137.

21 J. S. Bratton, 'English Ethiopians: British Audiences and Black Face Acts, 1835–1865', *Yearbook of English Studies*, 1981, pp. 127–142. Bratton connects the fanfaronade of this sartorial allure with livery worn in the eighteenth century by black footmen and pages, their presences having been kept alive on the early nineteenth-century stage 'as part of the background of exotic melodramas' (p. 139). The general trend after 1850 towards spectacular dress in British minstrelsy may also be connected with the traditional elaborate costume worn by black musicians in regimental bands. In both military and minstrelsy contexts a competitive spirit led to attempts at even greater 'unconventionality and *bizarrerie*', each further step towards outlandish extravagance signifying greater status for both regiment and troupe (Peter Fryer, *Staying Power*, 1984, p. 86).

22 The study of blackface minstrelsy in Britain outside of the halls and theatres has hardly begun. A notable exception is George Rehin's 'Blackface Street Minstrels in Victorian London and its Resorts', *Journal of Popular Culture*, vol. 15, no. 1, Summer 1981, pp. 19–38. See also 'Wandering Negro Minstrels', *The Leisure Hour*, vol. 20, 23 September 1871, pp. 60–602.

23 This description of minstrelsy is E. B. Marks' and is cited in Stearns, p. 56.

24 See Derek Hudson, *Munby, Man of Two Worlds*, London, 1972, p. 157–8. Munby noted in 1863 the exceptional presence of two female 'nigger' street singers in a five-person troupe, and said that 'they sang very well'. Also, H. R. Haweis, *Music and Morals*, 1875, pp. 499–501; P. A. Scholes, *The Mirror of Music 1844–1944*, 2 vols., 1947, 1, p. 514; 'Street Minstrelsy', *Household Words*, XIX, 21 May 1859, p. 579: 'Popular Street Tunes', *The Leisure Hour*, 1 March 1869, p. 159.

25 Reynolds, p. 10.

26 Peter Bailey, 'Custom, Capital and Culture in the Victorian Music Hall', in Robert Storch, ed., *Popular Culture and Custom in Nineteenth Century England*, 1982, p. 201.

27 See *Francis and Day's Album of G. H. Elliott's Popular Songs*, 1910 (with a critical appreciation by Charles Wilmott).

28 'I'll Be Busy All Next Week', written by W. J. Gilroy, composed by C. H. Linton,

sung by Miss Marie George: *Francis and Day's Second Book of Coon Songs*, London, n.d. [1904?]

29   Hugh Cunningham, *Leisure in the Industrial Revolution*, 1980, p. 29.

30   Bratton, pp. 135–142.

31   *Mohawk Minstrel's Magazine*, vol. 27, no. 81; The Walter Harding Collection of American Popular Song, Bodleian Library, Oxford, Box 177, 1880–1889 ('Haulie Boys' was described as 'a pseudo shantie with spiritual overtones'). 'The Dandy Broadway Swell' and 'Dandy Jim from Caroline' are typical examples of a minstrel stereotype originating with George Washington Dixon's 'My Long Tailed Blue' and 'Zip Coon' (Harding Collection, Boxes 170–172). (The attractive melody of 'Zip Coon' is better known today as the fiddle tune, 'Turkey in the Straw'.) Whites have, of course, been criticising black for foppishness since the early eighteenth century (Winthrop Jordan, *White Over Black*, North Carolina, 1958, p. 130). For the 'swell' song tradition, see Christopher Pulling *They Were Singing*, 1952, chapter two, and Peter Bailey, Chapter 3 in this volume.

32   'The Whole Hog or None' was written by George Ware (British Library, H. 1772. t. 27). For Hunter's 'Woman's Rights' see *Mohawk Minstrels' Magazine*, vol. 25, no. 77; the tunes of both songs were composed by Edmund Freeman, the Mohawk's Cellist.

34   Alexander Saxton, 'Blackface Minstrelsy and Jacksonian Ideology', *American Quarterly*, vol. 27, March 1975, pp. 3–28; Jules Zanger, 'The Minstrel Show as Theatre of Misrule', *Quarterly Journal of Speech*, vol. 60, February 1974, pp. 33–38; H. Wiley Hitchcock, *Music in the United States*, New Jersey, 1970 edn., chapter five.

35   Nathan Irvin Huggins, *Harlem Renaissance*, London, Oxford, New York, 1980 edn., chapter six.

36   Toll, pp. 87, 187.

37   Ibid., p. 27. See also Enkvist, chapter two; Sam Dennison, *Scandalize My Name*, New York and London, 1982, appendix I; and Mrs. A. Mathews, *Memoirs of Charles Mathews, Comedian*, 1839, 3 vols. Note: S. J. Arnold published a rebuttal of Mathews, memoirs entitled *Forgotten Facts in the Memoirs of Chas Mathews, Comedian*, 1839.

38   See Enkvist, chapters one to five.

39   John Abbott, *The Story of Francis, Day and Hunter*, 1952, p. 5.

40   F. J. Klingberg, 'Harriet Beecher Stowe and Social Reform in England', *American Historical Review*, vol. 43, 1938, pp. 542–52.

41   Douglas Lorimer, *Colour, Class and the Victorians*, Leicester, 1978, p. 203.

42   'The Whistling Coon' was written by Sam Raeburn. (*Francis & Day's Second Book of Coon Songs*.)

43   'Happy Am De Boys Down Der'. Sung by Fred Duriah and composed by Warwick Williams (*Mohawk Minstrels' Magazine*, vol. V, no. 15.)

44   'Carryin' de Corn in de Barn', written by Harry Hunter and composed by Alfred Lee (*Mohawk Minstrels' Magazine*, vol. 28, no. 82.)

45   *Mohawk Minstrels' Magazine*, vol. 31, no. 93.

46   See for example, 'Lucy Song', *Ethiopian Serenaders' Negro Melodies*, 1846. See also 'Jumbo Jim', 'Julia Johnson', 'Bowery Gals' in Dennison, pp. 121–122.

47   *Mohawk Minstrels' Magazine*, vol. III, no. 9. For Will S. Hays, see Sigmund Spaeth, *A History of Popular Music in America*, 1960 edn., pp. 155, 158–9.

48   Richard Dyer, *Light Entertainment*, 1973, p. 41.

49   Michael Pickering, 'Bartholomew Callow: Village Musician', *Musical Traditions*, no. 5, Spring, 1986.

50   Robert Roberts, *A Ragged Schooling*, 1978, p. 111.

51   See Lorimer, *passim*.

52   Paul Oliver, *Songsters and Saints*, Cambridge and London, 1984, p. 276.
53   George Rehin, 'Harlequin Jim Crow: Continuity and Convergence in Blackface Clowning', *Journal of Popular Culture*, vol. IX, no. 3, Winter 1975, pp. 682–701; Richard Moody, 'Negro minstrelsy', *The Quarterly Journal of Speech*, vol. 30, 1944, pp. 321–28.
54   Huggins, pp. 253–4.
55   Ibid., p. 254.
56   Clifford Geertz, cited in Barbara A. Babcock, ed., *The Reversible World, Symbolic Inversion in Art and Society*, Austin, 1978, p. 14.
57   Victor Turner, 'Variations on a Theme of Liminality', in Sally Moore and Barbara Myerhoff, eds., *Secular Ritual*, Amsterdam, 1977, p. 43.
58   Lorimer, p. 15.
59   S. L. Bethell, *Shakespeare and the Popular Dramatic Tradition*, London, 1944, p. 29 *et passim*, and Peter Davison, *Contemporary Drama and Popular Dramatic Tradition in England*, 1982, particularly chapters one and two.
60   Dyer, pp. 23–4.
61   Ann Purser, 'George Inns and the Candy Floss Show', *The Stage and Television Today*, 11 December, 1969.
62   Dyer, p. 23.

Chapter five

1   J. Hollingshead, *Good Old Gaiety*, 1903, p. 35; H. Hibbert, *Fifty Years of a Londoner's Life*, 1916, p. 51.
2   *New York Times*, quoted *Era*, 18 April 1891.
3   See *Era* review, 21 April 1878, 'she is the low comedian *par excellence* of the music hall boards'; and also *Era* review 11 November 1882, which credits her with originating female low comedy.
4   H. Scott, *The Early Doors*, 1946, pp. 205, 207.
5   M. Vicinus, *The Industrial Muse*, 1974, p. 262; E. Lee, *Folk Song and Music Hall*, 1982, p. 96.
6   *Era*, 4 July 1896.
7   In 'Variety Patter', *The Idler* vol. I, March 1892, pp. 121–135.
8   *British Music Hall 1840–1923*, Senelick *et al* Hamden, Conn., 1982.
9   *Era*, 27 July 1879.
10   See 'Some of Miss Jenny Hill's Reminiscences', *The Sketch*, 15 November 1893, p. 136.
11   *Era*, 23 July 1887.
12   *Era*, 20 December 1890.
13   *The Sketch*, 15 November 1893.
14   Bracketed dates in the following pages refer to the issues of *Era* in which the cards quoted appeared.
15   See *Era*, 25 January, 15 March and 12 April 1886.
16   See reviews quoted in *Era*, 8 February 1880, 6 January 1883, 12 February 1887.
17   *Era*, 27 April 1889.
18   *Era*, 22 September, 6 October and 8 December 1888.
19   *Ent'racte*, 5 July 1879.
20   In 'A Community of Friends' *Music Hall: The Business of Pleasure* 1986.
21   G. Mellor, *The Northern Music Hall*, Newcastle-upon-Tyne, 1970, pp. 141–2.

22 See *Era*, 18 July 1891 and C. Stuart and A. Park, *The Variety Stage 1895*, p. 131.

23 Hibbert, *Fifty Years*, p. 51.

24 *Sporting Times*, 5 April 1884.

25 *Era*, 21 June 1884.

26 See Pepys's diary entry for 14 January 1667–8.

27 See C. Williams, *Madam Vestris*, 1923, p. 193.

28 *Era*, 5 May 1894. I am grateful to Peter Bailey for this reference.

29 See *Era*, 26 May 1880.

30 *Era*, 3 June 1872 and 25 January 1872.

31 Quoted from H. Chance Newton, *The Idols of the Halls*, 1928, republished 1975, p. 111.

32 *Jackdaw*, 16/23 May 1879, quoted in *Era*, 22 June 1879.

33 *Era*, 1 July 1882 and 28 April 1883.

34 *Era*, 19 September 1891.

35 *Era*, 18 June 1876 and 22 June 1879.

36 *Era*, 4 April 1875.

37 See Pepys's diary entry for 7 March 1666–7.

38 *Era*, 15 November 1884.

39 *Era*, 25 October 1891, quoting from the Manchester *Star*.

40 *The Early Doors*, p. 207.

41 *Era*, 23 March 1889.

42 Words by John P. Harrington, music George Le Brunn.

43 *Era*, 16 August 1890.

44 *Idols of the Halls*, pp. 110–112.

Chapter six

1 Martha Vicinus, *The Industrial Muse*, 1974, pp. 144, 192.

2 Joe Wilson, *Tyneside Songs and Drolleries. Readings and Temperance Songs*, Newcastle nd [1890], reprinted East Ardsley 1970.

3 C. E. Catchside-Warrington, *Tyneside Songs*, Volume I, Newcastle 1911, p. 3. Volume III was also called *Tyneside Songs*, but Volumes II and IV were issued as *Album of Tyneside Songs*.

4 A 1906 cutting in Newcastle Central Reference Library maintained that 'Aw Wish' was 'a ditty which every Tynesider knows'. I must thank Douglas Bond and the staff in the Library for their continuous help and support in the preparation of this study.

5 See Dave Harker, *Fakesong: the manufacture of British 'folksong' 1700 to the present day*, Milton Keynes and Philadelphia 1985, pp. 146–9, 157–9, 165–6.

6 C. E. Catchside-Warrington, *Album of Tyneside Songs*, Volume II, Newcastle 1912, p. 2.

7 Ibid, Third Edition, p. 2.

8 This paragraph draws heavily on Ray Stephenson's articles, 'Geordies on Wax', in *Northumbriana* magazine, No. 22, pp. 21–2, No. 26, pp. 38–9 and No. 27, pp. 45–6.

9 According to Stephenson, in *Northumbriana* no. 27, p. 45, Catchside-Warrington wasn't above exploiting other brother masons, and earned the nick-name of 'Catchy'.

10 Interview with Alex Glasgow.

11 C. E. Catchside-Warrington, *Tyneside Songs*, Volume I, p. 4. This was reprinted in Volumes II and III, but did not appear in Volume IV.

12 *Album of Tyneside Songs*, volume IV, Newcastle nd [?1927]. For Reay, see *Grove's Dictionary of Music and Musicians*, 1954, etc.

13 John Stokoe, *Songs and Ballads of Northern England*, Newcastle and London 1893, and reprinted Newcastle 1974, p. 197. Stokoe 'collected and edited' the pieces, which were then 'harmonised and arranged for pianoforte by Samuel Reay, Mus. Bac. Oxon.'

14 See David Harker, 'John Bell, the Great Collector', in John Bell, *Rhymes of Northern Bards*, Newcastle 1971 ed., pp. iii–liii, and Harker, *Fakesong, loc. cit.*

15 *Allan's Illustrated Edition of Tyneside Songs and Readings*, 'Revised Edition', Newcastle 1891, reprinted Newcastle 1972, with an introductory article by David Harker, 'Thomas Allan and "Tyneside Song."'

16 *Op. cit.*, p. 475.

17 Wilson, *Tyneside Songs*, p. xxxvi.

18 Allan, *op. cit.*, p. 476.

19 William Andrews, *North Country Poets*, London 1888, Volume I, pp. 72–6. Vicinus, *op. cit.*, follows a similar line.

20 *Joe Wilson's Temperance Songs, Readings, and Recitations, in the Tyneside Dialect, Comic and Sentimental*, Newcastle nd [?1874.], No. 3, a 36-page 'Copyright' booklet, price 2d, is held in Newcastle Central Reference Library.

21 *Tyneside Songs, Ballads and Drolleries, by Joe Wilson*, Newcastle nd [?1873], can also be found in Newcastle Central Reference Library.

22 No. 2 is in Newcastle Central Reference Library.

23 Allan, *op. cit.*, p. xv.

24 Richard Welford, *Men of Mark 'Twixt Tyne and Tweed*, London and Newcastle 1895, Volume I, pp. 645–50.

25 *The Monthly Chronicle of North-Country Lore and Legend*, Newcastle and London (1887–91), 1889, pp. 130, 276; G. D. H. Cole, *British Working Class Politics*, 1941, pp. 25–37; and Maurice Milne, *The Newspapers of Northumberland and Durham*, Newcastle nd [?1970], pp. 63–83

26 Milne, *op. cit.*, p. 70.

27 Ibid., p. 69.

28 Ibid., pp. 73.

29 Ibid., pp. 38–9.

30 Eric Hobsbawm, *Industry and Empire*, Harmondsworth 1969, p. 117–18.

31 Percy Corder, *Robert Spence Watson*, 1914, p. 210.

32 Hobsbawm, *op. cit.*, pp. 154–5, 161.

33 Karl Marx and Frederick Engels, *On Britain*, Moscow and London 1953, p. 464.

34 Hobsbawm, *op. cit.*, pp. 109–33, 127–8.

35 Marx and Engels, *op. cit.*, pp. 464–70.

36 A. L. Lloyd, *Folk Song in England*, 1967, p. 368, was wrong when he surmised that Wilson 'fully shared' the conditions of the Newcastle working-class community.

37 All biographical information on Wilson derives from the 'Life of Joe Wilson' in the 1890 edition of his *Tyneside songs*, pp. xvii–xlii, unless stated otherwise.

38 For Corvan, and his key role in the development of the NE concert hall, see Dave Harker, 'The Making of the Tyneside Concert Hall', in Richard Middleton and David Horn, *Popular Music 1*, Cambridge 1981, pp. 27–56.

39 Cutting dated 28.2.1891, in Newcastle Central Reference Library: the 'Life of Joe Wilson' thought it was St Peter's. Alex Glasgow also went this route.

40 The striking miners of 1844 seem to have been some of the last to use this format –

see Dave Harker, *The Pitmen Determined to be Free: Songs and Verse of the Great Strike of NE Pitmen in 1844*, forthcoming. The purely commercial trade was moribund by the 1850s – see Harker, 'The Making of the Tyneside Concert Hall'.

41   No. 6 is in Newcastle Central Reference Library. The 'Life of Joe Wilson' mentions that these 'numbers' sold at 6d for five stitched together.

42   Joe Wilson's *Tyneside Songs and Ballads*, [Newcastle] 1864, No. 6, p. 46.

43   See Peter Bailey, *Leisure and Class in Victorian England*, 1978, pp. 106–23, for the Working Men's Club Movement.

44   For Fife, see Welford, *op. cit.*, Volume II, pp. 226–35.

45   *Newcastle Daily Chronicle*, 24.12.1891.

46   *Newcastle Daily Chronicle*. 3.1.1865.

47   Allan, *op. cit.*, p. 392.

48   *Newcastle Daily Chronicle*, 15.2.1875. This phrase was missed out from the report reprinted in the 'Life of Joe Wilson', by Allan.

49   *Newcastle Daily Chronicle*, 15. 2.1875.

50   *Newcastle Daily Chronicle*, 6.6.1865.

51   Some of Corvan's songs are now available in Keith Gregson, *Corvan, a Victorian Entertainer and his Songs*, Banbury 1983. For Corvan's use of music, see Richard Middleton, 'Articulating musical meaning/reconstructing musical history/locating the "popular"', in Richard Middleton and David Horn, *Popular Music 5*, Cambridge 1985, pp. 5–43.

52   For Ridley's songs and life, see David Harker, *George Ridley, Gateshead Poet and Vocalist*, Newcastle 1973.

53   See Bailey, *op. cit.*, pp. 61–2.

54   Advertisement in *Chater's Tyneside Comic Almanack*, 1867.

55   See Bailey, *op. cit.*, pp. 119–22, and note 36 on p. 212.

56   There is a lengthy run of Fordyce broadsides in the Madden Collection, Cambridge University Library.

57   Wilson's song, *Perfesshunal Lodgers* – Wilson, *op. cit.*, p. 235 – gives some idea of his feelings; and the cutting dated 7.11.1890, 'A Smart Retort', in Newcastle Central Reference Library, shows how Wilson was taunted because he was knock-kneed.

58   Allan, *op. cit.*, p. 519.

59   Advertisement in *Joe Wilson's Budjit*, No. 2, p. 6.

60   *Joe Wilson's Comic Christmas Pantomime. Pilferini*, Newcastle 1869 – copy in Newcastle Central Reference Library.

61   Cutting, dated 7.11.1890, Newcastle Central Reference Library.

62   Allan MSS, Newcastle Central Reference Library.

63   *Tyneside Songs, Ballads and Drolleries*, ?1873 edn, 'Note'.

64   For Harrison, see Allan's 1891 *Tyneside Songs*, pp. 513–15.

65   Lloyd, *op. cit.*, p. 368 and J. S. Bratton, *The Victorian Popular Ballad*, 1975, p. 93, give 1874, which is wrong.

66   *Newcastle Daily Chronicle*, 15.2.1875, and 16.2.1875.

67   A copy of the 'Subscription List' form is in the Allan MSS, Newcastle Central Reference Library.

68   *Newcastle Daily chronicle*, 24.2.1875.

69   Cutting, Newcastle Central Reference Library, dated 25.5.1893. However, R. J. Wilkinson published *Joe Wilson's Tyneside Songs, not published in any other collection*, in Newcastle in 1895, 'With Sketch of his Life, and Remarks by his brother, Thomas Wilson, etc.'

70   Allan MSS, Newcastle Central Reference Library.
71   Cuttings in the Allan MSS. The *Newcastle Weekly Chronicle* giveaway picture of Joe
       Wilson had been ready as early as October 1890! .
72   Cole, *op. cit.*, pp. 85–6.
73   Allan MSS, Newcastle Central Reference Library. Wilson wrote several uncom-
       plimentary songs about the police!
74   Wilson, *Tyneside Songs*, pp. xix-xx. All other Wilson songs referred to below can be
       found in that edition, and will not be cited separately here, if their titles are quoted.
75   Wilson, *Tyneside Songs*, p. 339. Bratton, *op. cit.*, p. 93, mistakenly describes Wilson's
       language as equivalent to the 'pitmatic' adopted by Tommy Armstrong later in the
       century. In fact, there had been several variants of 'Newcassel' idiom put into print
       for over 60 years before Wilson started to write songs 'phonetically' – see, for
       example, Dave Harker, *'The Original Bob Cranky?'*, in the *Folk Music Journal*, London
       1985, pp. 46–82.
76   Wilson, *op. cit.*, p. 1.
77   For example, Wilson *op. cit.*, pp.16, 32, 72.
78   Wilson, *op. cit.*, pp. 53, 63, 221, 262, 331.
79   For the keelmen, see David Harker, 'Popular Song and Working-Class Conscious-
       ness in North-East England,' unpublished PhD thesis, University of Cambridge,
       1976.
80   Wilson, *op. cit.*, p. 59.
81   Wilson, *op. cit.*, pp. 101, 185, 187, 219, 192–3. See Hobsbawm, *op. cit.*, pp. 154–5,
       161.
82   Wilson, *op. cit.*, p. 208. See David Kynaston, *King Labour*, 1976, pp. 19–20.
83   Wilson, *op. cit.*, pp. 118, 193, 61, 117, 129, 8, 7. Compare Corvan's *Oot o' Wark; or,
       The Year '62*, in *A Choice Collection of Tyneside Songs*, Newcastle nd [?1863] (the second
       edition of Allan's work).
84   Wilson, *op. cit.*, pp. 61, 139, 207, 95, 125.
85   Compare Bailey, *op. cit.*, pp. 80–1.
86   See above. See also the *Newcastle Daily Chronicle*, 24.9.1867 and 5.12.1867.
87   W. H. D. [awson], *Jarrow Chronicle*, 4.9.1869.
88   Wilson, *op. cit.*, pp. 79, 339, 83. See also Harker, 'The Making of the Tyneside
       Concert Hall,' and Bailey, *op. cit.*, pp. 19–20.
89   Wilson, *op. cit.*, pp. 84, 87–91.
90   Wilson, *op. cit.*, p. 69, and see above, for Engels.
91   Wilson, *op. cit.*, pp. 71–2, 166.
92   Wilson, *op. cit.*, pp. 22, 90.
93   Wilson, *op. cit.*, pp. 7–8.
94   Wilson, *op. cit.*, pp. 5–6.
95   Wilson, *op. cit.*, pp. 128, 176, 127. The word 'seem' means 'suit'.
96   Wilson, *op. cit.*, p. 15.
97   Wilson, 1890, p. xxiii. For a discussion of Robson's work, see Harker, 'The Making
       of the Tyneside Concert Hall,' and Harker, *The Pitmen Determined to be Free*.
98   Corvan wrote and published *£4 10s, or, the Sailor's Strike* and a deliberate parody of a
       Robson song, *The Funny Time Comin*, which are to be found in South Shields Public
       Library. Interestingly, Gregson, op. cit., chose to ignore these militant songs.
       Bailey, op. cit., note 31, p. 222, records that at least one London Concert Hall
       housed a benefit performance for the NE strikers in 1871.
99   *Newcastle Daily Chronicle*, 19.9.1871.
100   Alex Glasgow acknowledges this in a letter to the author, 1.5.1985. For the Whig

interpretation of the strike, and a selective use of the Wilson song, see E. Allan *et al.*, *The North-East Engineers' Strikes of 1871*, Newcastle 1971.

101 Karl Marx, *Capital*, Harmondsworth 1976, Volume I, pp. 333–8.
102 See Hobsbawm, *op. cit.*, p. 125.
103 Wilson, op. cit., pp. xxii–xxiii.
104 Allan, *op. cit.*, p. 474: Wilson, *op. cit.*, pp. ii, xxi; Vicinus, op. cit., p. 268.
105 *Newcastle Daily Chronicle*, 9.3.1865.
106 *Newcastle Daily Chronicle*, 18.4.1865.
107 Wilson, *op. cit.*, pp. 2, 136, 213, 321
108 Wilson, *op. cit.*, pp. 14, 76–8, 13, 134.
109 He seems to have been against rabbit-coursing, however, see *Newcastle Daily Chronicle*, 26.12.1891.
110 Vicinus, *op. cit.*, p. 269.
111 *Joe Wilson's Tyneside songs, not published in any other collection*, p. 12.
112 For example, Wilson, *op. cit.*, p. 372.
113 Wilson, *op. cit.*, pp. 280, 157.
114 Wilson, *op. cit.*, p. 368.
115 Wilson, *op. cit.*, pp. 211, 229.
116 Wilson, *op. cit.*, p. 410.
117 Alex Glasgow, letter to the author, 1.5.1985. Alex also observed that 'Academics and playwrights tell lies; the difference between them is that the latter own up.' Which, as I have shown in *Fakesong*, is true.
118 For an account of the Great Strike, see Alex Callinicos and Mike Simons, *The Great Strike*, 1985.

Chapter seven

1 Public Record Office, HO45/173738/4.
2 R. Williams, 'The analysis of culture', in T. Bennett, G. Martin *et al.* (eds.) *Culture, Ideology and Social Process*, Milton Keynes & Philadelphia, 1981, pp. 43–4.
3 *Era*, 19 Oct 1889, editorial; Select Committee on Licensing of Theatres and Places of Entertainment, 1892, Q. 4593, Johnson, and Q. 4726, Swanborough.
4 *Era*, 23 March 1867; 9 May 1891 and 19 Nov. 1892.
5 *Report from the Joint Select Committee of the House of Lords and the House of Commons on the Stage Plays (Censorship)* 1909, Q. 4881–3.
6 K. Roberts, *Contemporary Society and the Growth of Leisure*, 1978, p. 81–2.
7 Space prohibits full referencing, but the PRO files are listed under Board of Trade records, BT31; see John Hollingshead, *My Lifetime*, 2 vols. Sampson, Low and Marston, 1895, vol. 2, pp. 204–5; G. W. Altree, *Footlight Memories, Recollections of Music Hall and Stage Life*, Sampson *et al.*, 1932, p. 42; H. Chance Newton, *Idols of the Halls*, Heath Cranton, 1928, pp. 162–3; D. Hole, *The Church and the Stage, the Early History of the Actor's Church Union*, Faith Press, 1934, p. 96; 'Theatres of Varieties', *Times*, 24 January, 1910, p. 4.
8 This brief summary arises from interpretations in the following: C. Pulling, *They Were Singing and What They Sang About*, 1952; C. MacInnes, *Sweet Saturday Night*, 1967; R. Mander and J. Mitchenson, *British Music Hall*, 1965; Gareth Steadman Jones, 'Working class culture and working class politics in London 1870–1900, notes on the remaking of a working class' *Journal of Social History*, vol. 7, 1974, pp. 460–508; Martha Vicinus, *The Industrial Muse, A Study of Nineteenth Century British Working Class Literature*, 1974; P. Summerfield, 'The Effingham Arms and the Empire, working

class culture and the evolution of the music hall', in S. and E. Yeo (eds.) *Popular Culture and Class Conflict 1590–1914*, 1981, pp. 204–240; L. Senelick, 'Politics as entertainment, Victorian music hall songs', Victorian Studies, vol. 19, 1976, pp. 149–80; Standish Meacham, *A Life Apart, The English Working Class 1890–1914*, 1977: M. Chanon, *The Dream that Kicks, The Prehistory and Early years of Cinema in Britain*, 1981; I. Watson, *Song and Democratic Culture in Britain, an Approach to Popular Culture in Social Movements*, 1983.

9   S. Hall and P. Whannel, *The Popular Arts: A Critical Guide to the Mass Media*, 1964; J. Bratton, *The Victorian Popular Ballad*, 1975; B. Sharratt, 'The politics of the popular? From melodrama to television', in D. Bradby, L. James, and B. Sharratt (eds.) *Performance and Politics, Aspects of Popular Entertainment in Theatre, Film and Television 1800–1976*, Cambridge University press, 1980, pp. 275–95; Peter Bailey, *Leisure and Class in Victorian England, Rational Recreation and the Contest for Social Control 1830–85*, 1977; 'Will the real Bill Banks please stand up? Towards a role analysis of mid Victorian working class respectability', *Journal of Social History*, 1979, pp. 336–53; 'Custom, Capital and Culture in the Victorian music hall', in R. Storch (ed.) *Popular Culture and Custom in Nineteenth Century England*, 1982, pp. 180–201; H. Cunningham, *Leisure in the Industrial Revolution*, 1981.

10   S. McKechnie, *Popular Entertainment Through the Ages*, 1931, p. 146–7.

11   See section 4 of *Culture, Ideology and Social Process*, on Gramsci; Williams, *Marxism and Literature*, OUP, 1977, part 2.

12   Williams, *Marxism and Literature*, p. 136; Robert Cray, 'Bourgeois hegemony in Victorian Britain', in *Culture, Ideology and Social Process*, p. 246.

13   Peter Davison, *Popular Appeal in English Drama*, 1982, esp. Ch. 5, pp. 108–64, at p. 164; *Contemporary Drama and the Popular Dramatic Tradition in England*, 1982, esp. Ch.2, pp. 13–66, 'The Music Hall Tradition'.

14   See *Stage Year Book*, 1911, p. 92, and 1912, p. 38, on the 'dual license' arising from actions by the L.C.C.: I am grateful to the Keeper of Manuscripts and staff of the British Library Manuscripts Room for their cooperation in giving me access to unbound papers.

15   Anthony Caputi, *Buffo: The Genius of Vulgar Comedy*, Cornell, 1978, p. 20 and p. 63.

16   *Ibid*. Ch. 5, pp. 112–45.

17   *Ibid*. pp. 227–8.

18   Leo Hughes, *A Century of English Farce*, Princeton, 1956: Richard Bevis, *The Laughing Tradition, Stage Comedy in Garrick's Day*, G. Prior, 1981; Davison, *op. cit*.

19   Chanon, *Dream That Kicks*, p. 146: J. Montgomery, *Comedy Films 1894–1954*, 1954, rev. 1968, pp. 61–4, 90–5: Walter Kerr, *The Silent Clowns*, New York, 1975. 1975.

20   R. Findlater, *Joe Grimaldi: His Life and Theatre*, C.U.P., 2nd. ed. 1978, at p. 160.

21   A. Hippisley Coxe, *A Seat At the Circus*, 1951, rev. 1980, p. 213.

22   *Beeton's Book of Burlesques*, 1865, pp. 139–56. I am very grateful to Mr George Singer of Tunbridge Wells for this reference.

23   Whimsical Walker, *From Sawdust to Windsor Castle*, 1922 at pp. 220, 128.

24   See autobiographies by the following comedians, for example; George Mozart, *Limelight*, 1938; Harry Randall, *Old Time Comedian*, 1931; George Robey, *Looking Back on Life*, 1933; Billy Merson, *Fixing the Stoof Oop*, 1926.

25   M. Charney, 'Comedy High and Low', *An Introduction to the Experience of Comedy*, Oxford University Press, 1978, p. 60.

26   Bailey, 'Will the real Bill Banks', pp. 340–2.

27   William Brough, *Trying It On, A Farce in One Act*, 1853.

28   Tom Park, *A Domestic Mash, A Farce*, British Library manuscripts, Lord Chamberlain's Papers (hereafter Ld. Chamb.) ADD 53416, Oct. 1888, Lic. no. 293: Mark Melford, *Seaside Swells or the Prizefighter's Daughter, A Farce in One Act*, Ld. Chamb. ADD 53422, Jan. 1889, Lic. no. 22.

29   Arthur Barclay, *Shorthand, A Farce in One Act*, Ld. Chamb. ADD 53422, Jan 1889, Lic. no. 21.

30   Charles Wilmot, *The Curate, A comic Operetta*, Ld. Chamb. ADD 53413, Oct 1888, Lic. no. 23; see *Entr' acte*, 19 Aug 1905, similar piece called *The Curate's Dilemma, at the Canterbury Music Hall*.

31   R. K. Hervey, *Good Business*, Ld. Chamb. 53389 A–K, Nov 1887, Lic. no. 232.

32   Davison, *Contemporary Drama*, pp. 34, 53.

33   Vesta Tilley, *Recollections by Lady De Frece*,1934, p. 71.

34   See M. Pickering, Chapter 4 in this volume.

35   *Entr'acte*, 10 Aug 1878, South London: 18 Feb 1882, Summer and Winter Palace: 2 Feb 1878, Lusby's.

36   *Entr'acte*, 15 June 1878, Pavilion; 28 Jan 1882, Forester's.

37   *Entr'acte*, 25 Feb 1882, Queens Palace, and 25 March 1882, Gatti's.

38   *Era*, 10 Feb 1894, South London.

39   A. Roberts, *Fifty Years of Spoof*, 1927, p. 169.

40   *Entr'acte*, 13 April 1872, Gattis.

41   See eg. *Entr'acte*, 6 May 1905, reviews of Arthur Rigby's 'March of the Married Man', at Camberwell Palace, on illustrated songs having 'come to stay'.

42   See Davison, *Popular Appeal*, pp. 3, 9: *Contemporary Drama*, Ch. 2.

43   I am grateful to the Grand Order of Water Rats for allowing me to use this source at their archive in the Eccentric Club, St. James, especially to Mr A. Crooks, administrator.

44   *Performer*, 1 Nov 1922, p. 5, 'The passing of Wal Pink', by Fred Russell. I am grateful to Tony Barker of *Music Hall Magazines* for this reference: J. Parker (ed.) *Whos Who in Variety*, 1916: Roberts, *Fifty Years of Spoof*, p. 56.

45   See entry in Parker, *Whos Who*, and articles by Bert Ross in *Call Boy*, Dec 1966, March 1967: *The Music Hall*, 15 Feb 1890, p. 8, on Joseph Keegan, and his obituary, *Era*, 12 Oct 1901, p. 23.

46   Ld. Chamb. 55353, A–K, Feb–Mar 1886, Lic. no. 41.

47   *Era*, 6 Mar 1935, p. 3, obit.: *Era*, 30 April 1898, p. 20.

48   Some of Wal Pink's sketch scripts include directions indicating "Jimmy enters to music", but unfortunately we are not told if it is Joe Elvin's "latest hit", or tunes chosen simply to evoke the scene or his character. It seems likely that the tunes were songs associated with the comedian: see also G. Mozart, *Limelight*, p. 159.

49   See R. Findlater, *Banned, A Review of Theatrical Censorship*, 1967, on censorship, its opponents, and the 'new' dramatists: and *Select Committee 1909*, p. viii of Report on 'special laws' for the theatre, and evidence of Tree, Archer and Shaw in particular.

50   *Daily Telegraph*, 10 Oct 1889, p. 2, Crowdkr's; see also 8 Oct, p. 3, Bermondsey Star; 3 Oct, p. 8, Bedford and Trocadero.

51   *Times*, 24. Jan 1910, p. 4.

52   See e.g. William Archer, 'The County Council and the Music Halls', *Contemporary Review*, March 1895, p. 327. For earlier fears about the vulgaristion of the lower middle class, see Home Office memo, PRO, HO45/9575/80993. Occasionally moral purists attacked the halls later, see e.g. J. Cowen, 'Music Halls and Morals', *Contemporary Review*, Nov 1916, pp. 611–20.

53   A. Roberts, *The Importance of Being Another Man's Wife*, Ld. Chamb. 1913, vol. 26:
     Wal Pink, *Chips Off The Old Block*, Ld. Chamb. 1912, vol. 54.
54   Stoll to *Select Committee 1909*, Q. 5004–19, Q. 5061–7, Q. 5109–12; *Stage Year Book*,
     1909, p. 289–90, Melford prosecuted: Tozer to *Select Committee 1909*, Q. 4906–8.
55   See Parker (ed.) *Who's Who in Variety*, 1916 entry and also entry in R. Busby, *British
     Music Hall, An Illustrated Whos Who from 1850 to the Present Day*, Elek, 1976: *GPO*, Ld.
     Chamb. 1910, vol. 19: *Perkins MP*, Ld. Chamb. 1910, vol. 19; also *Persevering Potts*,
     Ld. Chamb. 1911, vol. 19.
56   C. Austin and C. Ridgewell, *Parker's Progress*, Ld. Chamb. 1911, vol. 35.
57   I am grateful to Mr Peter Honri for telling me of Sydney Race's annotated
     programmes covering the early 1900s, and to the staff in the local history archive of
     Nottinghamshire County Council Library, for making them so readily available.
     This entry was made for the Empire show, 16 June 1919.
58   Davison, *Contemporary Drama*, pp. 37–40.
59   Wal Pink, *Fishing*, Ld. Chamb. 1914, vol. 4; see also *Gardening*, Ld. Chamb. 1906,
     vol. 25.
60   British Library, Music Room, H.3981.j.25; H.3981.j.26; H.3980.m.81; H.3981.j.28.
61   Wal Pink and Harry Boden, *Another Winner*, Ld. Chamb. 1912, vol. 36; Pink, *Billy's
     Money Box*, Ld. Chamb. 1912, vol. 11.
62   Pink, *What's In A Name?* Ld. Chamb. 1912, vol. 54: *Era* review, 1 Feb 1913.
63   Pink, *Under Cross Examination*, Ld. Chamb. 1912, vol. 2
64   Pink, *Who Ses so?* Ld. Chamb. 1913, vol. 11.

Index